The Jonas Genre

An Ordinary Reading of the New Testament

Paul Kenneth Hubbard

THE JONAS GENRE

Interior design by Amanda Rooker

Contents

Preface

I've spent most of my adult life thinking about how to live out Christianity systematically. This is mostly because for most of my adult life Christianity has been breaking up from within. Despite the fact that Christianity outwardly (and apparently monolithically) proclaims itself to be true, inwardly it consists of hundreds of competing catholic and cultic truths. It seemed that the only way to practice this religion was to escape into the mindless mysticisms of traditionalism, liberalism, or fundamentalism. So I came to a crisis: was the system itself true, or was I just a prisoner of my own personal presuppositions, inherited from a time before the fall of Christendom? Was the New Testament an aggressive act of communication by God, or was it just another humanistic production of religious existentialism? If Christianity is only a contrived system, and I can have no final answers or conviction about the historical integrity of the New Testament materials, then I can have no final answers about forgiveness or eternal life or any other thing that it purports to address. And if I can have no final conviction about these things, then what is the point of embracing Christianity as if it were absolute truth and not my own parochial religion?

And so I prayed. I don't remember the exact words that I used. But I do remember the whole tenor of the conversation. It began very intentionally, much like the logic of the book of Job. "What is the point of religion if you can have no final conviction? If Christianity is not true, I don't want the 'opiate of the people.' I want to struggle with the harsh realities of a meaningless world, of hopeless philosophical ambiguity, and of my eventual, meaningless death, like all the other courageous secular existentialists. On the other hand, if your 'New Promise' is true, I have a right to hold you to your promise, especially in the light of the present condition of your church, which you said that you would defend.

If my convictions are ultimately based upon my own energy, because I *choose* to believe, whether rationally or irrationally, then this isn't much of a promise. And it isn't much of a religion. You said that you are a God that answers prayer? I don't want you to tell me why it's my fault or somebody else's fault that I don't have any final answers. I want answers. And if I can't have answers in this area, I thank you (if you are even listening) that this religious conservatism that I have embraced for these many years has given my life stability and a sense of accomplishment and even some joy, but now I think I am ready to face the absurdity of the cosmos and make preparations for the absurdity of my own death. Amen."

And so I set about to work. I opened the New Testament and my notebook and began making notes. The first thing that I tackled was the question about why I did not have any final conviction about my own forgiveness—and this apart from any consideration about whether the New Testament was true. This was a problem which seemed to be systemic to the New Testament itself. I attempted to merely string together a logical argument from biblical ideas. I succeeded, but not in the way I intended. My argument for my forgiveness did not derive from the Gospels. Nor did it derive from the works of Paul. Nor did it derive from the works of John. My argument for my own forgiveness came from the book of Hebrews. This argument was coupled with the fact that some pretty notorious people had achieved forgiveness, particularly David, despite his loathsome behavior concerning Uriah and Bathsheba.

So I had an adequate theological argument, and I had examples of men who I was sure were morally more reprobate than I. And though at first I thought this study about forgiveness was unrelated to the linguistic analysis that was to follow, it turned out to be crucial in understanding how that linguistic analysis should proceed. Yet unless I had conviction about the integrity of the New Testament itself, a promise of forgiveness was, of course, ultimately worthless. This problem was particularly aggravated by the fact that all the academic folks were saying that the New Testament materials *were* essentially worthless as historical witnesses to the phenomena of Christ.

Albert Schweitzer's *The Quest of the Historical Jesus*[1] stood, essentially, as the final answer to the ultimate integrity of the New Testament materials. He had concluded that the historical Christ simply could not be found. And there seemed to be no alternative to the biblical criticism of the modern establishment that seemed to effortlessly affirm his thesis in many different ways. So I set about to see if I could find one. I had the training in Greek. And I had read a generous selection of all the major writers. After reading J.P. Meyer's *A Marginal Jew*,[2] which is essentially a modern update of Schweitzer's thesis, I closed up the books and knew that I must look for an answer on my own. It had to be simple. It had to be verifiable. And it had to come from accessible sources—simple dictionaries, lexicons, and other reference books. And, of course, it had to come, primarily, from the original materials. If the New Testament was a communication to the common people, then any ordinary person, such as myself, should be able to substantiate it. It would take time. Even though I had a computer which would speed things up considerably, it would still take a great deal of time. Time to examine every word used by every author, if necessary. I had time. That was part of the bargain. I wanted answers. He wanted my time.

Over the next seven years or so, I worked nearly every day on the project. Sometimes for three or four hours. If there was a glitch or a question or an inconsistency, I would follow the rabbit hole until I found its end. I believed that there was substantial circumstantial evidence that Mark had not written first (the popular theory), but Matthew. But after a year of attempting to substantiate that Matthew was the literary source for Mark and Luke, I was at an impasse. I could see that all three of these Gospels were directly related to each other; that is, someone was copying from someone else, but I was at a complete loss as to how to prove it.

What really cracked the whole thing open for me was that I decided to read Matthew differently. Though I had read the New

---

1 Albert Schweitzer, *The Quest Of The Historical Jesus: A Critical Study Of Its Progress From Reimarus To Wrede,* English edition, trans. William Montgomery (London: A. & C. Black, 1910).

2 John P. Meyer, *A Marginal Jew: Rethinking the Historical Jesus* (New York: Doubleday, 2001).

Testament scores of times over the years, my reading of Matthew had always been part of reading the larger whole. And after all these years, I had no idea what Matthew was doing in his Gospel. I realized that I didn't know how the Synoptic Gospels were related because I didn't really know what any of them were doing. Were they just passive patchworks of unsubstantiated verbal traditions, which had already begun to degrade into confusing variants of cultural prejudice? Or were they aggressively taking a primary template and consciously making a coherent literary creation? As soon as I read Matthew with this question in mind, I was devastated. I don't mind telling you that I cried about this. I don't know why, exactly. It was a complicated emotional thing. I thought I had known these books. But I didn't know them. And I didn't know the men who wrote them. I had never even thought to let them communicate to me on the level of one person to another. What a superficial, chauvinistic fool I had been. After all these years, I didn't know Matthew.

As soon as I allowed that there could be a deliberate, coherent structure and form to Matthew, I began to understand what Matthew was trying to do. I began to know him as an author. He was not some charlatan of the late first century who had taken one of the apostles' names and surreptitiously inserted yet another rambling record of what had already, somehow, become an orthodoxy of community myth. Here was a man who wrote with authority. He wrote with authority because he was there. And based on the indirect evidence I saw in Mark and Luke, he was almost certainly Matthew the tax collector whom the Synoptics describe. Even his style of writing had the appearance of a man of numbers and facts. He was a proud conservative. His life was a complex compromise between his religion and his political philosophy. Once I saw the structure of Matthew, with just a few taps of a literary chisel the structure fell away to reveal much of the raw data. And it looked a lot like the presumed Aramaic version that Matthew was supposed to have written from the very beginning.[3] The appearance of John made it quite clear that even the pericopes themselves – the short vignettes which form the building blocks of the first three Gospels – must also be part of the form. And these pericopes looked very much like information that would have been recorded on separate pieces of

3 More will be said about this in the text itself.

writing material that would have been accessible to a tax collector.

The message of Matthew was intense—so intense that I had to admit that Matthew contrived his structure and form to convey an implicit theological *commentary* upon the raw data. It was such an imposition that I had to look for a word to describe what, for John, was overt editorial commentary throughout his Gospel. When I looked for the summary, literary key that would describe what Matthew was doing, I found it in the enigmatic symbol of his story. For all the "signs" that John gives us in his gospel, Matthew gives just one: the sign of Jonah.[4] I had never seen anything comparable to the literary structure of Matthew, but then, he claimed to be telling the most important story that was ever told. Since Mark and Luke employed the pericope form but also mirrored (with somewhat less intensity) Matthew's structure, there were now three such literary units with the same form and structure. It should now be called a genre. And if it is a genre, it must be called the Jonas Genre.

If I assumed that Matthew authored the Jonas Genre template, what could account for the fact that his pericopes were out of order with Mark and Luke for the first part of his story? There was nothing left to do but to line up the three accounts side by side to see what I could see. I color-coded the text to make the expected patterns more visible. The answer leapt off my charts. *Mark was combining Matthew and Luke.* There was a lot of complexity here, of course, because Luke (and Mark) had already been looking (presumably) at both Matthew's earlier Aramaic version and Matthew's Greek version. But Mark was also looking at Luke. The fact of synthesis seemed crystal clear. One day I was struggling to explain this to my wife, who knows no Greek. Yet with one look at my Greek charts, she tossed off casually, "It looks like Mark has zippered together Matthew and Luke." She had seen exactly what

4 *The Online Bible* (http://www.onlinebible.net/), the software used for this research, used the KJV translation, hence the KJV quotations throughout. Words and phrasing have been modernized only when original colloquialisms would unnecessarily obstruct the meaning for the modern reader. The KJV renders the name "Jonah" in the Old Testament (never "Jonas") and "Jonas" in the New (never "Jonah"). Though in the Hebrew, the word almost certainly ends in a "ah" sound; the nominative in the LXX and in the NT is ιωνας (*ionas*).

I saw. But she said it so matter-of-factly and so easily. It was a wonderful confirmation!

Then came the objections. The "what ifs." I went back to the data over and over again. A plausible argument, however strong, was just not going to be good enough for me. I wanted scientific conviction. Yet no matter how I ran the data, it always worked out the same. There are many other charts, graphs, and supporting research that are not in this book because they are all redundant confirmations. But I needed to do them to convince myself. Considering the seriousness of my prayer, I had no intention of stopping my inquiry until I overturned every objectionable stone I could find.

One of the most serious objections to my conclusions had nothing to do with the data. But it had everything to do with a very obvious *prima facie* objection that I myself would have had if someone else had done the work. And the objection was this: how is it that I had found what so many generations of academics have not been able to find? I'm just an ordinary person. Yet my conclusions struck at the very heart of the quest for the historical Jesus. If what I had found was true, we were no longer separated from the historical Christ by layers of unstable verbal traditions and cultural myths. I was no further removed from Christ than by one man's literary effort. If I can understand Matthew, I can understand Christ. If I can understand any one of these primary authors, I will have *contact* with the historical Christ. I may not understand him completely. But I will have contact.

As I said, I did have a computer to use. And the computer was a relatively new thing. None of the other reputable authors writing about the literary relationship of the Synoptics in past generations had had this technology at their disposal. Even *with* a computer it took me hundreds of hours to make the literary analysis. I had time on my hands to do this work. Almost all candid academics complain that they never have enough time for pure research. Also, my life was on the line. This wasn't about getting tenure. This wasn't about money or career or notoriety. This was about life. Or death. If I did not find substantive answers from my research, I was determined to die the death of the post-Christian West. I would go willingly. No blubbering. No complaints. No opium.

This book was written for those who are looking for answers about the integrity of the New Testament materials, as I was. Upon being converted to Christianity, we often immediately begin exploring the extent of this religion. If the New Testament materials are true, then this religion should touch every part of our lives. And as we mature, emotionally and intellectually, this religion yawns before us as an ever-expanding landscape of moral and intellectual challenges into which our lives may grow and flourish. Therefore, whether we experienced our initial conversion to Christianity as a child or as an adult, as emotional or intellectual, we will always be constantly growing and changing. The challenge of conversion will always continue. But today's Christian faces something new and quite beyond the ordinary challenges. Today's Christian faces an enormous, monolithic consensus—in the universities and in general culture—that the New Testament materials are not reliable witnesses to the historical Christ. It is said that the apostles didn't even write the records which ordinary history attributes to them, or that their records are primarily mythical, or that the early church suppressed or destroyed dissenting Gospels. These are very serious arguments. The integrity of the New Testament materials must be established before we can go anywhere with its religion.

There are many people I would like to thank for helping me with my research and with the publication effort. First, my wife, Jeanne, who very helpfully spent countless hours listening to the progress of my research and never complained when I crawled out of bed at four in the morning day after day after day. She offered me consistent encouragement whenever I needed it. Second, Margaret Novak, who argued with me a very long time ago about how the Gospels came to be written. Her argument provoked me to begin this study. And I thank a great many others who also argued with me and showed me that I didn't know what I was talking about. I never told them that. But now I do. Third, Christine Lonto, for inspiring me to write about my discoveries in terms that everyone could understand. Fourth, my editor, Amanda Rooker, for having worked so thoroughly and so hard to tell me what I did not want to hear. She swept away many of the obstacles that hindered the telling of this research story—obstacles that I myself erected. Finally, I would like to thank the folks who put together the online Bible program (http://www.online bible.net/), which I used for this project. I could not have done this research without it. It was free and it was powerful. And I think everyone should put a copy in their tool bag.

Introduction

If we want to understand any written work, we must first know its genre. Is it a joke? Is it satire? Is it history? Is it fantasy? If we get the genre wrong, every subsequent conclusion we draw may also be wrong. And the question of genre is no less crucial for the Synoptic Gospels in the New Testament than it was for Jonathan Swift's *A Modest Proposal*[1] or H.G. Wells' *War of the Worlds*.[2] The literary materials with which we have to deal are ordinary literary materials, just as the carpenter's son was an ordinary man.

Even a cursory reading reveals that the Synoptic Gospels assume that one's senses give a fairly reliable account of the world and that God may truly communicate with us using ordinary language. John the Baptist said that Jesus came to tell us what he, and only he, can see and hear—to repeat the very words of his own Father.[3] Luke is clear about the ordinariness of his Gospel and how his Gospel should be read: "Forasmuch as many have taken in hand to set forth in order a declaration of those things which are most surely believed among us, Even as they delivered them unto us, which from the beginning were eyewitnesses, and ministers of the word; It seemed good to me also, having had perfect understanding of all things from the very first, to write to you in order, most excellent Theophilus, That you might know the certainty of those things, wherein you have been instructed."[4]

---

1 *A Modest Proposal* was a satirical pamphlet written by Jonathan Swift in 1729. Swift proposes that the Irish could mitigate their poverty by selling their children as food for the rich.

2 The 1938 radio broadcast of *War of the Worlds* caused considerable public panic, since many people, tuning in late, missed the opening credits and thought that they were hearing a newscast.

3 Jn 3:32, 34.

4 Lk 1:1-4.

So if the Synoptic authors make their appeal primarily on the basis of what they have seen and heard, what is their appeal? They make the same appeal as John in his Gospel, although in a slightly different genre. John says directly, "These things are written, that you might believe that Jesus is the Christ, the Son of God; and that believing you might have life through his name."[5] The Synoptics say more indirectly, "This is my beloved Son: hear him."[6] If we look at the New Testament as a whole, we will see that it is also a *collective* argument of a specific religious community—the apostolic community. The Synoptic authors seem very aware of this community and give every evidence that they understand that their message is just a part of this collective argument—-a part of the larger whole of God's gospel. And so should we if we are to understand the distinct literary nature of the Synoptic Gospels.

We must allow that the Synoptic Gospels are not intended to be a comprehensive revelation. And it is important to do this because the collective argument of the apostolic community claims that God has already spoken to us in almost every possible genre. He has even written a book himself, they say. It was a very short book, written on two pages of stone, with his own finger—the Mosaic tablets. John will soon write a Gospel that claims Christ speaks directly into the soul of man, as soon as the soul comes into the world.[7] And Paul has written an extensive theological apologetic in his letter to the Romans that creation itself is a powerful, conclusive witness: "Because that which may be known of God is manifest in them; for God has showed it to them. For the invisible things of him from the creation of the world are clearly seen, being understood by the things that are made, even his eternal power and Godhead."[8]

Therefore, the primary message of the Synoptic Gospels is this: that *having* spoken to us in every conceivable venue and genre, God has now spoken to us through a direct representative of himself—his only son. Look at how the Synoptics convey this idea: "Hear another parable:

5 Jn 20:31.

6 Mk 9:7b.

7 Jn 1:9. "That was the true Light, which lighteth every man that cometh into the world."

8 Ro 1:20.

There was a certain householder, which planted a vineyard, and hedged it round about, and digged a winepress in it, and built a tower, and let it out to husbandmen, and went into a far country: And when the time of the fruit drew near, he sent his servants to the husbandmen, that they might receive the fruits of it. And the husbandmen took his servants, and beat one, and killed another, and stoned another. Again, he sent other servants more than the first: and they did to them likewise. But last of all he sent to them his son, saying, They will reverence my son."[9]

Yet the Synoptic Gospels strongly imply that God's message to the world does not reside primarily in the *words* of Jesus, but in the drama of his life. This explains why Mark leaves out so much of the teaching material that Matthew and Luke include. It is not so much *what* Jesus said as it is that *he* said it. Yes, the people thought that his teaching was astonishing. And his healing power was certainly astonishing. Nevertheless, the Pharisees and Sadducees ask Jesus for a "sign from heaven." This is how Matthew fields this question: "An evil and adulterous generation seeks after a sign; but there shall no sign be given to it, but the sign of the prophet Jonas: For as Jonas was three days and three nights in the whale's belly; so shall the Son of man be three days and three nights in the heart of the earth."[10] Essentially, Matthew says, the media is the message.

The Synoptic Gospels claim to be ordinary, eyewitness accounts, speaking in ordinary language and ordinary literary conventions, about an extraordinary drama. They claim that this drama is the consummate revelation of God to the world. They claim that God has spoken directly to us, uniquely, in the person of his own Son. Yet they also claim that the drama of the Son's life is not entirely unique. It conforms to a specific genre. And that genre is the Jonas Genre.

Similarly, this book concentrates not so much on what was said but how and why it was said. First we will take a look at some of the general features of the Synoptic Gospels. What is the setting? What was happening in the church? What is the structure? What do they say? How do they say it? And what is their form? Granted that each Synoptic author is attempting to express what he has seen and heard, how has

9 Mt 21:33–37.

10 12:39–40.

he formed that expression? Are the Synoptics three variant transcriptions of a body of apostolic sermons? Do they simply and randomly record a stream of community stories about Christ? Are they a biography in any sense of the word? Perhaps they are something entirely different.

Next we will compare the Gospel of John with the Synoptics—not to understand why John is different, but to shed even more light upon the Synoptic similarities. Then we can generate a more plausible hypothesis about how the Synoptic Gospels are interrelated: Who wrote first? Why were the second and third Gospels, which mirrored so much of the structure and form of the first, even written? If the structure and form of the Synoptic Gospels reside in a source outside the Synoptic tradition itself, why didn't John follow it?

Having laid the groundwork for a hypothesis which accounts for 1) the historical witness of Matthew's relatively brief Aramaic proto-Gospel, 2) a possible Matthean motive for having written both an Aramaic Gospel and a subsequently expanded Greek revision, and 3) the apparent order and interrelationship between all three Synoptics regarding both of these versions, we will ask some specific questions about what the authors are saying. It is essential to prove the interrelationship between the Synoptic Gospels, certainly not for the academic exercise, but because for material that is so similar in both content and form, the Synoptic editor's specific variations upon a template gives the final, crucial information we need to have in order to know his intent. These Synoptic variations are the author's theological intonations that inform every sentence, much like Christ's spoken intonations, necessarily missing in written manuscripts, which would have greatly clarified his own intent behind his words. And in matters which definitively establish the integrity of an author writing about an event absolutely unique in our civilization and absolutely fundamental to our own lives, we must hear these intonations. We must know the author's full intent. Otherwise we will be as confused as the apostles said they were about Christ, asking "Where is the historical Christ?" until the end of time.

Having presented considerable linguistic evidence that fixes the order in which the Synoptic Gospels were written, we will attempt to understand more about Matthew's genre by taking a close look at his structure and themes. Ultimately we will discover that the genre of the Synoptic Gospels is an intentionally contrived, broken literary simile that points the reader elsewhere for a fuller explanation of its content, and that the only logical place to which the Synoptic genre points is to Paul. The Synoptic genre is an extended parable or theater script which presents, as a quasi-play, a living, Hosean-like dramatization.[11] Although the Synoptic Gospels attempt to rigorously conform themselves to what was seen and heard, they are a religious dramatization. Christ said that there would be no sign given to an evil and adulterous generation but the sign of "Jonas the prophet."[12] Much like Hosea's prophetic method, in which he "acted out" much of the content of his prophecy, Christ's entire career was a parable.

Circumstantial evidence will indicate that it was Matthew who first saw that Christ's teachings and acts of power were conforming to a highly stylized, repetitive, theatrical pattern: the pattern of the prophet Jonah. Furthermore, Matthew developed this special Jonas Genre to retell this historical parable in the same literary mode in which Christ had presented himself to Israel: again, part ordinary history, part Greek play, and part prophetic parable. It will be seen that Luke and Mark have conformed their material to the contours and characteristics of Matthew's Jonas Genre, but in different "dialects" of artistic interpretation, freely re-paraphrasing the representative dialogues, and in some cases, the representational events of Matthew.

Having stabilized the genre and the order of the Synoptic Gospels and the thematic structure of Matthew, we will ask: What was Mark's intent? Luke is, of course, much less a mystery. Though he follows the contours of the Jonas Genre, he adds a great deal of his own material that could easily be examined for specific editorial intent—a fertile area for future research. But Mark very rarely adds completely new material. So why attempt an "official" Gospel which essentially repeats 90% of the content of one that is already written? If our theory is correct, then a great deal of the author's intent may be expressed in artistic variations

11 Hosea, an Old Testament prophet, takes a prostitute for a wife, by which he had children. His family then prophetically signifies various aspects of God's relationship with Israel. See especially Hos 1.

12 Mt 12:39–40.

upon a theme—in this case, Matthew's Jonas Genre template. Then the message *is* the media; that is, the message resides in *how* the material is presented. If Mark closely follows Matthew's content, what is his "intonation" of the implicit themes of Matthew?

As we examine Mark with these expansive ideas of editorial license, we find that there is much more to the Jonas Genre than that of a broken simile that encourages us to look to Paul for a more comprehensive theology of Jesus. One of the main sub-themes of Matthew, for example, is Peter's fall from grace. Thirty years after the death of Christ, Matthew finds it necessary to graphically present this embarrassing fall as if it were indispensable to the gospel story. Matthew could have easily ignored the whole tawdry affair of Peter's incomprehensible betrayal.

What has this to do with the story of Jesus? Matthew seems determined to present Peter as typological of Israel's ongoing rejection of its Messiah. And there appears to be more. Peter's typological role seems to be taken up in an even larger editorial program in which Matthew sets the stage for the theological and ecclesiastical ascendency of Paul as an antipode to Peter's fall. This kind of agenda may be shocking to modern critics who assume that the Synoptic gospels are merely passive historical accidents of religious existentialism. But for the Synoptic authors, the resurrection of Christ was not the end of the story; it was just the beginning.

These authors seem to be saying that the drama of the post-ascension, apostolic church partakes of the very substance of the historical Christ. In this sense, the act of writing the story is part of the story itself. And Peter and Paul's ongoing response to Christ is just as much a part of the story. If this is true, how does Mark portray all this? Mark follows Matthew so closely because Matthew's story is apparently the necessary context for Mark's own message. As we examine Mark's message, we will see a fuller exposition of Peter's crucial role in the continuing gospel storytelling not only of his typological fall, but his typological rehabilitation.

1

The Setting of the Synoptic Gospels

The Gospel writers clearly did not, at first, understand who Jesus was and what he was doing. Like many biblical scholars today, they initially thought Jesus was just another good man who was eventually destroyed by his own popularity and the envy of the religious establishment. But in time, they all realized that it was not that simple. For one thing, this man had some kind of death wish from the beginning. Jesus believed that it was his destiny to be humiliated and destroyed.[1] And when Peter attempted to persuade Jesus to give up what Peter perceived as self-destructive foolishness, he was severely reprimanded: "But [Jesus] turned, and said to Peter, Get behind me, Satan: you are an offence unto me: for you savor not the things that be of God, but those that be of men."[2] When Peter again attempts to impede this destiny, by drawing his sword when the soldiers come to apprehend Christ in the Garden of Gethsemane, Jesus more gently chides him: "Put up again your sword into his place: for all they that take the sword shall perish with the sword. Don't you think that I cannot now pray to my Father, and he shall presently give me more

---

1 He tells this to the disciples in three different pericopes in the Synoptic Gospels.
2 Mt 16:23.

than twelve legions of angels? But how then shall the scriptures be fulfilled, that thus it must be?"[3]

If we look at Peter's early sermons in Acts and the first group of Paul's letters, we do not find any well-developed theological arguments—for example, that Christ is God. What we *do* find is a community grappling with the extraordinarily unlikely fact that God was tearing away the kingdom of God from Israel and giving it away to the whole Gentile world. This convulsive struggle is evident in Acts, which haltingly transitions from the gospel of the circumcision to the gospel of the uncircumcision, reflecting tremendous tension within the early Jewish and Gentile Christian communities. It is evident in the story of the Jewish and Gentile widows in Acts 6,[4] in Peter and Paul's conflict at Antioch,[5]and in the Jamesean/Pauline theological conflict over justification.[6] This is why our discussion of the setting of the Synoptic Gospels must begin with Paul himself.

Paul's initial and enduring missionary strategy was to begin at the synagogue. Not only does he struggle with the failure of this strategy, he struggles in Romans 9–11 with the script that God has apparently written for his own nation: "What shall we say then? That the Gentiles, which followed not after righteousness, have attained to righteousness, even the righteousness which is of faith. But Israel, which followed after the law of righteousness, has not attained to the law of righteousness?"[7] But eventually Paul is convinced that this missionary strategy has failed because it did not sufficiently conform to the radical purposes of his calling in God: we read late in Acts that Paul eventually abandons this missionary strategy and begins to go directly to the Gentiles. "Then Paul and Barnabas waxed bold, and said, 'It was necessary that the word of God should first have been spoken to you: but seeing you put it from you, and judge yourselves unworthy of everlasting life, lo, we

3 Mt 26:53–54.

4 Greeks here are being treated as second-class citizens of the Kingdom, who participated at the pleasure of, or who were tolerated by, the Circumcision Party within the Jerusalem Church.

5 Gal 2:11–14.

6 This dramatic tension can be seen by comparing Ro 4:2 with Jas 2:21, and Ro 3:28 with Jas 2:24.

7 Ro 9:30–31.

turn to the Gentiles.'"[8] But the transition is not easy. Three chapters later in Acts, we find Paul right back in the synagogue: "Now when they had passed through Amphipolis and Apollonia, they came to Thessalonica, where was a synagogue of the Jews: And Paul, as his manner was, went in to them, and three sabbath days reasoned with them out of the scriptures, opening and alleging, that Christ must have suffered, and risen again from the dead; and 'that this Jesus, whom I preach to you, is Christ.'"[9]

Then comes a passing, seemingly accidental event which turns out to be pivotal in Paul's ministry. After being driven out of one synagogue after another, his disciples leave him in Athens, in hiding, attempting to protect him from the Jews. Paul finds himself passively waiting and alone. Then the Spirit drives him into the wilderness of an entirely Greek audience within the Areopagus, where Luke records Paul's short, representative sermon. For the first time, Paul's argumentation is entirely independent of the Jewish Scriptures and remains entirely within the circle of Greek thought.[10] It is an argument that we will see again in Romans, in which he addresses both Jews and Greeks.[11]

In Ephesus, again, something entirely new happens. Paul *extracts* the believing Jews from the synagogue: "And he went into the synagogue, and spoke boldly for the space of three months, disputing and persuading the things concerning the kingdom of God. But when many were hardened, and believed not, but spoke evil of that way before the multitude, he departed from them, and separated the disciples, disputing daily in the school of one Tyrannus. And this continued for two years; so that all they which dwelt in Asia heard the

---

8 Acts 13:46.

9 17:1-3.

10 17:16–34.

11 That is not to say that Paul does not allude to or even quote from the Old Testament, but the allusions and quotations are from the more general passages (of the Psalms, for example) to make a general, theological point. Nevertheless, in the very next vignette, Luke has Paul right back in the synagogue at Corinth. Likewise, when Paul leaves Corinth, he sails to Ephesus and heads straight for the synagogue (Acts 18:18–19).

word of the Lord Jesus, both Jews and Greeks."[12]

By the time Paul comes to Troas, on his final, fateful pilgrimage to Jerusalem, we see that the disciples have been fully extracted from the synagogue, meeting from house to house. They even meet on a different day of the week: "And upon the first day of the week, when the disciples came together to break bread, Paul preached unto them, ready to depart on the next day; and continued his speech until midnight.[13]... I kept back nothing that was profitable to you, but have showed you, and have taught you publicly, and from house to house."[14]

Luke, therefore, has been intentionally taking us on an unusual voyage. It is not just a voyage from Peter's Jewish gospel to Paul's Gentile gospel. Luke is showing us a small part of a radical transition that Paul *himself* has made during his whole ministry. In Acts, Luke represents this as Paul's departure from the synagogue. It was a seemingly impossible crossing for Paul. He says in the last part of his argument in Romans, "For I could wish that myself were accursed from Christ for my brethren, my kinsmen according to the flesh."[15] And yet by the time Paul writes Philippians, he has crossed over this impossible barrier: "But what things were gain to me, those I counted loss for Christ. Yes, doubtless, and I count all things but loss for the excellency of the knowledge of Christ Jesus my Lord: for whom I have suffered the loss of all things, and do count them but dung, that I may win Christ."[16]

Luke was in an ideal position to see a literary parallel that Paul surely could not, at first, have seen — that the drama of Paul's life looked very similar to the life of Jonah the prophet. Paul was never intended to get bogged down in the synagogue. Like Jonah, he was intended to preach a message of repentance far beyond the boundaries of Israel.

---

12 Acts 19:8-10

13 20:7

14 20:20. Although based on Acts 8:3, it appears that prior to Paul's conversion, some Jews were already meeting "house to house," perhaps in addition to synagogue attendance. "As for Saul, he made havoc of the church, entering into every house, and haling men and women committed them to prison."

15 Ro 9:3.

16 Phil 3:7–8.

But he had to learn this for himself. Late in his ministry, Paul recounts what Jesus had said, which he had found so difficult to do: "Depart: for I will send you far away to the Gentiles."[17] Like Jonah, he resisted this call. For many years his ministry stalled in the dispersed synagogues of the Jews. Like Jonah, Paul was eventually thrown out of Jewish culture and handed over to the sea of unsympathetic Roman law and to the devouring beast of Nero. And just as the missionary vision of Jonah is completely radicalized in the belly of the whale, so the most radical part of the transformation of Paul's own vision, captured in the writing of Philippians, occurs while sitting helplessly in a Roman prison. Yet Matthew, while watching Paul's career from the relative safety of the Jerusalem enclave, was in a position to see an additional, historical parallel that even Luke, at first, may not have seen. Matthew may have suddenly realized that he had personally witnessed this whole drama somewhere before, that there was an eerie connection between the career of Paul and the career of Jesus himself. And this realization would have completely radicalized his own understanding of the gospel.[18]

Papias, a church father writing early in the second century, says that "Matthew composed the 'logia' [a compilation of Jesus' sayings] in the Hebrew tongue and everyone interpreted them as they were able."[19] This indicates a document with very little editorial commentary, a kind of stand-alone "New Torah" of the Prophet Jesus. This New Torah would have been the original from which all satellite copies were made. Indeed, if Paul finds those who "knew only the baptism of John" at Ephesus[20] a decade or so after the death of Christ, this "New Torah" may have proclaimed a mighty, messianic prophet, but one with a baptism of no clearer significance beyond that of John the Baptist. It could certainly not have been a literary and theological preparation for

17 Acts 22:21.

18 This word "radicalized" is chosen advisedly. Simon Zelotes and Judas Iscariot were *already* radicals, perhaps blinded with a fierce conservatism of their own sort. One drops out of history and the other betrays it. It would have been Matthew's analytical, pragmatic, and ordinarily conservative mind that would have provided the raw material for an extraordinarily convulsive radicalization.

19 Eusebius, *The History of the Church*, 3.39; cf. 3.24. 20 Acts 18:25.

what is to become Paul's baptism in Christ.

Paul's baptism was far more radical than the baptism of John. It was a baptism of death to self and resurrection *to* Christ as Lord and *in* Christ as savior from sin. And the coming up out of the waters of this baptism was a resurrection from sin and death and from the judgment and wrath of God. It was a resurrection to a new, eternal life in the Spirit. Unlike John's baptism of mere repentance, Paul's baptism in Christ was a baptism in the Holy Ghost, a far more radical baptism, which we now see clearly portrayed in the opening pages of Matthew's extant Gospel in the mouth of John himself.[21]

Imagine the setting that Luke gives us in Acts as a place to construct a potential scenario for Matthew's sudden radicalization.[22] Matthew was probably at Jerusalem when Paul came with his obeisance offering to the Jerusalem church sometime around 59 A.D., at the Feast of Pentecost. Things are relatively quiet. Matthew has seen some sort of détente emerge between the Romans; the Sanhedrin; and James, Peter, and John. Then, suddenly, the religious authorities became extremely agitated and very aware of the arrival of Paul—the shorn-headed,[23] traveling preacher of *Asia*—as if he were the primary, troublemaking apostle of the Nazarenes.

But by Paul's own assertion, he was practically invisible during the temple visit: he was not "disputing nor raising up the people, nor arguing in the synagogues or in the city."[24] So one must wonder: if Paul was so notorious as to be recognized in a crowd, why did it take as long as the last day of the feast to recognize him? And how is it that "some Jews from Asia" so easily stir up the local crowds and the local religious establishment to such a fervor that Paul can only escape Jerusalem—and that barely—by eventually appealing to Caesar? To make matters even more suspicious, when Paul finally arrives in Rome, why do the

21 Acts 19:2–5; Mt 3:11. "I indeed baptize you with water unto repentance: but he that cometh after me is mightier than I, whose shoes I am not worthy to bear: he shall baptize you with the Holy Ghost, and with fire."

22 Acts 21:15–25:12.

23 21:18–26. Paul had probably shaved his head with the four men who were at charges with him. And this, of course, would have made him far more difficult to recognize, even for his friends.

24 24:12.

Jews there seem completely unaware of who Paul is?[25] Everyone in the church seemed to know that trouble was waiting for Paul if he were to continue on to Jerusalem.[26] Even James seemed to know.[27] And here it was.

Though it appears in the Acts narrative as a providential rescue, it seems like Paul's arrest was a complete setup. For example, after Paul's defense, why the outcry "crucify him," if they did not already know who he was and why he must die? If the Sanhedrin was already divided over the resurrection issue,[28] where did the cohesiveness of the "plot of the 40" come from, which vowed to kill Paul, if it were not the product of a prior conspiratorial action?[29] *Someone* must have already told the centurion (Chief Captain Lysias), who fortuitously rescues Paul in the temple precincts, that a notorious criminal was there: the Egyptian ringleader of the murderous *Sicarii*.[30]

By the time Paul makes his defense before Felix, the Jews from Asia are nowhere to be found, because they have already executed their part in the conspiracy. Tertullus' complaint to Felix bears a striking resemblance to James' more moderate objection to Paul: that he was a "mover of sedition" among Jews throughout the world.[31] Matthew had heard the Sanhedrin, whom Tertullus represented, say that Paul was the "ringleader of the sect of the Nazarenes." But wait: Paul wasn't the *ringleader* of the sect, was he? Weren't James, Peter, and John?[32] Then why had the Sanhedrin left them alone? Was it, perhaps, because their theology had become effectively neutralized, while Paul's theology

---

25 28:17–22. 26 20:22–23.

27 21:22: "…the multitude surely must come together: for they will hear that you have come."

28 23:6–7. 29 23:12–13.

30 21:27–38. Perhaps what we are seeing here is how a complex plan to have Paul murdered began to work at cross-purposes with itself. If Lysias had been pre-briefed that Paul was an armed, murderous Egyptian, Lysias could have (and would have) easily killed him first and asked questions later. Yet if he had not arrived to apprehend Paul when he did, the crowds themselves would have almost certainly killed Paul.

31 Compare Acts 24:5 with Acts 21:20–21.

32 Gal 2:9. "And when James, Cephas [Peter], and John, who seemed to be pillars, perceived the grace that was given to me, they gave to me and Barnabas the

continues to become more and more radical? Is this not why, after two years of subsequent imprisonment, someone is still attempting to assassinate Paul and not James or Peter?

Matthew must have seen all this. Perhaps he concluded (rightly or wrongly) that this was a setup to do away with Paul by the "thousands of Jews who believed, who were zealous for the law,"[33] almost all of whom were of the Jamesean party. If we are to judge by Matthew's unusual typological use of the Old Testament,[34] surely Matthew's prophetic mind could not have missed the parallels between the life of Jesus and the life of Paul. Just as Christ had set his face to go to Jerusalem, so Paul had set his face to go to Jerusalem, even though in every city the brothers prophesied that "bonds and afflictions" awaited him there. Just as the religious establishment had sold Christ out by means of the mob, so Paul was being sold out by the Jerusalem establishment by means of the mob. Paul goes before Herod Agrippa II just as Christ went before Herod Antipas. Paul goes before Caesar just as Christ went before Pilate, rejected and sacrificed by his own people.

To summarize, Matthew had been a silent historical witness to the increasing tensions between the Jerusalem church and the church at Antioch, Paul's home base. He saw the increasing tensions between the Circumcision Party and Paul. Matthew almost certainly saw that James' letter to the dispersed Jewish Christians flatly contradicted much of the force of a central tenet of Paul's theology, that we were free from the law in a way that was utterly unimaginable to him. He saw the embarrassing moral failure of Peter and Barnabas at Antioch.[35] He saw how John Mark had humiliated Paul by rejecting his mission and had

---

right hands of fellowship; that we should go unto the heathen, and they to the circumcision."

33 Acts 21:20.

34 For example, about the slaughter of the innocent children in Bethlehem, he quotes Jeremiah: "Then was fulfilled that which was spoken by Jeremy the prophet, saying, 'In Rama was there a voice heard, lamentation, and weeping, and great mourning, Rachel weeping for her children, and would not be comforted, because they are not.'" This refers to the deportation of the children of Israel to a foreign country, not to their murder *in situ*. The connection is not the context but the *typology* of mothers weeping for their children. More will be said about this later.

35 Gal 2:11–13.

returned to the church at Jerusalem.[36] At some point after the Jerusalem conspiracy failed to kill Paul, Matthew may have emerged from his own Jonah-like spiritual catharsis, just as Paul had done.

If, under these conditions, Matthew suddenly goes over to the Pauline theological camp, it is easy to imagine what such an emotional catharsis must have done to his theology. Though he had been a publican, he was suddenly no longer a second-class citizen of Judaism. And, doubtless, he would never go back to what would be increasingly viewed as an Egypt of circumcision theology to sit in the back of the synagogue.[37] He perhaps saw clearly, albeit prophetically, how God was destroying the church at Jerusalem. Thinking about Christ's apocalyptic predictions in a new way,[38] he could have seen how God would physically destroy Jerusalem at the hands of the Romans, thereby eliminating any hope of reconstituting the old Israel. He could have seen how the Jews had nearly succeeded in killing Paul and how diffident the Jerusalem church was towards this persecution. He remembered Paul's letter to the Galatians: "But though we, or an angel from heaven, preach any other gospel unto you than that which we have preached unto you, let him be accursed."[39]

As a corollary to Matthew's theological transition, he would have quite logically theorized that the Jerusalem church was content with a functionally dead Jesus because she was still clutching the old but now deadly wine of Judaism—and that his own Aramaic Gospel had become a kind of golden calf for a church who should have been making an exodus from a nation under judgment. From a Pauline perspective, it would have appeared that the Jerusalem church was in the very process of returning to the Egypt of a works righteousness, from which they had been just delivered. And Christ was "dead in vain."[40]

---

36 Acts 13:13; 15:36–39.

37 Thereby anticipating John's witness that Jerusalem *was* now, typologically, Egypt (Re 11:8).

38 Which we may see in chapter 24, which seems to treat of the fall of Jerusalem as distinct from the *parousia* (appearing) of Christ at the end of the world.

39 Gal 1:8.

40 2:21. "I do not frustrate the grace of God: for if righteousness come by the law, then Christ is dead in vain."

If this all is true, Matthew would have seen that his first Aramaic Gospel[41] insufficiently addressed the convulsive nature of the divorce between God and the Old Israel, and the ongoing exodus of the lost sheep of Israel from a land of bondage. And he therefore *re-wrote* his Gospel in Greek, the language of Paul's ultimate audience. Among the major restructurings, such as the inclusion of the genealogy, the visit of the Magi, and the temptation in the wilderness, his own calling to be an apostle was also now included. Mark and Luke ensure that the reader understands that it was Matthew who hosted the feast[42] where Christ's own unusual missionary strategy is revealed: "I am not come to call the righteous, but sinners to repentance."[43] Immediately following is the explanation to John's disciples that Christ is the bridegroom – therefore, how can his disciples fast? When we examine the thematic structure of Matthew, we will see that this is not just an indirect, disconnected assertion that Christ is God. This is a deliberate employment of the marriage imagery to set the stage, in the second half of Matthew's Gospel, for the increasingly tense account of the divorce proceedings between God and the Jews.

Mark's Gospel emphasizes the humiliation and suffering that would soon be the lot of every believer in the midst of a hostile Roman community. But Peter, James, and John were no longer suffering. They were being left alone. Paul was suffering. A theme very strongly emphasized in Matthew's re-written Gospel is the ripping and tearing in the psyche of every believer who must leave his very *house and home* for the sake of Christ. To become a Paulinist destroyed the possibility of the Jamesean accommodation with the Jerusalem establishment.

But in practical terms, this would also mean the repudiation of the Mosaic system (eventually Hebrews is written and makes this point uncompromisingly clear). For believers, this meant that they would be mutually repudiated by their family and their community. Matthew and Luke both record Christ's teaching about division in the same household, but Matthew's account is stronger. He says: "a man's *enemies* (**εχθρος**) shall be they of his own household."[44] If this line of

41 We will say more about this later.

42 Mk 2:14–15; Lk 5: 27–29.

43 Mt 9:13.

conjecture is true, when Matthew, son of Alphaeus, walked out of the Jerusalem church to become a Paulinist, he had to stand up to the "pillars of the church": Peter, John, and quite possibly his own cousins, James and Judas, also sons of Alphaeus.

Even without this conjectural hypothesis of emotional catharsis accompanying the production of Matthew's Greek Gospel, the Synoptic documents appear to stand near the conclusion of a violently convulsive theological evolution. In Paul's epistles, many of which appear to be written before the Synoptics,[45] we see the evolutionary convulsion of believers who were grappling with the radical demands of Christ: complete surrender to the spiritual death and rebirth of baptism *in* Christ, humiliation, suffering, and physical death. Paul's religion, and, as we shall see, the Synoptic religion, was a *disproportionate* religion which tore to shreds the old wineskins of religious conservatism, moderation, and accommodation. Somehow, a more flexible conceptual material must be woven into the very fabric of the law in order to contain the fermenting wine of this new covenant. Perhaps Paul's metaphor for resurrection itself was, in part, motivated by this need to transform and transcend, yet contain and not utterly destroy. Second Corinthians elaborates: "For we know that if our earthly house of this tabernacle were dissolved, we have a building of God, an house not made with hands, eternal in the heavens. For in this we groan, earnestly desiring to be clothed upon with our house which is from heaven: If so be that being clothed we shall not be found naked. For we that are in this tabernacle do groan, being burdened: not for that we would be unclothed, but clothed upon, that mortality might be swallowed up of life."[46]

We shall see that this catharsis does not end with Paul's justification by faith (in Christ crucified) apart from works. Paul's crucifixion theology matures into a kind of *incarnational* theology. Paul's understanding seems itself to be progressively "clothed upon" by the understanding that Christ has descended into the depths of creation by

---

44 Mt 10:36.

45 Since there are no apparent, direct quotations from them, except very late: such as 1 Tim 5:18/Lk 10:7 (αξιος…ο εργατης του μισθου αυτου).

46 2 Cor 4:1–4.

means of incarnation, to draw all of creation upwards into an eternal weight of glory. This goes far beyond fixing things broken by Adam's fall. This is a program which reaches back before Adam's rebellion, before Lucifer's rebellion, and before the foundation of the very cosmos. In 1 Corinthians, the dead shall be recreated *incorruptible*.[47]

This theme also clearly appears in Romans, where the entire creation is in the process of redemption from the futility of entropy[48] and winds its way through the "Prison Epistles" (Ephesians, Colossians, Philemon, and Philippians): "Let this mind be in you, which was also in Christ Jesus: Who, being in the form of God, thought it not robbery to be equal with God: But made himself of no reputation, and took upon him the form of a servant, and was made in the likeness of men: And being found in fashion as a man, he humbled himself, and became obedient unto death, even the death on the cross."[49]

This incarnational theology also evolved in John: "And the Word was made flesh, and dwelt among us.[50]" It reaches a sophisticated maturity[51] in Hebrews: "Forasmuch then as the children are partakers of flesh and blood, he also himself likewise took part of the same."[52] And it is endued with full regalia in John's Apocalypse, in which all of creation is renewed and subject to the "King of Kings and Lord of Lords."[53] The immortal, incorruptible, and invisible has intersected with the mortal, corruptible, and visible. This is something far beyond Paul's Christ "crucified for our reconciliation." It is but a prelude to the exaltation of man himself to a place intended at the very thought of creation. Through incarnation, God has descended to the lowest depths of creation in order to transposition her to glory. All creation is taken

47 1 Cor 15:52. "In a moment, in the twinkling of an eye, at the last trump: for the trumpet shall sound, and the dead shall be raised incorruptible, and we shall be changed."

48 Ro 8:20–21. "For the creation was made subject to vanity, not willingly, but by reason of him who hath subjected the same in hope, because the creature itself also shall be delivered from the bondage of corruption into the glorious liberty of the children of God."

49 Phil 2:5–7.

50 Jn 1:14.

51 Heb 6:1a. "Therefore leaving the principles of the doctrine of Christ, let us go on unto perfection…"

52 2:14a. 53 Re 19:16.

up into the body of Christ. Humanity has become worthy of this transposition because it has partaken of the divine nature. Humanity has partaken of the divine nature because the Son emptied himself and took upon himself the nature of humanity and created a fellowship of priests and kings in his own flesh.

If the previous literary scenario is true, Matthew has realized not only that Christ presented himself as a parable, but that all history has been parabolic to what has come upon his own generation. Matthew has realized that Paul is leading the church in a *true* exodus from a bondage of sin and death and has almost certainly written his Gospel as a theological prelude to such a Pauline exodus. Hebrews will soon be written, which will tell of a corresponding "eisodus" (entrance)[54] into the sabbath rest of a righteousness far better than that of Abel and a citizenship in a heavenly city far beyond mortal Adam's dreams.[55] Matthew has called it the kingdom of heaven. Its sign is the sign of Jonas.

54 Heb 10:19 first employs this term in a theological context: "having therefore, brethren, boldness *to enter* into the holiest by the blood of Jesus." Towards the end, Peter understands exactly what this means: "For so an *entrance* shall be ministered unto you abundantly into the everlasting kingdom of our Lord and Savior Jesus Christ" (2 Pe 1:11).

55 1 Cor 15:45. "And so it is written, The first man Adam was made a living soul; the last Adam was made a quickening spirit."

2

The Structure of the Synoptic Gospels

One significant structural characteristic of the Synoptic Gospels is that they all claim to be prologues, or introductions, with limited boundaries. Mark says that his story of the birth and death of Christ is just the beginning: "The beginning of the gospel of Jesus Christ, the Son of God."[1] Matthew emphasizes the same thing: "The book of the generation of Jesus Christ."[2] Luke categorizes his Gospel as that which relates to "...all that Jesus began both to do and teach until the day in which he was taken up."[3] The replacement of Judas invokes the same criteria which delimits the Synoptic genre itself. He must be a man who can witness to all that Jesus did "beginning from the baptism of John, unto that same day that he was taken up from us."[4] A second distinguishing structural feature is that their material is arranged in relatively short narrative or teaching vignettes no more than a few paragraphs in length. These paragraph-long vignettes are called *pericopes* (Greek, "to cut around"). And this is because they look as if

1 Mk 1:1.

2 Mt 1:1.

3 Acts 1:1.

4 1:22.

they have been cut out of a larger context. In each Gospel, these sections are strung together in various ways, but the content of each of the pericopes stays essentially the same. At the end of many teaching pericopes comes an *aphorism*, like the one-line summation of an Aesop's fable or a saying of Confucius. For example, "… render to Caesar the things that are Caesar's and to God the things that are God's."[5] Or: "But many first will be last; and last will be first.[6] These *aphoristic pericope conclusions*, or *APCs*, sometimes wander about each of the Gospels. Sometimes they become attached to a completely different pericope. But they give us a kind of literary landmark when we compare the Synoptic Gospels to each other.

Where did these pericopes come from? Many of the pericopes having to do with the discourses of Jesus must have come from the obvious source: Jesus himself. And one of the most distinguishing features of many of these pericopes is that they are parables. They start off with something such as, "The kingdom of heaven is like…," as in, "The kingdom of heaven is like unto a certain king, which made a marriage for his son."[7] But even many of the non-discursive pericopes have the same general character. For example, the walking on the water pericope and the feeding of the five thousand pericope seem to be parabolic dramatizations.

This idea accords well with Christ's teaching about himself as a prophet. He said that his life was a religious dramatization of his message. For example, when the religious establishment asked Jesus for a sign that he was the Christ of the Old Testament prophecies, he said that no sign would be given except that of Jonas the prophet. Then he explained: "For as Jonas was three days and three nights in the whale's belly; so shall the son of man be three days and three nights in the heart of the earth." [8] As Hosea dramatized his message with symbolic actions, so Christ is in the midst of a symbolic act on both occasions when he alludes to Hosea 6:6 ("I will have mercy, not sacrifice"): the feast at Levi's, at which sinners were present, and the cornfield incident. And like the parables themselves, these dramatizations— the healings, the

5 Mt 22:21.
6 19:30.
7 22:2.
8 12:40.

walking on water, the last supper, etc.— are compartmentalized and not necessarily related to anything that goes before or after.

One can see the literary challenge of this problem in the Synoptics. For authors who seem determined to have a minimum narrator/ reader dialogue, they must constantly editorialize in order to stitch pericopes together. The Synoptic authors all appear to be confined to source material that has been transmitted in pericope form. This accounts, of course, for many of the similarities in the Synoptics. But they also seem to know that the pericope remains an enigma standing by itself. Though they have consciously confined their story to the pericope form, the *way* they stitch them together will bring out their meaning. This also accounts for many of the differences in the Synoptics.

You can easily see this literary stitching. Mark uses "immediately" 50 times. Luke uses "and it came to pass" 50 times. This is roughly once every 23 sentences. Even as a seasoned writer, Luke has difficulty with this literary challenge. Consider the literary transition at 11:14, for example. Here the pericope of the Lord's Prayer (and a little commentary) is stitched together with a pericope about demon possession with a rough, jerky, one-liner connective: "And he was casting out a devil, and it was dumb. And it came to pass, when the devil was gone out, the dumb spoke; and the people wondered." Or consider 16:18, when Luke suddenly brings in, "Whoever divorces his wife and marries another commits adultery." There seems to be no logical explanation for this intrusion within the pericope of the unjust steward before, or within the pericope about Lazarus the beggar after.

Consider Matthew's favorite literary stitching, "and this was to fulfill..." Many of Matthew's references to the Old Testament do not clearly reveal his larger editorial intent beyond a mere generalization that Jesus is the fulfillment of many Old Testament prophecies. The reader says, "So what?" to many of them. For example, what does it mean that a virgin shall be with child (Isaiah 7:14)? What has this to do with the Matthean storyline? Or the call out of Egypt (Hosea 11:1)? Or the slaughter of the innocents (Jeremiah 31:15)? Matthew seems to mention these Old Testament prophecies not to explain but to *maintain* the literary connections between pericopes in his Gospel.

A third distinguishing feature of the Synoptics is that they are enigmatic. The editorial dialogue between author and reader is sparse and somewhat guarded. And this dialogue slowly deteriorates from "let the author explain" to "let the reader understand." And though we are given somewhat of an insiders' view, which often includes private explanatory dialogue between Jesus and the apostles, Mark says that Jesus brokered all of his public teaching by means of parables[9]—some of which were left uninterpreted even for us. And it is clear from the Synoptic template that these parables were not all self-interpreting. To employ a parable as a teaching method is to employ simile. When a simile is working well, with but a few hints on how the parabolic connections should be plotted, the parable could yield fairly complex and illuminating conclusions about the object of instruction. Yet the start-up connections that show the relationship between the parable and the reality are consistently and decidedly sparse.

It is commonly supposed that Jesus taught in parables in order to clarify things. Yet all three Synoptics record that Jesus said that a big part of why he taught in parables was to *obscure* something. Consider, for example: "And the disciples came, and said to him, Why do you speak to them in parables? He answered and said to them, Because it is given to you to know the mysteries of the kingdom of heaven, but to them it is not given."[10] The Synoptic authors do not apologize for this. And in many cases, they *repeat* this mode in their own narratives by including parables without interpretation and narrative vignettes that raise unanswered questions for *us*. It is very often the case, therefore, that due to a lack of editorial interpretation and incomplete clues of context, we as readers find ourselves on the receiving end of a broken simile. The parables themselves are used in such a way as to force the reader to look elsewhere for clarification. Although many of them seem very plain, many others remain an enigma.

---

9 Mk 4:34.
10 Mt 13:10–11.

It is also commonly supposed that the Synoptics—Matthew, Mark, and Luke—are stand-alone theological essays about the good news of Christ. There is indeed considerable good news in *Paul's* epistles, but if the Synoptic Gospels are read without any Pauline preconceptions, their news does not appear unequivocally good. Nor is it clear how the Synoptic material relates to the good news in Paul's epistles. For example, Paul teaches that three things abide: belief, hope, and love.[11] But in the Synoptics, belief (**πιστευω**) occurs only 24 times, and it is unclear what the *object* of such belief should be, except that it seems to be related to Jesus' ability to heal physical infirmity.[12] Paul says that through "hope" that we are saved.[13] Yet in the Synoptics, the verbal form of hope (**ελπιζω**) rarely occurs, and the noun (**ελπις**) is not used at all! The last and "greatest" of Paul's three abiding religious principles fares no better: "love" (**αγαπη**) is mentioned only twice in the Synoptics.[14]

It is odd that the Synoptics are rarely (if at all) quoted elsewhere in the New Testament. But it is also odd that key theological terms so common elsewhere in Paul, who is at least nominally representative of key concepts throughout the whole New Testament, are rarely mentioned, or otherwise vaguely defined, in the Synoptic Gospels. In one of Paul's key summary passages we read, "For the kingdom of God is not meat and drink; but righteousness (**δικαιοσυνη**), and peace

---

11 1 Cor 13:13.

12 Both Mark and Luke include one instance in which "belief" also includes a faith in Jesus' ability to control the forces of nature, but the pericope is offered without theological comment, just a question: "What manner of man is this, that even the wind and the sea obey him?"

13 Ro 8:24.

14 In Matthew, the verbal **αγαπαω** is used seven times, but taken together this amounts to little more than a re-articulation of what has already been said in Leviticus 19:18b: "thou shalt love your neighbor as yourself." It is true that Matthew and Luke both once include Jesus' injunction to "love your enemy," but there is no theological commentary offered for this except that the original commandment in Leviticus is simply too lax for the kind of stringent righteousness that God expects. Seven times Matthew records Jesus as increasing the rigorousness of the law with the introductory "You have heard that it was said…but I say to you..." This injunction to love your enemy, which seems psychologically and morally impossible, is one of them.

(ειρηνη), and joy (χαρα) in the Holy Ghost."[15] On these topics again, the Synoptics are functionally silent. Matthew mentions "righteousness" six times, but with no direct commentary on what it might mean—except to say that unless our righteousness *exceeds* that of the scribes and Pharisees, we will be unfit for that kingdom. This is not good news. It is discouraging, even forbidding news. Mark doesn't mention the term. Luke mentions it once without commentary.

The theme of "peace" in the Synoptics is also a vague problem. The term is only used twice in Matthew, and in one of these uses, Jesus is recorded to have said that he did *not* come to bring peace, but a sword.[16] Mark offers no help, with only one non-theological use. Luke uses the word 13 times, but except for another variant of Jesus bringing "division" not peace, the word is used in a general, ambiguous, and undefined way.

Finally, "joy" is mentioned only 15 times in the Synoptics, but it is again unclear what the believer has to be joyful about. It would be reasonable to suppose that the disciples may have been joyful about "salvation" (σωτηρια), except that this term too is absent from Matthew and Mark. Luke makes three vague references to salvation in Zacharias' prophecy[17] and another passing use by Jesus to Zacchaeus.[18] Luke also has it (σωτηριον) in Simeon's prophecy over the Christ child and in John the Baptist's composite quotation of Isaiah 40:4-5a.[19]

The Synoptics, therefore, include no theological development of the very word "salvation," a concept of the highest importance to the rest of the New Testament. The disciples were said to be joyful at Jesus' appearance after his death, but no more than Elisha was joyful when

---

15 Ro 14:17.

16 Mt 10:34.

17 Lk 1:69.

18 19:9.

19 Compare Lk 3:4–6 with Isaiah: "Every valley shall be exalted, and every mountain and hill shall be made low: and the crooked shall be made straight, and the rough places plain: And the glory of the Lord shall be revealed, and all flesh shall see it together: for the mouth of the Lord hath spoken it." But then John the Baptist tacks on a little bit of Is 52:10: "The Lord hath made bare his holy arm in the eyes of all the nations; and all the ends of the earth shall see the salvation of our God."

Elijah was translated to heaven so long ago.[20] And this is because the disciples' reaction to Jesus' reappearance was confused and complex, which probably explains why the Synoptic Gospels never mention the theological *significance* of Jesus' resurrection.

In fact, when read in isolation, the entire Synoptic storyline leaves the reader with a sinking feeling. The resurrection is just one of many forbidding subjects opened up and left unresolved. The mood becomes bleak. For example, six times Matthew records Jesus' teaching that in the end of the age there will be eternal "weeping and gnashing of teeth"[21] for those who do not find the kingdom. And this is coupled with Jesus' teaching that successfully rich men and those who are righteous by Mosaic standards possess only a *shadow* of the righteousness required of the kingdom. This produced an understandable exasperation in Jesus' own disciples: "When his disciples heard it, they were exceedingly amazed, saying, Who then can be saved?"[22]

---

20 Childhood Sunday School lessons convey a sense of finality when Elijah is carried off. But there is more to the story. At Elijah's "translation," Elisha tears his clothes – a sign of extreme anguish. Besides this, there is considerable doubt as to what is going on. Fifty of Elijah's student prophets offer to send out a search party to look for Elijah. And Elisha *agrees*: they suggested, quite innocently, to Elisha that "maybe the Spirit of the Lord has taken him up, and cast him upon some mountain, or into some valley. And he said, You shall not send. And when they urged him till he was ashamed, he said, Send. They sent therefore fifty men; and they sought three days, but found him not" (2 Kgs 2:16-17). Likewise in the Synoptic Gospels, the reaction to the disappearance of Jesus' body is complicated. For example, in Luke's account, the primary reaction to Jesus' appearance from the grave is *fear*: "And as they thus spoke, Jesus himself stood in the midst of them, and said to them, Peace to you. But they were terrified and affrighted, and supposed that they had seen a spirit" (Lk 24:36-27). When the women meet Jesus in Mt 28:9-10, they are afraid: "Jesus met them, saying, 'All hail.' And they came and held him by the feet, and worshipped him. Then said Jesus unto them, Be not afraid: go tell my brethren that they go into Galilee, and there shall they see me." When the disciples finally see him, they too worship him, but there is also *doubt*: "Then the eleven disciples went away into Galilee, into a mountain where Jesus had appointed them. And when they saw him, they worshipped him: but some doubted" (Mt 28:16–17).

21 Mt 8:12; 13:42; 13:50; 22:13; 24:51; 25:30.

22 19:25.

Taken as a whole, the Synoptic Gospels are a literary tragedy which ends in the humiliating death of its main character.

One man, wanting to join Jesus' religious order, asks Jesus if he could please wait a few days before moving on while he goes to his father's funeral to pay his last respects. But Jesus *denies* his request: "follow me, and let the dead bury their own dead."[23] On another occasion, a woman comes in abject humility to the disciples of Jesus to beg them to heal her daughter. But Jesus *ignores* her. Still desperate, the woman breaks through the inner ring of Jesus' disciples and begs him directly. Jesus still refuses with a seemingly rude remark: "It is not right to take the children's bread, and to throw it to dogs."[24] Jesus finally relents and heals her, but only after she has accepted her inferior cultural status.[25] One day, surrounded with disciples, someone breaks into Jesus' inner circle and tells Jesus that his own *family* are standing on the perimeter of the crowd, trying to tell him something important—we do not know what. Yet Jesus appears to disrespectfully ignore them and says: "My mother and my brethren are these which hear the word of God, and do it."[26]

---

23 Mt 8:22.

24 15:26.

25 Supposing an African American mother forces her way into a doctor's waiting room in the South before the civil rights movement. She persistently begs the receptionist to have the doctor look at her daughter, near death. With reluctance, the doctor emerges from his examination of a rich white women to attend to this disturbance and says, "It is not right to take the bread of medical care and throw it out to niggers." And she says, "Yes sir, Doctor. But even niggers eat the crumbs from the white man's table." Protestant commentators attempt to tone down the problem of Jesus' response by claiming that Jesus didn't say "dog." He said "little dog." But would it have mattered if the doctor had said "nigger," or "little nigger"—that is, with disdain, or with condescension?

26 Lk 8:20–21. When Jesus disappears from his parents' caravan back to Nazareth, his parents, half-crazy with anguish, finally find him in the temple chatting with religious leaders. His exasperated mother says, "Jesus—why are you treating us this way?" His reply? "Why did you seek me? Didn't you know that I must be about my Father's business?" In almost every culture, this kind of behavior in a child deserves a beating. With no other context, a part of us must wonder: is this kind of behavior right?

Jesus seems to be compassionate to the crowds, but he also seems to be something of a megalomaniac. He claimed that of all men who have ever lived, only he has seen and known the Father.[27] He claimed that he could absolve sin.[28] He claimed that unless men put him before every earthly affection—as far above them as love is above hate—and followed him to the death, they were disqualified as true disciples.[29] Far from worldly standards of humility, he claimed that while he was alive, he was the main event: "For you have the poor with you always, and whensoever you will you may do them good: but me you have not always."[30]

He was crucified for blasphemy: for making himself equal with God, for claiming to forgive sin, and for speaking disrespectfully towards the Temple at Jerusalem. In the end, Matthew has a chorus of passersby taunt this megalomaniac with a seemingly reasonable criticism: "You that would destroy the temple and build it in three days, save yourself. If you are the Son of God, come down from the cross."[31]

What sort of editorial behavior is this? If the Synoptics are attempting to build sympathy for their protagonist, why do they record his humiliation as central to the storyline, yet each one of them has a wholly unsubstantial and unsatisfying conclusion? The resurrection endings seem like clumsy additions to a storyline which the Synoptics authors seem determined to leave as an unfinished, enigmatic tragedy. Jesus' encounter with the two disciples on the road to Emmaus perfectly illustrates the disciples' sadness and confusion after the disappearance of the body—despite reliable reports of Jesus' reappearance.

As the resurrected Christ approaches these two and asks them for their analysis of the empirical events to which the Synoptics purposely confine themselves, their response is reasonable perplexity:

---

27 10:22.

28 Mt 9:6.

29 10:37.

30 Mk 14:7.

31 Mt 27:40.

> "And, behold, two of them went that same day to a village called Emmaus, which was from Jerusalem about threescore furlongs. And they talked together of all these things which had happened. And it came to pass, that, while they communed together and reasoned, Jesus himself drew near, and went with them. But their eyes were restrained that they should not know him. And he said unto them, What manner of communications are these that you have one to another, as you walk, and are sad? And the one of them, whose name was Cleopas, answering said unto him, Are you only a stranger in Jerusalem, and have not known the things which are come to pass there in these days? And he said unto them, What things? And they said unto him, Concerning Jesus of Nazareth, which was a prophet mighty in deed and word before God and all the people: And how the chief priests and our rulers delivered him to be condemned to death, and have crucified him. But we trusted that it had been he which should have redeemed Israel: and beside all this, today is the third day since these things were done. Yes, and certain women also of our company made us astonished, which were early at the sepulcher; And when they found not his body, they came, saying, that they had also seen a vision of angels, which said that he was alive. And certain of them which were with us went to the sepulcher, and found it even so as the women had said: but him they saw not.[32]"

At this point Luke tells us that "beginning at Moses and all the prophets, [Jesus] expounded unto them in all the scriptures the things concerning himself." Unfortunately, none of that exposition is recorded in Luke. The Synoptics leave us with the same emptiness of the Emmaus two. For all they knew, Jesus was a prophet as of old, calling his people back to faithfulness to God, who was martyred just like so many of the Old Testament prophets. His resurrection appears to be understood as nothing more significant than the appearance of Moses and Elijah at the Transfiguration or, perhaps, the mysterious translation of Enoch. As is often noted in critical literature, the resurrection itself is not witnessed.

---

32 Lk 24:13–24.

The witness is to 1) an empty tomb and 2) post-resurrectional appearances. But these are offered briefly and without theological comment. Matthew ends with the briefest appearance of Jesus to the women at the grave, and his brief, formal appearance to the eleven at Galilee in which they are given the "Great Commission." Then—nothing. No elaboration. No explanation. If Mark 16:9-20 is discarded due to historical problems,[33] Mark ends with the absence of the body of Jesus and the *announcement* of the resurrection to the women by a strange young man sitting within the tomb. The end.

Judged by the rules of classical rhetoric, the endings of the Synoptics would fail miserably as fitting conclusions to a normal story. A normal story is a page-turner: the reader forges ahead to see what new thing will happen next. Yet the Synoptic Gospels slowly grind to a halt. If Pauline presuppositions about what the resurrection of Christ might mean are rigidly excluded, then the "clumsy" addition of this feature does not really change the structure of the Synoptic storyline. Resurrection comes with no more explanation than walking on water or feeding five thousand. Though we have been conditioned to think of the Synoptic Gospels as telling us some good news about life, in isolation from any other theological commentary they read like an obituary. Miracle workers come; miracles workers go. We are happy for the resurrection of its main character, but the reader is still left with an unrestricted storyline that sounds like something out of Ecclesiastes: "the thing that has been, it is that which shall be; and that which is done is that which shall be done: and there is no new thing under the sun."[34]

---

33 The most reliable early manuscripts and other ancient witnesses do not include this passage. My own analysis shows it to be substantially inconsistent, linguistically, with the rest of Mark.

34 Eccl 1:9.

3

The Form of the Synoptic Gospels

The fact that the modern science of biblical criticism has not produced a believable theory about how the Synoptic Gospels came to be written and how they are related to one another is evidence of a science in crisis. The standard model of biblical criticism freely admits that it cannot find the historical Jesus in these materials.[1] This demonstrates how important these literary theories can be. The modern science of biblical criticism is in crisis because its literary theories are driven by presuppositions that place an enormous restriction upon what is possible to discover. It expects to see nothing more than religious prejudices blown about by ordinary historical processes; therefore, this is exactly what it has found.

All science is plagued by self-imposed restrictions.[2] But if we rule out, from the very beginning, the enormous possibility that God can

---

1 See, for example, Albert Schweitzer's *The Quest for the Historical Jesus*. A more down-to-earth primer on this subject is Charlotte Allen's lucid analysis *The Human Christ* (Free Press, 1998).

2 And the unbelievable theories which follow can only be overturned by what Thomas Kuhn has called "extraordinary research." See particularly his book, *The Structure of Scientific Revolutions* (Chicago: University of Chicago Press, 1962).

speak and act clearly in the midst of human events, then we will have just such an overwhelming restriction on what can be discovered in the New Testament materials. Modern language theory assumes that as soon as God speaks a word about himself in ordinary human language, it necessarily becomes tainted with distortion and falsehood. God may exist, but he is *functionally* silent, it is said, for this reason. The current model of biblical criticism has therefore discovered that the New Testament materials are merely humanistic religious sentiments because its presuppositions rule out the possibility that they can be anything more than this. If we rule out the possibility that God can speak about himself in ordinary human language, then we will hear and see only our *own* religious sentiments.

But if we look back at the process of revelation so-called in Old Testament history, we find no indication that the "word of God" is blunted by the process of being spoken into human culture. We find the prophets claiming that whatever the circumstances, whatever the foibles and failures of men, the "word of the Lord" will not be thwarted—even if false prophets arise claiming to be speaking his word. We see that all of Pharaoh's resistance was employed to say and do precisely what God wanted to say and do through the redemption of his people from bondage. We must therefore confront ordinary historical processes and ordinary human foibles, not uncritically expecting to see how God's revelation might have been blunted, but to see how God may have exploited those very weaknesses of our ordinariness in order to achieve an extraordinarily precise expression of his word. As the *logos* was incarnated without the limitations of sin in human flesh, so might God's disclosure of himself have been incarnated without distortion in human history and human words.

There is overwhelming evidence in the New Testament materials that the apostles only gradually understood the theological implications of what they had seen and heard. Far from merely expressing cultural prejudices, these documents chronicle ideas that have convulsively destroyed dearly held cultural prejudices, tearing apart the fabric of every Jewish psyche that came into contact with them. We see both these themes clearly treated at length in the Synoptic Gospels: the disciples' gradually breaking down an enormous wall of incomprehension, and the emotional convulsiveness of leaving all to follow what has been comprehended.

Paul becomes the figurehead in fully embracing the "scandal" of the cross. We see him transformed from a persecutor of the way of Jesus to its most zealous proponent. Like Moses and Christ, he is immediately driven into the wilderness,[3] and just as with Moses' extended stay in Midian and Christ's three days in the bowels of the earth, we are given no observations of Paul's spiritual convulsion. We see only the results. We see a man embracing a radicalized interpretation of Christ with utter abandonment. And we see his ongoing radicalization in the pages of his own epistles. We see the Jerusalem church grudgingly concede to Paul's "gospel of uncircumcision." We see the chief of the apostles (and Barnabas) chastised by him in righteous indignation for their hypocritical Jewish conservatism. We see Mark chastised and barred from the Pauline missionary team. We see Peter's concession of leadership to him by effectively elevating his writings to the level of "scripture."[4] In the New Testament materials, we do not see figures formed by cultural prejudices. We see figures relentlessly overturning tables, pulling down walls, and casting out cultural prejudices.

Matthew's intent is to describe what had been seen and heard. But Matthew's literary form is a theatrical parable that interprets Jonah the prophet. Matthew not only defines Christ as a kind of Jonah, he defines the apostolic reaction to Christ in terms of Jonah's reaction to his own call. He takes the reader on a guided tour through the same enigmatic circumstances that destroyed the apostles' assumptions about what they saw and heard—leaving them (and us) astonished and bewildered. Jesus did not come to restore the physical kingdom of David. He came to gather the lost sheep of Israel for an exodus from bondage. His Gospel indicates that Matthew believed Paul was not simply an apostle to the uncircumcised, but a type of Moses who had been chosen to deliver the people from a covenant of death to inherit a covenant of life and liberty. The old laws are left behind for a new law of righteousness through faith. And any attempt to mix the two covenants would be like

3 Gal 1:17.
4 2 Pe 3:16.

putting new wine into old bottles: they would burst.

Paul was God's prophet chosen to herald the divorce between God and Israel, foretold by Jeremiah and Jesus, and to proclaim a second marriage between God and the Gentiles, foretold by Hosea,[5] in which the casting away of Israel meant the salvation of the world.[6] The judgment of Israel had come, and that judgment was divorce. Concerning Jesus' teaching on divorce, only Matthew records the one exception: **πορνεια**, illicit sexual intercourse—a sin that everywhere represents spiritual adultery in Old Testament prophetic literature.

Exactly how the Synoptics, particularly Matthew and Mark, express this parable is the subject of later chapters, but here we must establish why understanding the Synoptic literary form is so crucial. If Matthew had no literary form—that is, if Matthew had simply dressed up a meandering, religious do-gooder with the cultural prejudices of the day, we would immediately see this. The standard, scientific model of how the New Testament materials were written assumes this very thing. But the minute you *read* Matthew, the standard model comes crashing to the ground. Matthew's literary form demonstrates to the reader that he has a very good idea of what is important and what is not important.

This is what makes Matthew so different than the pseudographic material that alleges to have come from the same period. In the pseudographic material, legendary stories run together as a confusion of unrelated data. Considering the substance of such a literary event, the critic does not feel a primary, pressing need to ask, "Did this really happen or not?" He simply shrugs his shoulders and asks, "What does it matter if did or it didn't?" There is no literary scheme or form included by the author to discern the sense of it all. Therefore, what is the point of telling such a story? It looks so unlike life— who *knows* if it is mythological or not? This applies to the Gnostic material as well. In the Gospel of Thomas, for example, there is no editorial stitching. There is no form. It is an unrelated list of the sayings of Jesus.

5 Hos 2:23; 1:10.

6 Ro 11:15.

It is an obvious reworking of much earlier material. As a witness to the historical Christ, it is nearly worthless.

Not so with the Synoptic Gospels. The Synoptic authors confidently and consciously take the literary license to create their own literary form, which is unashamedly displayed for all to see. And it does not take a linguistic expert to see that they are using this literary form to say something about Christ. In John, one gets a clear and candid admission about this license to impose such forms upon what has been seen and heard. John says that they believed that the spirit of Christ, who had been promised to them by Christ, was actively *directing* them to impose these forms: "These things understood not his disciples at the first: but when Jesus was glorified, then they remembered that these things were written of him, and that they had done these things to him… Howbeit when he, the Spirit of truth, is come, he will guide you into all truth: for he shall not speak of himself; but whatsoever he shall hear, that shall he speak: and he will show you things to come."[7]

Paul shows this same confidence about his own writing. He is utterly convinced that he received his radical theological form from the Spirit of Christ, not from the depths of his own psychology or from others.[8] The Psalmist says that God speaks through nature and history in a kind of low-level parable. Paul says that in a primary sense, this is all we need: "For the invisible things of him from the creation of the world are clearly seen, being understood by the things that are made, even his eternal power and Godhead..."[9]

The author of Hebrews says that although God has spoken to us in many different ways, God has spoken to us in the last days by his Son, and his Son has spoken to us through his apostles. The Son took upon himself the nature of ordinary flesh to speak of God, and the apostles took upon themselves the nature of an ordinary parable to speak of Christ. Christ told the apostles not to worry about how to say what they had seen and heard, because God would use the weaknesses of their ordinariness to achieve an extraordinarily precise expression of his word. All language is a parable, and all parabolic connections must be

7 Jn 12:16; 16:13.

8 Gal 1:1.

9 Ro 1:20a.

drawn from a temporary world. God would say precisely what he intended through the very imprecision of the parables that were chosen by those whom he had sent.

If the apostles had written independent, formless accounts immediately following the events, there would *be* no "Synoptic problem." The mistaken impression that Christ would physically return in the apostles' lifetime might have suppressed the motive to write such early independent accounts, with the exception of the early Aramaic Matthew. And if the Aramaic Matthew had survived, we probably would have seen just such an uncorrelated mass of inexplicable supernatural phenomena and pious platitudes. Like the Gnostic accounts, the Aramaic Matthew would have also been historically worthless because there would have been no criteria by which to understand it.

But John gives a much stronger reason that no independent account beyond this one example was ever written: John says that it took the apostles a long time to understand what had just happened.[10] John implied that the apostles *themselves* had very little criteria by which to comprehend what they had just seen and heard. Yet the Synoptic Gospels include some confident criteria - in terms of form. And there are *three* confidently different accounts that are obviously aware of each other *and are all using this same form.* The Synoptic author seems completely indifferent to a project of hyper-accurate research for the exact words of Christ. And this is probably because such exactitude would have little utility in the project of telling a parable. This is true even of Luke, who begins his Gospel as follows: "It seemed good to me also, having had perfect understanding of all things from the very first, to write to you..."[11]

The variations in the Synoptic authors' work are all about achieving a context, which gives a parable its proper sense. We can take any given grammatical formula of words, and by altering the context, even just a little, the solution to the formula changes radically. And to emphasize again: the power and meaning of just one word is often bound up in the very *intonation* of that word—something which cannot be directly transmitted in a written record. In our language, we may partially con-

10 Jn 12:16.
11 Lk 1:3.

vey a part of intonation with punctuation. If we put a question mark at the end of a statement, the intonation goes up. When we *italicize* a word, we slow down and emphasize the accented word. But there is no punctuation available to the apostles.

The apostles are not refined storytellers, but they are all very aware of what they are doing. They all know that there has been a slow unfolding of understanding about what has happened to them; and even as they write, they do not understand everything as they ought.[12] The apostles are well aware of the limitations of their own speech: "Likewise the Spirit also helps our infirmities: for we know not what we should pray for [or write] as we ought: but the Spirit itself makes intercession for us with groanings which cannot be uttered."[13] These are ordinary men, but they are not stupid. They know that we, as their readers, will also be conscious of the limitations of their speech. They expect us to make provision for the fact that their own mental furniture—by which their speech must be constricted—has become a crucial part of the context. To precisely express what they saw and heard, they must assemble their expression with the imprecise fragments of their own linguistic equipment. In one sense, what they have seen and heard is inexpressible: "And I knew such a man...How that he was caught up into paradise, and heard unspeakable words, which it is not lawful for a man to utter."[14] Nevertheless they believe that the Spirit of truth will overcome even this limitation: "For it is not you that speak, but the Spirit of your Father which speaks in you."[15]

Therefore it is naïve and unreasonable for us to expect that the apostles should have reconstructed the "exact words" of Christ, when such a formula is insoluble without the contexts that will necessarily be stripped away in such a process. It would be rude of us to believe that the apostles sin when they paraphrase, when the whole project of telling history is a project of paraphrase.[16] Why would we expect from them

12 1 Cor 8:2. "But if any man think that he knows any thing, he knows nothing yet as he ought to know."

13 Ro 8:26.

14 2 Cor 12:3–4.

15 Mt 10:20.

16 History writing—and even modern journalism—is not, like archeology, an act of reconstruction; it is an act of abbreviation, which, itself, is an enormous activity of interpretation. The essence of what has happened is as much tied up with what is left out of a story as it is with what is chosen to be in the story.

what we ourselves cannot do? We would be expecting from them the same kind of dead and motionless formula which the law itself had become. In the giving of the law, no context was given; hence it logically spawned volumes of commentary. It also spawned volumes of human behavior that attempted to conform itself to the letters of those commentaries, while completely ignoring the more demanding spiritual intent behind them. Why should we indict the apostles for presenting a living spirit because we were expecting an historical cadaver?

The differences between multiple accounts of the same dialogues in the Synoptic tradition prove that they are *representational* of Christ's words. The ultra-literalism of the modern world sees this as a "corruption" imposed upon the "actual" words of Christ, yet the apostles all assume this license. A photograph means nothing without the context in which it was taken. Words are meaningless until they are given a context or form. The apostles, each in his own way, construct a representative historical form in which to place Christ's words. As this historical form is parabolic, so his words are also, in many cases, representative. They must be. Human history is not just about words. Nor is it about mechanical "events." It is about the parabolic relationship of each detail of that which is seen and that which is heard to the whole story of humanity.

4

The Parallax of John

The term *Synoptic* ("seen together") is a misleading term. A more appropriate term for three interdependent Gospels from slightly varying perspectives would be *stereoscopic*. In our own vision, the offsetting of our two eyes by three inches floods our minds with depth. We do not have a "Synoptic problem" as much as we have a stereoscopic *solution*. If you have ever tried to reach out and touch something at a distance with one eye closed, you would immediately remember why stereoscopic vision is a blessing, not a curse. Yet even with stereoscopic vision, you cannot tell the distance of a clothesline, because the clothesline is horizontal along the same axis on which our two eyes are displaced. If we could have a third eye displaced on a *vertical* axis, the depth of the clothesline would immediately appear.

And this is exactly what we have in the case of John. Here we have an account which loosely follows the structure of Matthew but uses a completely different literary form. But in John we have more than a sight along the vertical axis of history. John provides something akin to the sense of touch itself: "That which was from the beginning, which we have heard, which we have seen with our eyes, which we have looked upon, and our hands have handled, of the Word of life."[1]

If the Gospel of John is placed alongside the Synoptic Gospels, differences immediately appear. Yet these differences in setting, structure, and form appear only after John is accepted as essentially similar to the Synoptics: his genre, scope, global editorial motive, and theological orientation are, essentially, the same. And although John incorporates many unique narrative elements, they do not significantly outnumber the unique elements that Luke introduces into the midsection of his Gospel (9:51–18:14, not found in Matthew or Mark).[2] Though there is very little synchronous phraseological activity outside the "Passion Week" narrative, John's *vocabulary* correlates very strongly with the Synoptics (see Figure 1).

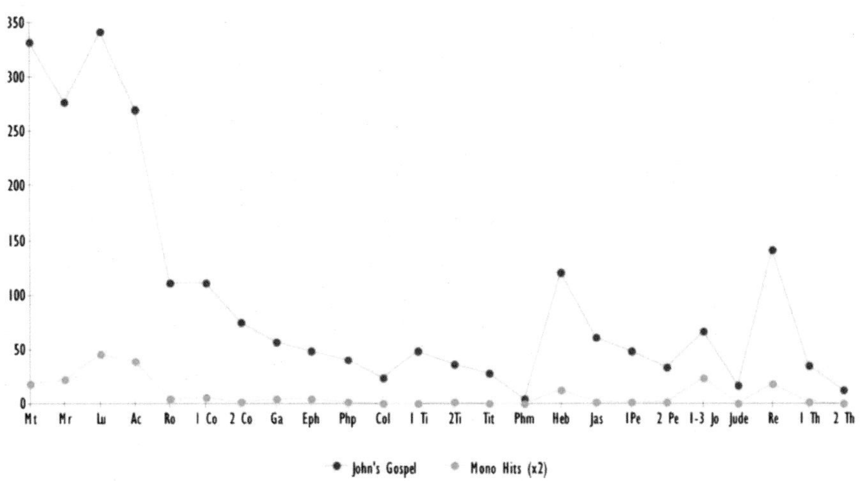

Figure 1. Vocabulary Print of the Gospel of John[3]

The overlap in technical terms required to relate an eyewitness account of the same historical event will certainly account for much of

1 1 Jn 1:1.

2 This includes the stories of the good Samaritan (Lk 10:29–37), the prodigal son (15:11–32), the rich man and Lazarus, the healing of ten lepers (17:11–19), and many others.

3 "Mono Hits" refers to words that John and only one other book share. They are doubled ("x 2") on the chart only for the purposes of making the display clearer.

John's Synoptic correlation, but there is considerable correlation with non-technical terms—words that could easily be employed in any genre. In the following tables, the first column shows the Greek word, its meaning, and the number of times John uses it in his Gospel. The second column lists the number of times the word is used in the **Syn**optics and **Acts**, with which John seems to be closely related.

Table 1. Technical Terms

επαυριον "the next day" 5	12 SYNACTS
περαν "the other side" 8	15 SYN
εκειθεν "thence" 2	26 SYNACTS
απαντησις "meet" 1	6 SYNACTS
πυρετος "fever" 1	5 SYNACTS
εμβαινω "entered" 4	14 SYN
αναπιπτω "sit down" 3	7 SYN
πεντακισχιλιοι "five thousand" 1	5 SYN
ανακειμαι "reclining guests" 3	10 SYN
κλασμα "fragments" 2	7 SYN
κοφινος "baskets" 1	5 SYN
δακτυλος "finger" 3	5 SYN
αναβλεπω "received sight" 3	21 SYNACTS
αυλη "fold" 3	8 SYN; 1 Re
δαιμονιζομαι "demon possessed" 1	12 SYN
μυρον "ointment" 3	9 SYN; 1 Re
κωμη " village" 3	24 SYNACTS
συνεδριον "Sanhedrin" 1	21 SYNACTS
συνανακειμαι "sat at table" 1	8 SYN
ισκαριωτης "Iscariot" 5	6 SYN
πωλος colt" 1	10 SYN
αναπιπτω "sit down" 3	7 SYN
κρανιον "skull" 1	3 SYN

Table 2. Non-Technical Terms

εμβλεπω "looking upon" 2	10 SYNACTS
πριν "before" 3	11 SYNACTS
ποτε "when" 2	14 SYN; 1 Re
κατω "beneath" 3	8 SYNACTS
διαλογιζομαι "consider" 1	14 SYN
διασκορπιζω "dispersed" 1	8 SYNACTS
απαρνεομαι "deny" 1	12 SYN
θαρσεω "be of good cheer" 1	7 SYNACTS
διαμεριζω "parted" 1	10 SYNACTS
πληρης "full" 1	15 SYNACTS; 1 II John
βοαω "cry" 1	9 SYN; 1 Gal
συκη "fig tree" 2	11 SYN; 1 James; 1 Re
ανα "apiece" 1	8 SYN; 2 I Cor; 3 Re
επανω "over" 1	14 SYN; 1 I Cor ; 2 Re
χωλος "lame" 1	13 SYNACTS; 1 Hebrews
υγιης "whole" 7	6 SYNACTS; 1 Titus
ισος "equal" 1	5 SYNACTS; 1 Phil; 1 Re
κατηγορεω "accuse" 2	17 SYNACTS; 1 Ro; 1 Re
ποταμος "floods" 1	6 SYNACTS; I II Cor; 8 Re
εντελλομαι "commanded" 4	11 SYNACTS; 2 Hebrews
λιθοβολεω "stoned" 1	7 SYNACTS; 1 Hebrews
ληστης "thieves" 3	11 SYN; 1 II Cor1013
θυω "kill" 1	10 SYNACTS; 2 I Cor
αλειφω "anoint" 2	5 SYN; 1 James
θνησκω "be dead" 6	6 SYNACTS; 1 I Tim
δειπνον "supper" 4	8 SYN; 2 I Cor1013; 2 Re
σιτος "wheat" 1	10 SYNACTS; 1 I Cor; 2 Re
υστερον "afterwards" 1	10 SYN; 1 Hebrews
απαγω “led away" 2	13 SYNACTS; 1 I Cor
παιδισκη "maiden" 1	7 SYNACTS; 4 Gal
ακανθα "thorns" 1	9 SYN; 1 Hebrews
χιτων "coat" 1	8 SYNACTS; 1 Jude

Though John's prologue is very different from the Synoptic Gospels, which begins with introductory Christological statements and extends through the cleansing of the temple, his Passion Week ending is very much the same. He also begins with the ministry of John the Baptist that is the fulfillment of Isaiah 40:3 - and with the Spirit's descent upon Christ. But except for the feeding of the five thousand, the walking on water, and the confession of Peter, his Gospel does not follow the pericope structure of the Synoptic template.

What is not so obvious is that, like Matthew, John has arranged a teaching block and a healing block of material. Matthew's Aramaic version may, perhaps, have been constructed around a number of extended soliloquies, but Matthew's Greek version delivers the bulk of his teaching in the Sermon on the Mount. John delivers the bulk of his teaching by means of individual interviews, such as the interview with Nicodemus, the interview with John the Baptist, and the interview with the woman at the well.

And John continues to teach by means of an interview-oriented symbol and soliloquy method even in his healing block, especially in the cure of the lame man at Bethesda, the feeding of the five thousand, the cure of the blind man in Jerusalem, and the raising of Lazarus. John, therefore, helps to distinguish the fact that there is not so much a "Synoptic Gospel" and a "Johannine Gospel," but a Synoptic *template* to which John more loosely adheres. It can therefore be said that Matthew, Mark, and Luke are parallel accounts which are sometimes complementary, and that John is a complementary account which is sometimes parallel.

In contrast to the Synoptic template, John is full of editorial dialogue between himself and the reader.[4] John carries many interpretive speeches by Christ, both public and private. The Synoptics claim that only *one* sign will be given by Christ: the sign of Jonas the prophet—specifically, his three-day ordeal in the belly of a fish. John is full of

4 For example, see 2:21–25, 5:18, 6:6, 7:39, 12:16, etc.

"signs." The Synoptics bring misunderstanding into sharp contrast. But John is reluctant to allow misunderstanding to develop. "Then said the Jews, Forty and six years was this temple in building, and will you rear it up in three days? *But he spoke of the temple of his body* [emphasis added]."[5] "When therefore the Lord knew how the Pharisees had heard that Jesus made and baptized more disciples than John—*though Jesus himself baptized not, but his disciples* [emphasis added]."[6]

Whereas the theatrical *timing* of the temple cleansing is all-important as it is related in the Synoptic structure, for John it is ordinary chronological information. Matthew groups data unchronologically to form the sections of his dramatic parable—the composite Sermon on the Mount and the healing block which immediately follows. In John we see interpretive, selective signs and attendant soliloquies that function as theological commentary upon key chronological episodes, which are conspicuously absent in the Synoptics.

The Gospel of John has no thematic turning point in which the disciples come to a crucial understanding of who Jesus is.[7] This is because John is constantly telling us who he is. What other reason would the Synoptic author have for leaving out such important interpretive episodes as the raising of Lazarus and Jesus' friendship with that family, which were so much a part of the historical data presented by John? And why leave out the meeting with Nicodemas? In this meeting we find a key theological truth which every Sunday School child knows: "For God so loved the world, that he gave his only begotten Son, that whosoever believes in him should not perish, but

5 Jn 2:20–21.

6 4:1–2. But sometimes John subtly allows the reader to work things out independently. "Many of the people therefore, when they heard this saying, said, Of a truth this is the Prophet. Others said, This is the Christ. But some said, Shall Christ come out of Galilee? Has not the scripture said, That Christ will come of the seed of David, and out of the town of Bethlehem, where David was?" (7:40–42). John's confidence that the reader will work this out would be very nicely explained by the fact that Matthew and Luke have *already* explained how Jesus came to be born in Bethlehem in considerable detail, and that John is assuming that his reader is already aware of this detail.

7 See Mk 8:27. We have said that John carries the "confession of Peter" which parallels this (see Jn 6:67–69), but it is not so highly dramatized here as it is in the Synoptic template.

have everlasting life."[8] Yet this same truth finds *veiled* expression in multiple parables in the Synoptic Gospels. Why leave out the meeting with the woman at the well, in which Jesus tells the woman that he *is* the Messiah? Why leave out the healing of the man born blind—to which John devotes forty-one sentences? The answer, again, is probably that these scenes were not necessary to the thematic structure of the Synoptic template. In John, Jesus' cleansing of the apostles' feet is pivotal. But in the Synoptics, the cleansing of the temple is pivotal.

John therefore provides a kind of vertical parallax we need to understand the episodic nature of the Synoptic template: the inexorable march to Jerusalem and the great betrayal of Peter. The contrast of John's signs and soliloquies has also stabilized the parabolic structure of the Synoptic template. Through John, we may understand more clearly how the Synoptics variously use the parables of Christ to condition the way we understand the sacrificial death of Christ, the nature of righteousness, and God's terrible divorce from Israel. Though parables are scattered throughout Luke and Mark, they arrive suddenly but more logically, fully and forcefully in Matthew after an extended editorial contrivance of increasing conflict between Jesus and the establishment, which makes them more thematically necessary. Yet the vertical parallax of John helps us to understand that even the parable form is not essential, since this form is entirely absent in his Gospel.

Though a very strong theme embedded in the Synoptic Gospels is apostolic incomprehension, the Synoptics present this idea against the backdrop of a dual audience within the storyline: the twelve apostles - and everyone else. A specific call of twelve apostles, private interpretations of the parables, private teaching, and especially the private viewing of the glory of Christ at the Transfiguration bring the reader of the Synoptics deep inside the inner workings of the so-called messianic secret. Unlike the Synoptics, John does not clearly distinguish these two audiences for editorial dialogue. Since John has omitted this literary device,[9] he must make a lengthy transition during his extended

8 Jn 3:16.

9 18:20. "Jesus answered him, I spoke openly to the world; I ever taught in the synagogue, and in the temple, whither the Jews always resort; and in secret have

Last Supper, table-talk section (13:1–16:33) - from the audience of "the Jews" to the audience of his beloved followers. Of the three Synoptics, the sudden arrival of parables in Matthew (13:1) seems to more clearly create this "dual-audience" characteristic, which more directly pushes the reader to identify more closely with the incomprehension of the apostles themselves. Since Luke seems to more loosely follow the dual-audience device, he encounters the same editorial difficulty as John and must use Peter to help sort things out: "Then Peter said unto him, Lord, do you speak this parable to us, or to all?"[10] In Matthew, the reader feels more pressure to decide which audience he belongs to: those who have eyes to see or those who do not. It is here that the reader feels more keenly the editorial commentary's deterioration from "let the author explain" to "let the reader understand."

The parallax of John, therefore, helps to distinguish that this dual-audience characteristic is also not absolutely essential to telling the Gospel. Mark, for example, seems unable to bear the full brunt of the literary pressure which Matthew allows. By means of his artful elaborations in pericopes that deal specifically with the nature of belief, Mark, seemingly betraying his sympathy with the reader, relieves much of the enigmatic tension that this literary device creates. He knows what the reader is feeling: "And immediately the father of the child cried out, and said with tears, Lord, I believe; help my unbelief!"[11]

One would have supposed that this tortured belief would have been put into the mouth of one of the apostles in the inner circle. But Mark accentuates the apostles' lack of belief. In Mark, examples of belief, when they occur, almost always come *outside* the apostolic circle. It is true that in the Synoptic template, Peter appears to be making a stupendous confession about the Sonship of Christ in the middle of the story. Yet at the end, his repudiation of Christ is catastrophic. In Mark, Peter is not so much the typological traitor as he is the universal emblem of unbelief.

In the Synoptic template, the healing of a blind man is left in its parabolic, suggestive state; that is, it is easy for the reader to suspect that Matthew, for example, believes that Jesus is using this healing as

I said nothing."

10 Lk 12:41.

11 Mk 9:24.

as representation of Israel's blindness. But John leaves no doubt. He reworks the blind man healing episode to achieve an irony that even a child can understand. John extracts the ironic conclusions for us twice: once in the mouth of the blind man; once in the mouth of Christ: "The man answered and said to them, 'Why herein is a marvelous thing, that you do not know from whence he is, and yet he has opened my eyes'...Jesus said to them, 'If you were blind, you would have no sin: but that you now say, 'we see'; therefore your sin remains.'"[12]

The irony of this kind of blindness occurs repeatedly in John. In the Nicodemus pericope, Jesus asks, "You are a teacher in Israel and you do not understand these things?"[13] At the woman at the well episode, John again toys with his prey: "The woman answered and said, 'I have no husband.' Jesus said to her, 'You have well said, I have no husband: For you have had five husbands; and he who you now have is not your husband: in that you have said truly.'"[14] Though the Synoptic template lacks the persistent theological commentary of John, Matthew is filled with both implicit and explicit typological illumination, which understands the history of the Jews as a mere foreshadowing of the drama of Christ. Matthew's contrived Sermon on the Mount more intently exhibits an implicit allusion to the giving of the law by Moses. The central thesis of the Synoptic template—that the significance of Jesus' death is somehow parabolically illustrated by the prophetic life of Jonah the prophet— is reflected with considerably less intensity in Luke, and the thesis statement itself is lacking in Mark. The inexorable march to Jerusalem to encounter a Jonah-like, sacrificial death has itself been achieved by a kind of chronological paraphrase consistent with the method by which the present structure of Matthew was itself contrived. Without John's chronology of the temple clearing, we would never know that Matthew has taken some chronological liberties.

John is twelve chapters of sign/soliloquy introduction to an extended section of table-talk with Christ. John shadows the Synoptic

12 Jn 9:30, 41.
13 3:10.
14 4:17–18.

template, but because it contains so much theological commentary, John appears also to be a kind of *hybrid* genre, which also combines some of the features of Paul's more theological letters. In contrast, Matthew is an episodic, dramatic parable that follows the Son of Man through a reenactment of the human drama—the Eden-like temptation, the flight to Midian, the exodus from Egypt, the giving of the law, the fall and disgrace of Israel (in the person of Peter), the return of King David's heir in triumphal entry, and the sacrifice of Jonah for the salvation of the world.

Thus John's "vertical" perspective helps to distinguish the setting, structure, and form of the Synoptic template. But if the Synoptic Gospels are variations upon a template, and that template has originated substantially *within* the Synoptic tradition, who originated it?

5

The Interrelationship of the Synoptic Gospels

The standard theory of biblical criticism claims that Mark wrote first. Matthew and Luke then follow Mark and add a great deal of teaching material. As evidence for Marcan primacy, this standard model claims that Mark became a kind of secretary to Peter and recorded his "memoirs," based upon Papias' comment that Mark was the "interpreter" of Peter. But Mark's secretarial role, if any, seems to have occurred very late—towards the end of Peter's career in Rome.[1]

Just as we saw the anguished concern in Paul's later writing about "grievous wolves" entering the flock after his decease,[2] so too we can see that same anguish in Peter's concern for false prophets which will "bring in damnable heresies" after his decease.[3] When Peter wrote this, the Pauline letters were in circulation, yet they were undefended against those "unlearned and unstable who wrest them, as they do also the other

1 "The church that is at Babylon, elected together with you, salutes you; and so does Mark my son" (1 Pe 5:13).

2 Acts 20:29. "For I know this, that after my departing shall grievous wolves enter in among you, not sparing the flock."

3 2 Pe 2:1.

scriptures, unto their own destruction."[4] Peter's first epistle had been written by Silvanus,[5] a missionary protégé to Paul, who likely became Peter's secretary after Paul's death. Mark, whom Paul requested Timothy to bring with him to his cell in Rome[6] (probably from Paul's diocesan seat at Ephesus), arrives in Rome to witness Paul's end, and then rejoins Peter who has also come to Rome and is now possibly in chains.[7] Early in Peter's second epistle, he indicates that his purpose is "to endeavor that you [his congregation] may be able after my decease to have these things always in remembrance … the power and coming of our Lord Jesus Christ."[8]

And this is, after all, what Mark's Gospel is about. Perhaps this is why Mark is constantly using the historical present[9] to portray the events of Christ's visitation. A child uses the historical present unconsciously because while he tells the story of what happened, it happens all over again in his mind and he is once again present. But a seasoned author uses the historical present to bring his audience closer to things which are long past. Did Peter succeed in getting the good news of Christ's visitation on parchment by the hand of Mark before he died? The circumstantial evidence says no. And the linguistic evidence (fully examined in a later chapter) demonstrates that Mark is almost *entirely* a synthesis of the data which Matthew and Luke present and shows very little literary dependence on any other source but these two writers. Yet, though Peter may not have been directly able to put his people in remembrance of the power and coming of the Lord Jesus, he may have extracted a promise from Mark to do so. And in the act of doing so, Mark may very well have embedded an apologetic for the late conversion of Peter, thus functionally becoming the "interpreter" of Peter.

The standard model of biblical criticism has attempted to account for the common teaching material in Matthew and Luke omitted by

4 2 Pe 3:16.

5 1 Pe 5:12.

6 2 Tm 4:11.

7 1 Pe 5:13.

8 2 Pe 1:16.

9 The historical present refers to the employment of the present tense when narrating past events.

Mark by assuming a "teachings" source document called "Q."[10] The idea behind such a document is not without merit. Indeed, Matthew's Aramaic version is just this sort of document. Such a teachings compendium would likely emerge early since merely recording the sayings makes no theological demands upon their recorder. But it would be difficult to imagine a community setting and an author other than Peter that could produce such a "sayings" document with sufficient authority to compel the level of textual agreement we see between an apostle (Matthew) and a well-known and widely respected secretary to the Apostle Paul (Luke). And it is difficult to imagine how Mark, a non-apostle and still a very young man, for whom such an early protégé-like association with Peter seems unlikely, could have written *before* the formation of such a primitive collection. If there were any Q document, it must not have been widely circulated outside the Jerusalem enclave, since Paul does not seem even to be aware of the apparently more polished Synoptic tradition until the early 60s, when he apparently quotes one of its APCs: "The laborer is worthy of his reward."[11]

Besides this, the theory of a teaching *logia* called "Q" conjures up the image of a relatively random collection of independent moral maxims. But many of these so-called teaching pericopes are not about disconnected moral principles but are teachings *about Christ*, many of them alleged to be from his own mouth. For example, the pericopes on the nature of discipleship, division in households, the blessedness of the disciples, and the lost sheep – these are all unintelligible as moral platitudes apart from how they relate to Christ. The standard model asks: "where did Matthew and Luke get their teaching material?" Perhaps a better question would be: why does Mark omit so much of it, after having acknowledged Jesus as an important teacher even more emphatically than Matthew?

For example, Mark has the disciples call Jesus "teacher" four times. In Matthew, the disciples never address him as teacher. Matthew, editorially, refers to Jesus as teacher eight times. Mark does this fourteen times. As Mark sets up his narrative for the feeding of the five thousand, he says that Jesus is moved with compassion for the multi-

10 This comes from the German *quelle,* meaning "source."
11 1 Tim 5:18b.

tudes because they were as sheep not having a shepherd. Matthew too tell us that Jesus is moved with compassion on this very occasion. So what does Jesus do to alleviate the situation upon which his compassion is fixed? Matthew says, "He healed their sick.[12]" Yet Mark says, "And he began to teach them many things."[13] In the pivotal confession of Peter, Matthew says that Jesus now begins to "show" his disciples that he must go to Jerusalem to suffer.[14] But Mark says, "And he began to *teach* them [emphasis added]."[15] In the three-way temple cleansing pericope, Mark departs from Matthew and Luke to say that Jesus "*taught,* saying, is it not written… [emphasis added]"[16]

In a very visible editorial narrative stitch, Mark says that Jesus was *habitually* teaching the people: "And he arose from thence, and came into the coasts of Judea by the farther side of Jordan: and the people resort unto him again; and, as he was accustomed, he taught them again."[17] How does Matthew's account read? "And it came to pass, when Jesus had finished these sayings, he departed from Galilee, and came into the coasts of Judea beyond Jordan; And great multitudes followed him; and he healed them there."[18] Mark repeats four times that what astonished the people most about Christ was his *teaching,*[19] and he uses the verb "to teach" seventeen times versus Matthew's thirteen times. However, Matthew contains more teaching *content,* despite the fact that he mentions healing proportionately more than Mark.[20] Mark is the reverse; he mentions teaching more often but has more healing

12 Mt 14:14.

13 Mk 6:34.

14 Mt 16:21.

15 Mk 8:31. 16 11:17. 17 10:1. 18 Mt 19:2.

19 "And they were astonished at his doctrine for he taught them as one that had authority, and not as the scribes" (1:22). "And when the Sabbath day was come, he began to teach in the synagogue: and many hearing him were astonished" (6:2). "And they were astonished out of measure, saying among themselves, Who then can be saved?" (10:26). "And the scribes and chief priests heard it, and sought how they might destroy him: for they feared him, because all the people was astonished at his doctrine" (11:18).

20 Matthew repeats this phrase five times: και εθεραπευσεν αυτους (and he healed them).

content. This narrative emphasis seems the very opposite of what one might expect.

Therefore let it no longer be said that Mark has less regard for Christ's teaching ministry than do Matthew and Luke. This is not true. Mark has *more* regard for this teaching ministry than do Matthew and Luke. It seems constantly on Mark's mind. When the disciples are seemingly overcome by a storm at sea, they wake Jesus and plead for help. In Matthew, they say, "Lord, save us!" In Luke they say, "Master, we perish!" In Mark, they say, "*Teacher!* Don't you care that we perish?! [emphasis added]" Some other reason for Mark's omitting a mass of teaching material must therefore be sought. If Mark's Gospel is a relatively late synthesis of Matthew and Luke (and even John), then perhaps Mark omitted so much of the Synoptic teaching material because school was, simply, out of session. Perhaps the apostolic community was already well-acquainted with this new Torah-like teaching material.

Much like Mark, John gives scant room to this new "sayings" compendium and concentrates on anchoring the interregnum Christ into the world in which we live. John begins his Gospel, in many ways, where Matthew's ends: at the supper table, lying on Jesus' breast. John has Jesus enter Jerusalem shortly after the *middle* of his gospel. And for what purpose so early? Not for the symbolic cup and bread of Matthew's Last Supper, but for the table talk itself. And it is talk of a relationship with Christ that has far advanced beyond the relationship presumed in the Sermon on the Mount.

Mark begins his Gospel where John ends: "Let us rise and go."[21] The table talk of John is over in Mark. The final examination has arrived. It is time to put all the moral training gained from the New Torah to the test. It is time to *endure* the test. It is time for decision. It is time for courage. It is time to act upon belief. And this is something no teacher can teach. Fear brings paralysis; Mark writes about the Lord of action in the face of fear. Mark's excessive use of the historical present is, quite possibly, also due to the fact that the history of Christ's typological trial is *now* being presented to his church. While emphasizing the teaching role of Jesus, even more so than Matthew, Mark nevertheless retains a mere sketch of the New Torah, because the time for teaching is over for

21 Jn 14:27.

many of his flock. The immediacy of their coming trial is linked with the immediacy of his Gospel, which invokes "immediately" (**ευθεως**) forty times. Mark is apparently attempting, emotionally, to compress forty years (from the 30s to the 70s) in order to stitch together "back then" with "right now."

If Mark was written late, it may be presumed that Mark's congregation would soon be "salted with fire"[22]—perhaps an allusion to the coming Roman persecution. Yet Mark admonishes, "Have salt in yourselves." Every good chef knows that salt is not so much an additive as it is a catalytic agent. It releases the flavor of the food which is salted. And it also acts as a connective between the different foods that are blended in the same pot. In vain we tediously look between the lines of Mark for solutions to some burning theological controversy. We may invent them. But they will be figments of our own imagination. The linguistic evidence that is presented in the next section will show that Mark is both a conservative follower and a creative craftsman in blending disparate accounts. His gospel is the salty connective between Matthew and Luke. Much of the potatoes and carrots have been set aside, because now it is time to eat meat. Mark is feeding his congregation the Word of Christ, and that word is … suffering.

And Jesus, of course, knows what his congregation must go through. We will see Mark's fast-paced Gospel pause to include relatively more material again and again to demonstrate this. He takes the time to record the conversion of one of the lawyers even after Jesus enters Jerusalem. For Matthew's intense argument, it would have been unthinkable to include this detail. Mark takes the time to say that Jesus looked upon the rich young ruler "and loved him."[23] He takes the time to use just the right word when Jesus takes up the children: he "enfolds them into his arms."[24] He creates the atmosphere of Christ's very presence. Specifically, he creates the smell of the sacrifice of Christ. Like Salome, Mark anoints Matthew's Jonas Genre with sweet spices, that its aroma might penetrate every thought before the Roman Christians of Mark's congregation lose their own lives in a baptism of death. He ends his Gospel on a note of fear because his congregation is now looking

22 Mk 9:49-50.

23 10:21.

24 10:16.

into a gospel outcome that can have no happy ending.

It is often erroneously claimed that many three-way synchronous passages show signs that Matthew and Luke have elaborated upon the shorter Mark. This is simply not correct; the reverse is true. Except for Matthew's "typological illumination," in which he quotes Old Testament examples to illustrate an event's significance,[25] when there is elaboration in synchronous passages, Mark is the elaborator. How can this be, if Mark's Gospel is so much shorter than Matthew's? Because Mark has not only left out teaching material, he has also left out a prologue and much of the temptation of Christ in the wilderness. In all, Mark has left out thirty-eight Synoptic sections, fourteen of which are *not* teaching pericopes.

Mark is also much more efficient in covering the same literary territory with fewer words than Matthew. Though Marcan Greek sometimes *seems* crude, it is much more sophisticated than Matthew's. Mark's words are bigger. While Matthew and Luke's average word length are 5.05 and 5.07 characters per word respectively, Mark's average word length is 5.14[26] characters per word. Secondly, Mark is more densely packed with words. Mark starts off with more new words per verse and rarely drops below the pace of Matthew. In terms of the number of raw words, the length of Mark equals the length of Matthew *minus* the length of Romans. But if we compare the "significant word vocabulary" of Mark and Matthew—that is, words that are used 50 times or less—we find that Mark's significant word vocabulary is 94% as large as Matthew's! In other words, with 38% fewer words, Mark covers approximately the same vocabulary territory as Matthew.

Said another way: in the same number of sentences, Mark will use 34% more significant words than Matthew and 25% more words than Luke. This is particularly noteworthy in that many of Matthew and Luke's new words have more to do with technical terms associated with parables that Mark omits than with the ordinary business of editorial diction. It is true that Mark has a number of unusual constructions

---

25 That is, Matthew seems to see characters and historical themes portrayed in the Old Testament documents as mere prototypes or foreshadowings of the drama of Christ's life and of the age which, he appears to believe, has begun with Christ.

26 This length is consistent throughout his Gospel.

which appear awkward or clumsy. But so does *The Adventures of Huckleberry Finn*. Mark's "clumsiness" results from his intentionally coarser language, his use of ellipsis,[27] his use of the historical present, his excessive use of "immediately" as a one-word editorial stitch, and the contrasting effect of his more dense verbiage.

From a literary standpoint, Mark has acres of space in which to elaborate. But why does Mark decide to elaborate in these fairly highly structured pericopes? In almost every example of Marcan elaboration, he emphasizes Jesus' healing power and our complex response of belief concerning this power, especially in the context of fear. Every one of these pericope elaborations deals with Jesus' complete power to cure that which afflicts the individual and that which no power on earth can cure: leprosy, demon possession, death, hunger, epilepsy, blindness. In this way, Mark answers the questions of his congregation as if they were John the Baptist's doubtful questions from prison: "Is this really the one, or should we look for another?" Although Mark does not include the pericope of John's question to Jesus,[28] his editorial emphasis in his expanded pericopes *is his answer*: "This is what I [or my source] saw: 'The blind receive their sight, and the lame walk, the lepers are cleansed, and the deaf hear, the dead are raised up, and the poor have the gospel preached to them.'"[29]

We are no longer thinking about what Matthew and Luke are *not* doing. We now are attempting to understand what Mark *is* doing and how this purpose operates within the parameters of Matthew's presumed template. Mark emphasizes the *compassion and power of Christ to heal us despite our equivocating response to him*. In a Gospel which has left out 38 sections of Matthew, making it 38% shorter, Mark takes the pericope of Jairus' daughter and a woman's faith[30] and tremendously expands it. It is not only 270% longer than Matthew's account; if its *relative* length were expressed in Matthean standards, we would have a pericope of 600 words: 435% longer than Matthew! This stupendous ex-

27 Or omission.
28 Mt 11:1–6.
29 11:5.
30 Mk 5:21–43.

pansion elaborates upon the compassion and power of Christ and our equivocating response to him.

Surely Mark is attempting something very similar to what John has achieved in his Gospel. John's Gospel is about believing that Christ is the Son of the living God and abiding *in* him. John uses seven "signs" to authenticate the person of Christ, and there is no more convincing sign in the New Testament than the raising of Lazarus from the dead. In this story, this family is of special, affectionate importance to Jesus. John makes no secret of this. The weight of Mary's suffering in the midst of her incomprehension is excruciating. It is incomprehensible to think that John has not intentionally created this literary tension. Jesus wept. But his weeping was not entirely like ours. He was sorrowful, troubled, and *angry*. He was angry for what sin had done to his poor, favorite little lamb. But he is troubled and sorrowful because Martha and then Mary have both equivocated on the very brink of belief. And this, Mark also seems to say, is what we really want to know. We want to know what Jesus thinks and feels—and what he will do—about our equivocation.

In contrast, when we read Matthew's account of Jairus' daughter and a woman's faith, we are not sure what Jesus thinks or feels. From the flow of Matthew, we know that Jesus can do these sorts of things already. In fact, through narrative ellipsis, Mark and Luke assume that we remember that the woman was healed, but Matthew's more terse account will brook no omission. He must assure us with the facts: "And the woman was made whole from that hour."[31] But what the individual reader really wants to know is this: is this Gospel something that only happens to these historically faceless, lucky souls, or can it really happen to me? Will he heal *me*? What must I do to be healed? Will Jesus accept my wretched, pitiful belief? Listening to James' lecture on faulty, double-minded faith, how can we be sure?

Yet if I can know the look upon his face or the intonation of his words, I can then know with a surety in my own soul that Jesus *does* accept me and that his healing *can* happen to me. This is exactly what Mark does. Just as John chooses seven signs to capture the pathos of

31 Mt 9:22b.

what is going on, Mark chooses seven healing events.[32] By taking the time and the space to create the *atmosphere* of these healing events, he puts a true face on the woman with an issue of blood, and he puts true blood into the very words of Christ. Jesus asks, "Why do you make a tumult and weep?" "I'm here now." "Do not fear, only believe." "How can the children of the bridechamber be distraught when the bridegroom is present?" At the end of Matthew's Gospel, Jesus says in the historical present, "I am with you until the end of the age."[33] Mark adopts this use as the distinguishing tense of his Gospel. And Mark will take the anti-type of Peter (which Matthew, presumably, has created) and make him typological for our complex response of belief, apart from the works of which James is so apparently proud. Mark will prove to us that if Jesus will accept Peter's fearful, equivocating, disloyal response, then he will accept us.

Again, the point of this line of reasoning is not to arrive at an academic conclusion about the date and sources of Mark. The purpose of this line of reasoning is to definitively establish (if it is possible) the *perspective* of Mark so that we can understand with confidence his intent. For if Matthew and Luke, two of the most powerful men in the early church, are using Mark as a source, and upon examining his extended pericopes say, "This is a waste—all this about what Jesus thinks and feels is just opinion and can be exchanged for a teaching pericope," then we won't have any confidence in it, either. If Matthew and Luke gloss over these expansions as so much sentimental salt, won't we be tempted to do the same? But if Mark is *following* Matthew and Luke, and so far we have every indication that he is, then we no longer have data about what *isn't* important to Matthew and Luke. We now have data about what *is* important to Mark.

If we are right about Mark, then in these expanded pericopes, Mark is practically shouting to us, "Are you looking for my perspective? Well, here it is. I am taking great liberties in expanding these pericopes. My Gospel is not insider information about what, ex-

32 Jesus in the synagogue at Capernaum (Mk 1:21–28), the healing of Peter's mother-in-law (Mk 1:29–31), the healing of a leper (Mk 1:40–45), the Gerasene demoniac (Mk 5:1–20), Jairus' daughter and a woman's faith (Mk 5:21–43), an epileptic boy healed (Mk 9:14–29), and the healing of blind Bartimaeus (10:46–52).

33 Mt 28:20.

actly, Peter spoke to the young girl in the upper room. Peter made no secret about all his 'privileged' knowledge of the inner three. He has already disseminated this knowledge far and wide in the Christian church. You don't need me for this knowledge. But you do need me to put you in *remembrance* of these things. These accounts tend to drift out of the mind the minute they are left unattended and un-exercised. But persecution and suffering is an exercise that calls up the very essence of why this particular story was originally part of the Gospel. You have forgotten the very essence of Jesus' power over disease and death. Your mind retains these accounts as theological abstractions. It is my commission from Peter to put you in remembrance of these things. So I will tell this pericope again. My way. I will try to make it hard to forget the essence of Christ's compassion and power over death—even at the threshold of your own death. Half-hearted attachments to theological abstractions will do you no good in the amphitheater when they are overcome by terror. They certainly didn't work for Peter in the courtyard, and they won't work for you. So I want you to read closely."

And if we do read closely, we will see very little evidence that Mark has written first. The evidence all runs in the opposite direction: that Mark has written last. An early date for Mark doesn't even fit the editorial dialogue of Mark. Mark explains to his audience why the Jews are always washing their hands.[34] Although Abraham is mentioned thirty times in the Gospels, only one of those times is in Mark, since his audience was not as conversant with Abraham's patriarchal status. His reference to his one-time fellow citizens as **Ιεροσολυμιτης** (Jerusalem-ites)[35] demonstrates his emotional distance from the Jews. **ο εστι** ("which is") is a note of editorial translation or explanation used only by Mark. He uses it to explain Aramaisms: *boanerges*,[36] *corban*,[37] *ephpha-*

---

34 Mk 7:3–4. "For the Pharisees, and all the Jews, except they wash their hands oft, eat not, holding the tradition of the elders. And when they come from the market, except they wash, they eat not. And many other things there be, which they have received to hold, as the washing of cups, and pots, brasen vessels, and of tables."

35 1:5.

36 Mk 3:17.

37 7:11.

tha,[38] and the fairly basic Jewish concept of **παρασκευη**, "the day before the Sabbath."[39] Mark explains how many *quadrans* (Latin) a *lepton* (Greek) is worth.[40] Only Mark uses **κεντυριων** (a Latin loanword) for the **εκατονταρχης** (centurion) at the crucifixion. Though Matthew and John use **πραιτωριον** without comment, Mark finds it necessary to explain that the hall into which Jesus was taken was indeed called the "Praetorium"—not that his readership was unfamiliar with the word, but that they were unfamiliar with how this familiar term was used in foreign districts (i.e., Palestine). But a work explaining Jewish terms surely could not have occurred before the transition to Gentile Christianity.

Mark's rupture with Paul occurs in approximately 50 A.D.— quite possibly over taking the gospel unreservedly to the Gentiles. Yet Paul and Mark have apparently reconciled at least by 62 A.D. It is extremely unlikely that Mark was written before such a reconciliation. Though Paul is still calling Mark a member of the circumcision party as late as the Roman imprisonment,[41] if we are to judge by the editorial evidence above, this is a Gospel to the uncircumcised. But why would a member of the Judaizing party be writing a Gospel to the uncircumcised? The Aramaisms in Mark are there because Mark is a Jew. But it may very well be that Mark's Latinisms[42] appear *because he is now head of the Roman congregation* that he has inherited from Peter. Peter's gospel of the circumcised[43] is now, perhaps, moot.

So then, hypothetically, let us assume that Matthew's Gospel is familiar to Mark's audience. Paul has died and Mark has seen Paul's leadership entourage disintegrate "because they have loved this present world."[44] And Mark has long been thinking of how he had fail-

38 7:35.

39 15:42.

40 12:42.

41 Col 4:10–11.

42 This must also include subtle indicators such as Mark's word choice for "purple." **πορφυρα**, a purple of Latin origin, was derived from fish, and Mark uses it to describe the robe in which Jesus was mocked, whereas Matthew uses **κοκκινος**, a purple derived from grain by the Jews of Palestine.

43 Gal 2:7.

44 2 Tm 4:10.

ed to see the bigger picture of God tearing away the kingdom from the Jews and giving it to the Gentiles through the messianic figure of Paul.[45] And he may have seen that he had failed Paul, as his master Peter had failed Christ. Peter himself had eventually found his end in Rome, after his long struggle with the truth to which Paul had so unambiguously submitted. If Peter is now dead, Mark would be seeing the threat of false teachers, ignorance, worldliness, lack of perseverance, and the Roman congregation's complete underestimation of the fiery trial which would soon overtake them—which Peter foresaw in his two epistles.

Nero had burned Rome to presage the coming slaughter of innocents. Burning Christians had already begun to light up Nero's garden parties. The futile rebellion against Rome had already begun in Palestine. John's Gospel, written as early as 61 A.D.,[46] does not adequately address the rapidly deteriorating existential situation of the church (which is redressed by the book of Revelation). Armed with the template of Matthew, the supplementary material of Luke, and oral information from various sources, Mark would have had tremendous impetus to write. Even John's pastoral imperative — to "abide" in Christ—would have been now dated. Mark's Gospel must now address the more pressing need for an unwavering, courageous faith of *action* and the moral imperative of submission to humiliation.

And this humiliation will go far beyond the humiliation we see in Paul's earlier books, like 1 and 2 Thessalonians, which refer to a ghetto created for Jews who had embraced the Pauline gospel. A Christian must now prepare his face to be spat upon in a new way. Mark's Gospel is not about an impossible ideal of Christian behavior. It is about the very essence of what following Christ involves. Christians must submit

---

45 Even in relating the husbandmen parable, Mark is vague—still reluctant to face the finality of this historical reality. He says that "God will come and destroy the husbandmen, and will give the vineyard unto others" (Mk 12:9). Luke adds that "and whosoever shall fall on this stone shall be broken: but on whomsoever it shall fall, it will grind him to powder" (Lk 20:18). Matthew, however, is unequivocal and adds further: "Therefore say I unto you, The kingdom of God shall be taken from you, and given to a nation bringing forth the fruits thereof" (Mt 21:43).

46 The dating of John will be addressed in the third book of this series, *A Vesture Dipped in Blood.*

to Jesus' washing their feet, yes. But now Christians must submit to Christ spitting into their eyes.[47] Only by losing their lives in abject humiliation will Christians be ready for Christ to lay upon their eyes the hands of power.

Mark's Gospel has an intensity and pathos not found in Matthew. Mark's perspective is suffering. Teachings about "how should we then live," so characteristic of the New Torah, have significantly diminished relevance to a Christian who will soon be looking down the throat of a lion. Mark is also about how *not* to follow Christ. He omits the small measure of Peter's success in taking his few faithful steps on the water.[48] He omits how the church is built upon the rock of the confession of Peter that Matthew records,[49] because Peter represents the weakness of human flesh under the true pressure of living and confessing the obedient life. Peter was willing to side with Christ – but only in an imaginary scene of all men denying him. But when the true test came, Peter couldn't even stay awake for an hour while Christ was tried - or to be a little chilly for an hour or so while Christ was tried - or to leave his comfortable, conservative, routine life as a fisherman to feed Christ's sheep when they were tried. Mark's Gospel illustrates how to follow Christ under pressure. Matthew's parable of the ten virgins creates a *sense* of urgency in the soul. In Mark's Gospel, such a parable is entirely superfluous because the urgency of having the lamp lit is *now*.

Matthew, Hebrews, and the Pauline epistles have all indicated how the Jewish community persecuted, rejected, humiliated, marginalized, ostracized, and randomly killed Christians. Now an even greater menace looms on the horizon. It is Rome. For Matthew, the forty-day temptation in the wilderness is reminiscent of Israel's wandering in the desert. It symbolizes not only the church's time of testing in the world, but also the Christian's time of testing in the world. Matthew builds climax into his pericope by inferring that just after the forty-day fast, the devil comes with his threefold temptation of Christ, a kind of final

47 Mk 8:22–26. A rare Marcan addition, inserted just before Peter's confession.

48 Mt 14:30–31.

49 16:17–19.

examination. Not until near the end of Matthew's pericope do we learn that this is not just any devil. It is *Satan* himself. For Mark's congregation, that period of trial, presumably, is almost over. Therefore he omits the substance of the pericope and begins at its climatic conclusion, not with an unspecified **διαβολος**, but with Satan. He also adds that Jesus was "with the wild beasts (**θηριον**)." Popular sentimental exegesis often portrays these "wild beasts" fawning over Jesus in St. Francis fashion. But the wild beasts of the Roman amphitheater were anxiously awaiting a meal of human flesh. Mark's Gospel ends where his congregation may very well now stand: at the doors of fear and death.

6

The Odd Man Out Is Mark

At this point we must convincingly resolve the basic interrelationship between the Synoptic Gospels once and for all. Otherwise the phenomenon of the Synoptic Gospel will remain an impenetrable circular argument. We may generalize about genre and form and intent, but our literary generalities and our theological deductions and our existential applications will remain unsubstantiated and tentative until we know who originated the template of the Synoptic gospel. Let us assume that we know nothing of the strong *prima facie* case for an earlier Aramaic version of Matthew with which all three authors are extremely familiar. We then have before us three documents which display such a close textual and literary relationship that there can be only two possible scenarios. The first scenario is that one of the Synoptic authors is the source and the other two authors independently follow him. The second scenario is that one of the Synoptic authors is the source, the second author follows him, and the third author follows both. But how can we tell who is the source and who are the followers?

Imagine that you are a social science professor. You have been teaching your students about a special current event, and for the final examination you have asked your students to write a lengthy in-class essay concerning this event. You have already given them many writing assignments to practice for this final examination. You have even written a model essay weeks before the examination and have given a copy to each of the students. You have told them that even if they just *memorize* the model essay and recreate it on the day of the examination, they will get a passing score for the course. But if they give evidence that they have mastered the material, bringing in original ideas of their own which develop the model essay that you have supplied, they will receive a much higher grade.

A few days after the examination, you find yourself grading all these examinations. You slog through paper after paper, which, unfortunately, monotonously and mindlessly recreate your own model essay. Then suddenly you come across a paper that is simply electric with originality. Student "J" loosely follows the chronological structure of your model essay but recreates much of the historical nature of the current event of study by means of a series of extended dialogues between representative personalities of the period. A very clever and original narrative device. You give the student a high grade.

As you begin slogging through papers once more, your boredom and disappointment are again interrupted by another highly original and masterful piece of writing. Student "T" takes an approach which is completely different. Instead of conjuring up representative personalities of the period, he contrives representative *events*, in which the chronology of your model essay is relatively unimportant. But there is more. This student strings these representative episodes together in such a way that his whole essay becomes a thinly veiled allusion to a well-known Greek play that several of your students have just studied in another class. Instead of direct commentary about what your selected current event might mean, he achieves a very strong literary implication that *the meaning of the current event is synonymous with the moral of this Greek play.* And there is still more. This student not only creates an amazingly artistic structural parallel between your current event and a Greek play, he ignores the underlying philosophical position of your model essay (which you thought was so cleverly concealed), and he slants the nature of this structural parallel to convey the philosophical position of his Greek drama professor! And this is particularly irritating to you, not only because you personally find the philosophical position of your colleague crude, naïve, and just plain embarrassing to men of such high academic credentials, but also because you resent the fact that this student is using your classroom and a relatively mundane academic assignment to evangelize *you,* apparently, with your colleague's philosophical position!

Still smarting from this breach of interpersonal decorum, you soon come across two more papers by student "L" and student "M," which follow the same format as student T. Of course, your first thought is plagiarism. But perhaps there is another explanation. Perhaps these two other students are part of the same political activist group and have all conspired, *prior* to the class, to follow this particular format in order to make some kind of political statement in their assignments. But as you place all three papers side by side, you realize that this theory will not do. They follow each other too closely. A prior agreement to follow this format in the writing of their examination papers could not have produced the kind of close textual similarities you see. They must have been looking at each other's papers *during* the examination.

But this is not just a simple case of cheating. Although their structure and wording are very close in virtually every paragraph, they rarely appear to copy from each other for more than twenty or thirty words. And strangely, the *variations* in format and wording achieve an originality that far surpasses the bulk of mediocre, hackneyed papers of the rest of the class. So why, from students of such originality, was there any in-class cheating at all, you wonder?

The only idea that comes to mind is that these three students are so intent upon using every opportunity to make a political statement that they simply do not *care* about what you consider to be "acceptable student behavior." The really irritating thing about these three students is that they seem to be paying no attention whatsoever to the very thing that seemingly motivates all other students and the very thing that gives your own position such enormous power in their lives: the purely utilitarian concern over their academic standing. Two of these students care so little about your power to negatively affect their academic futures, and care so much about how well this third student has made their common political statement, that they have completely ignored the invitation to plagiarize *your* model essay in order to shamelessly plagiarize one of *theirs*—during the course of the entire examination!

Finally, another vague thought, which you have been subconsciously attempting to ignore suddenly comes into focus: student J is part of this political conspiracy! You are ashamed to admit to yourself that you completely missed what he was doing the first time around. He makes the same basic political statement by using a very different format. Even worse, the more you think about it, the more you realize that there is a distinct relationship between his format and the format of these three students (which one might call, hypothetically, the "Synoptic" format). Confused and embarrassed, you nevertheless know your duty. Though this seems peevish, your pride pursues this duty. You would confront the students directly with the charge of cheating if you were not so ashamed of the moral superiority of their innocent political enthusiasm. Surely someone of your literary ability could immediately sort out which student was the source and which two were plagiarizing him.

You lay all three side by side by side and begin your analysis. You stare at them for an hour. Students T and L agree together on a considerable amount of material that student M has omitted. But L and M similarly sequence the first half of their essay differently than student T. Yet the essays of student L and M reflect the overall literary effect achieved by student T, but with considerably less intensity. All that you can come up with are these confusing generalities. If only there were some convincing clue that would stabilize your investigation.

Wait! Don't you remember seeing student T turning in his paper first? This would mean that he *had* to have been the source and student L and student M must be following accounts. But you can't remember for sure. You do not want to take the risk of going to these students with an analysis based entirely on generalities and vague memories. If you guess wrong, you will reveal to these students that one of the reasons that you cannot make a final determination on who is the source and who is the follower is because you don't really understand their philosophical position very well. You have dismissed this position often enough in casual conversation with other sympathetic colleagues by means of defective psychological assumptions, but now you realize that you are unable to understand the philosophical interrelationship between these three papers because you don't really know these students very well either.

Then it suddenly strikes you that there *is* a way to construct a foolproof determination about who is the source and who are the followers. It will take time and a considerable amount of effort, but the method is simple and scientific. You remember from your literary training that the interrelationship between similar texts can often be directly determined by the elements of syntax, grammar, style, and vocabulary of one author that appear in other authors. This was particularly applicable to a student who had plagiarized other texts. The importations of these characteristics showed up as internal inconsistencies, or distinct clashes, with the known writing characteristics of the student.

You remember also a problem like this in a class you once took as an undergraduate in manuscript science. You recollect that you learned how to categorize manuscripts into "families" based on internal characteristics alone. You were able to determine the relative dates of the manuscripts by the process of elimination: if two manuscript families "accidentally" agreed together against a third, this agreement made it more likely that the "odd-man-out" manuscript was not the source for the other two. Based on these guidelines, almost immediately you discover the source student. And not only this: you see that the main reason that the source student himself had sometimes seemed to be the odd man out was because one of the students had not only been following the source, he had also often blended together the essays of *both* students, occasionally making the source student *appear* to be the odd man out.

The problem with a parable is that you must leave it just as it gets interesting. You must cross over from one arm of the parabola to the other—across the void of imagination—from the understandable world of the story to the complicated world of true life. But Matthew, perhaps, would have told you that there is nothing more interesting than true life, and that the purpose of a parable is not to create meaning but to momentarily concentrate the essence of that meaning.

As we cross back over from imagination to our literary analysis of the Synoptic Gospels, let's hold on to the most important part of the parable. Our imaginations created a confidence in us that the proud professor really *could* develop some relatively ordinary rules and find the mystery source student. Why can't we have that same confidence now? Whether we are attempting to determine the authenticity of the Donation of Constantine, the interrelationships of the Synoptic Gospels, or the nature of simple plagiarizing between students, the literary procedures we use will be the same ordinary science our proud professor would have used. True science is completely neutral. It doesn't care whether we use it to find our keys or to find a murderer.

But if we *had* continued the parable of the proud professor, we would have found him discovering—bit by bit—the powerful mechanics of simple odd-man-out rules in literary analysis. And we would have found him thinking out loud, so that the reader could understand that the main reason that such a list of rules has never been developed for larger-scale literary units before now was because there was no high-speed computer technology to rigorously apply them. And even *with* computer technology, such a comprehensive analysis would require considerable manual effort, since the computer technology of literary pattern recognition is still being developed. Programmers know how to get answers, but they are still learning how to ask the right questions, especially in this area.

True science always requires considerable work. And for psychological and philosophical reasons that are not difficult to imagine, we would have found the proud professor doing this work in order to arrive at a few, relatively simple conclusions. If we could, even now, step back inside this parable and walk over to the professor's desk to see exactly what rules he had used to arrive at those conclusions, we would have found a list that looked something like this:

Odd Man Out Rules

In multiple texts in which interdependencies exist…

OMO1 *Unless a deviation rationale can be formulated for the majority texts, the minority text is probably not the source.*

OMO2 *The text that includes significantly more material and other interesting details which the majority texts simultaneously omit or corrupt is probably not the source.*

OMO3 *The text that continually appears as a composite of other texts will sometimes exhibit redundancies and other inexplicable narrative difficulties.*

These rules work in true life as well as they would have worked in the parable. The standard model of biblical criticism is a theory in crisis because it does not play by the rules—by this simple set of rules or by any other set. A theory in crisis will always be characterized by "stopgap" patches brought in to fix things up when its assumptions and conclusions do not agree very well with the actual data that is observed. Before too long, the theory becomes a hopelessly complex tangle of props, patches, and implausibilities. Since the mind cannot bear such a theoretical contraption, the theory begins to detach itself from the phenomena and acquires a life and internal balance of its own. It becomes an orthodoxy of personal myth protected by its own guards and eventually becomes re-enforced by groupthink. But true science is characterized by simplicity, elegance, and independent stability.

Despite what we have said about the need for considerable manual effort, the evidence that Mark is not the source has lain upon the surface of the data as clearly as the retrograde motions of the planets had lain on the surface of the data of celestial mechanics prior to Copernicus. *In almost every pericope in which there is substantial three-way agreement, Mark has a more elaborate account.* Mark expands seven healing pericopes against Luke the physician: Jesus in the Synagogue at Capernaum,[1]

The Healing of Peter's Mother in Law, The Healing of the Leper, The Gadarene Demoniac, Jairus' Daughter and a Woman's Faith, An Epileptic Boy Healed, and The Healing of Bartimaeus. Mark also expands Matthew's central teaching parable, The Parable of the Sower, and its interpretation. Mark even expands the pericope in which Matthew himself is called as an apostle (The Call of Levi).

But Mark also expands many key *narrative* pericopes such as The Sending out of the Twelve, The Return of the Twelve, The Feeding of the Five Thousand (the central narrative pericope prior to the week before the crucifixion), and The Cleansing of the Temple. Even in pericopes which Luke omits, Mark expands Matthew: The Death of John, What Defiles a Man, The Feeding of the Four Thousand, and The Anointing at Bethany.

Based on its assumption of Marcan priority, the standard model has already brought in a mysteriously wandering "Q" patch to explain why Matthew and Luke have "added" so much material to Mark. But the standard model also needs another sizable patch in order to explain why Matthew and Luke so mysteriously and simultaneously "abridge" so much of Mark[2]—especially when most of these Marcan pericopes strangely emphasize the same editorial concerns of healing and the complex nature of belief. The truth is that Matthew and Luke are not revolving around Mark. The truth is that Mark is revolving around Matthew and Luke.

A linguistic analysis of Mark should show that his literary behavior conforms to all three odd-man-out rules listed above. We should expect no less. We should accept no less. If this theory is true, then it really doesn't matter which three-way pericopes are selected for analysis because virtually all of them should conform to these rules. True science is repeatable. It does not matter which pericope is chosen for analysis; it does not matter who does the analysis—these literary units will always conform to this explanation. And virtually all of the rare excep-

1 To facilitate the clarity of designating various pericopes in the following discussion, the pericope titling conventions found in *Gospel Parallels*, edited by Burton H. Throckmorton Jr. (New York: Thomas Nelson & Sons, 1949), will be used hereafter.

2 This mystery is further compounded by the fact that so many of Mark's unique words are found clumped in his more lengthy pericopes and in his unique pericopes.

tions will have a clear extenuating circumstance to account for its "departure" from the predicted literary behavior. For example, when Mark includes a Matthean pericope that Luke omits, Luke becomes the odd man out at that level. But in almost every case in which Luke omits or severely truncates a pericope, Mark expands it.

For now, we will let stand the example that Matthew and Luke agree on so much material that Mark omits as the best example of **Odd Man Out Rule #1:** *In multiple texts in which interdependencies exist, unless a deviation rationale can be formulated for the majority texts, the minority text is probably not the source.* As we go on, it will be easy to see how, in the transmission of so much data, Matthew is the odd man out in cases to which his unique editorial agenda and intense literary style pertain; Luke and Mark depart from Matthew's typological use of the Old Testament in order to understandably pursue different narrative goals. Luke and Mark, for example, simultaneously omit Matthew's two quotations of Hosea 6:6 because they are so closely connected to Matthew's heated emphasis on the theme of Pauline righteousness. Luke and Mark simultaneously omit Matthew's development of Peter's role as a sophisticated anti-type of Christ, because this is far beyond the editorial agendas of both Luke and Mark. Matthew's "deviations" are especially easy to understand if Luke and Mark are working from *two* editions of Matthew.

Mark further compounds the issue by creating a few instances where Matthew appears to be the odd man out by occasionally favoring Luke's account for reasons other than those that motivated Luke to depart from Matthew. But many of these instances are inconsequential, since much of Mark's preference for Luke is at the level of *phraseology* and not important facts.[3] Mark's deviations (particularly his very noticeable elaborations), when they occur against Matthew and Luke's agreement, are much more difficult to account for if he were the source. While many of Matthew's deviations occur because of his intense literary agenda, many of Mark's deviations seem to revolve around *incidental* matters of fact. If Matthew and Luke are following Mark, or if Luke is a compound follower of Matthew and Mark, why the alteration or omission of these facts?

3 We will see this in the examples presented below.

For example, in recounting that "no man sews a piece of new cloth on an old garment," why would Matthew and Luke use a clumsier term like **επιβαλλω** (cast on), when Mark has "already" used the more precisely correct term **επιρραπτω** (sew)? Unless we place Mark as a follower and not the source, this question—"why would Matthew and Luke simultaneously alter so much Marcan data?"—will emerge again and again.

Odd Man Out Rule # 2 states that *the text that includes significantly more material and other "interesting details" which the other texts simultaneously omit or corrupt is probably not the source for the other two.* Perhaps the best example of this rule is the fact that in almost every pericope in which there is substantial three-way agreement, Mark has a more elaborate account. If Mark were the source, this would mean that Matthew and Luke are simultaneously omitting or abridging a large amount of Marcan material. But even in three-way pericopes in which Mark does not have considerably more material, interesting details appear in Mark that Matthew and Luke simultaneously omit or corrupt.

Consider the Plucking Ears of Grain on the Sabbath[4] pericope shown below. Matthew is (presumably) out of order with his Aramaic version and thus Luke and Mark. Matthew is here, apparently, using this event to set up the beginning of a series of confrontational incidents that lead to the beginning of parabolic teaching within a hostile environment. Matthew adds an extended point that the temple priest technically profanes the Sabbath by doing his job on the Sabbath. And by saying that "there is one here greater than the temple," Matthew implies the higher priesthood of Christ, who is simply doing his job. And that job is epitomized in Hosea 6:6, "I will have mercy and not sacrifice," which he repeats here. So this is almost certainly an editorial addition imposed upon the Aramaic version by Matthew in direct support of his new structural plan for the Greek version. But Mark and Luke omit this because their "deviation rationale" is that they simply do not aggressively follow Matthew's typological illustrations.

But look carefully at Mark's behavior. In the middle of a three-way, textually synchronous sentence ("they went into the house of God and

4 Mt 12:1-8.

ate the show-bread"), Mark inserts the interesting detail, "when Abiathar was high priest." If Matthew and Luke were following Mark, why would they omit this? The table below represents this oddity by color-coding the text. Blue represents material in which the text of all three authors agree exactly (or are synchronized). Black is verbiage unique to each author. Mark's interesting detail is underlined. Orange is Matthew/Luke agreement. Bright plum is Matthew/Mark agreement. Bright green is Luke/Mark agreement. The top portion of the table is the Greek text. The bottom portion represents a free rendering of the Greek text into English that attempts to maintain the color-coding of the Greek. Why all this color-coded complication merely to illustrate one interesting detail that Mark inserts? The reason for this is that this format will be used again in this section, and it will be very helpful to become familiar with the colors and with this method of comparing the three Synoptic Gospels.

Table 3. Plucking Ears of Grain on the Sabbath[5]

Matthew	Mark	Luke
ο δε ειπεν αυτοις ουκ ανεγνωτε τι εποιησεν δαβιδ οτε επεινασεν αυτος και οι μετ αυτου πως εισηλθεν εις τον οικον του θεου και τους αρτους της προθεσεως εφαγεν ους ουκ εξον ην αυτω φαγειν ουδε τοις μετ αυτου ει μη τοις ιερευσιν μονοις	και αυτος ελεγεν αυτοις ουδεποτε ανεγνωτε τι εποιησεν δαβιδ οτε χρειαν εσχεν και επεινασεν αυτος και οι μετ αυτου πως εισηλθεν εις τον οικον του θεου επι αβιαθαρ του αρχιερεως και τους αρτους της προθεσεως εφαγεν ους ουκ εξεστιν φαγειν ει μη τοις ιερευσιν και εδωκεν και τοις συν αυτω ουσιν	και αποκριθεις προς αυτους ειπεν ο ιησους ουδε τουτο ανεγνωτε ο εποιησεν δαβιδ οποτε επεινασεν αυτος και οι μετ αυτου οντες ως εισηλθεν εις τον οικον του θεου και τους αρτους της προθεσεως ελαβεν και εφαγεν και εδωκεν και τοις μετ αυτου ους ουκ εξεστιν φαγειν ει μη μονους τους ιερεις

5 Table footnotes are found at the end of the chapter.

But he said to them: have you not read what David did when he and those with him hungered - how he went into the house of God and ate the showbread, which was not lawful to him to eat, neither those with him except the priests only?	And he said to them: have you never read what David did when he had need and he and those with him hungered - how he went into the house of God when Abiathar was highpriest and ate the showbread, which was not lawful to eat, except the priests and gave also to those who were with him ?	And answering them Jesus said have you never read this - what David did when he and those which were with him hungered - how he went into the house of God and he took and ate the show-bread and gave also to those with him which was not law-ful to eat, except the priests only?

In this pericope, the colors seem randomly distributed, except for this notable addition by Mark. Yet even in this passage, there are tantalizing hints just below the surface that indicate Mark is a conservative but skilled *synthesizer*. But the synthesis that Mark achieves is not primarily a blending of different data. Mark primarily follows the overall narrative flow of Matthew, but often departs from this flow to import narrative details and phraseology from Luke. Observe the plum. It incidentally hints that Mark follows the "what," "when," and "how" of Matthew, but he will often switch to Luke's artful paraphrase of details in order to add depth. In this particular case, the detail that David *gave* the bread to those who were with him is missing in Matthew, but compared to Luke, it dangles just a little at the end of Mark's passage.

We have already seen a case when Matthew and Luke use the clumsier term **επιβαλλω** (cast on) when Mark has "already" used the more precisely correct term **επιρραπτω**. But in this next example, drawn from the woman who had a hemorrhage for twelve years, the opposite occurs: Matthew and Luke simultaneously use a more precisely correct word which Mark omits: **κρασπεδου**, a technical term for the border of a garment. Note also Mark's more elaborate account and his blending behavior.

Table 4. The Woman with an Issue of Blood

Matthew	Mark	Luke
και ιδου γυνη αιμορροουσα δωδεκα ετη προσελθουσα οπισθεν ηψατο του κρασπεδου του ιματιου αυτου ελεγεν γαρ εν εαυτη εαν μονον αψωμαι του ιματιου αυτου σωθησομαι	και γυνη τις ουσα εν ρυσει αιματος ετη δωδεκα και πολλα παθουσα υπο πολλων ιατρων και δαπανησασα τα παρ εαυτης παντα και μηδεν ωφεληθεισα αλλα μαλλον εις το χειρον ελθουσα ακουσασα περι του ιησου ελθουσα <u>εν τω οχλω</u> οπισθεν ηψατο του ιματιου αυτου ελεγεν γαρ οτι καν των ιματιων αυτου αψωμαι σωθησομαι και ευθεως εξηρανθη η πηγη του αιματος αυτης και εγνω τω σωματι οτι ιαται απο της μαστιγος	και γυνη ουσα εν ρυσει αιματος απο ετων δωδεκα ητις εις ιατρους προσαναλωσασα ολον τον βιον ουκ ισχυσεν υπ ουδενος θεραπευθηναι προσελθουσα οπισθεν ηψατο του κρασπεδου του ιματιου αυτου και παραχρημα εστη η ρυσις του αιματος αυτης
And behold, a woman having a flow of blood twelve years, having come from behind, touched the border of his garment, for she said in herself if only[1] I touch his garment, I shall be healed.	And a woman, who, having an issue of blood twelve years, and suffering much from many doctors, and having spent all her means but was not profited but rather became worse, hearing about Jesus, having come from behind <u>in the crowd</u>, touched his garment for she said in herself that if I but touch his garment, I shall be healed. And immediately the flow of her blood was stopped and she knew in her body that she was healed of her affliction.	And a woman, having an issue of blood for twelve years, who had consumed her whole life on doctors, not able[2] to be healed by anyone, having come from behind, touched the border of his garment and immediately[3] stopped the flow of her blood.

Often Mark simply prefers a different term. For example, in the healing of the paralytic, he uses **κραββατος** four times, yet Matthew and Luke use **κλινη**.

Table 5a. The Healing of the Paralytic

Matthew	Mark	Luke
και ιδων ο ιησους την πιστιν αυτων ειπεν τω παραλυτικω θαρσει τεκνον αφεωνται σοι αι αμαρτιαι σου και ιδου τινες των γραμματεων ειπον εν εαυτοις	ιδων δε ο ιησους την πιστιν αυτων λεγει τω παραλυτικω τεκνον αφεωνται σοι αι αμαρτιαι σου ησαν δε τινες των γραμματεων εκει καθημενοι και διαλογιζομενοι εν ταις καρδιαις αυτων τι ουτος	και ιδων την πιστιν αυτων ειπεν αυτω ανθρωπε αφεωνται σοι αι αμαρτιαι σου και ηρξαντο διαλογιζεσθαι οι γραμματεις και οι φαρισαιοι λεγοντες
ουτος	ουτως	τις εστιν ουτος ος
βλασφημει και ιδων	λαλει βλασφημιας τις δυναται αφιεναι αμαρτιας ει μη εις ο θεος και	λαλει βλασφημιας τις δυναται αφιεναι αμαρτιας ει μη μονος ο θεος
ο ιησους τας ενθυμησεις αυτων ειπεν ινα	ευθεως επιγνους ο ιησους τω πνευματι αυτου οτι ουτως διαλογιζονται εν εαυτοις ειπεν αυτοις	επιγνους δε ο ιησους τους διαλογισμους αυτων αποκριθεις ειπεν προς αυτους
τι υμεις ενθυμεισθε πονηρα εν ταις καρδιαις υμων τι γαρ εστιν ευκοπωτερον ειπειν αφεωνται σοι αι αμαρτιαι η ειπειν εγειραι και περιπατει ινα δε ειδητε οτι εξουσιαν εχει ο υιος του ανθρωπου επι της γης αφιεναι αμαρτιας	τι ταυτα διαλογιζεσθε εν ταις καρδιαις υμων τι εστιν ευκοπωτερον ειπειν τω παραλυτικω αφεωνται σοι αι αμαρτιαι η ειπειν εγειραι και αρον σου τον κραββατον και περιπατει ινα δε ειδητε οτι εξουσιαν εχει ο υιος του ανθρωπου αφιεναι επι της γης αμαρτιας	τι διαλογιζεσθε εν ταις καρδιαις υμων τι εστιν ευκοπωτερον ειπειν αφεωνται σοι αι αμαρτιαι σου η ειπειν εγειραι και περιπατει ινα δε ειδητε οτι εξουσιαν εχει ο υιος του ανθρωπου επι της γης αφιεναι αμαρτιας

Matthew	Mark	Luke
τοτε λεγει τω παραλυτικω εγερθεις αρον σου την κλινην και υπαγε εις τον οικον σου	λεγει τω παραλυτικω σοι λεγω εγειραι και αρον τον κραββατον σου και υπαγε εις τον οικον σου	ειπεν τω παραλελυμενω σοι λεγω εγειραι και αρας το κλινιδιον σου πορευου εις τον οικον σου

But in this example, a case of an "interesting detail" may also be resolved as a case of literary synthesis. Because, strangely, this is the same term and the same expression used by *John* in his significantly different pericope in the healing of the lame man at the pool of Bethsaida. Jesus there says, "Rise, take your bed and walk" (Jn 5:8). You can already see a combination of plum and green in the middle account. It is a blending that occurs over and over again. But if we were to overlay John upon Mark (color-coded brown), we see a hint of yet another synthesis.[6]

Table 5b. The Healing of the Paralytic

Matthew	Mark	Luke
And Jesus, seeing their faith said to the paralytic: "take comfort, child, your sins are forgiven you." And behold some of the scribes said in themselves: "He blasphemes."	But Jesus seeing their faith says to the paralytic: "child, your sins are forgiven you." But there were some of the scribes there sitting and reasoning in their hearts, "why does this man thus speak blasphemy?" "Who is able to forgive sins except God?"	And seeing their faith he said to him: "man, your sins are forgiven you." And the scribes and Pharisees began to reason saying: "He speaks blasphemy." "Who is able to forgive sins except God only?"

6 This implies that John wrote before Mark. The full proof for this will be presented in another work, *A Vesture Dipped in Blood.*

Matthew	Mark	Luke
And Jesus knowing their thoughts, said[4] "why do you think evil in your hearts? For which is easier - to say 'your sins are forgiven' or to say 'rise and walk'? But that you may know that the son of man has power upon the earth to forgive sins" —he then[5] says to the paralytic:	But Jesus, immediately knowing in his spirit that they so reasoned in themselves he said to them: "why do you reason these things in your hearts? For which is easier - to say to the paralytic 'your sins are forgiven' or to say 'rise **and take up your pallet** and walk'? But that you may know that the son of man has power upon the earth to forgive sins" - he says to the paralytic:	But Jesus, knowing their reasonings, answered to them and said to them:[6] "why do you reason in your hearts? For which is easier - to say 'your sins are forgiven you' or to say 'rise and walk'? But that you may know that the son of man has power upon the earth to forgive sins" - he says to the paralytic:
"rising, take up your bed and go into your house."	"I say to you rise and take up your **pallet** and go into your house."	"I say to you rise and take up your bed going into your house."

The blending behavior that continually appears in Mark's account brings us to **Odd Man Out Rule #3**, which states that *the text which continually appears as a composite of other texts will sometimes exhibit redundancies and other inexplicable narrative difficulties*. Mark's synthesis of expression and content is so consistent and so close that many redundant expressions, omissions of assumed details, and other narrative difficulties occur within the *same* pericope. A good example of redundancy occurs at the juncture of Mark's pericope of The Healing of Peter's Mother-in-Law and The Sick Healed at Evening (Table 6). Mark includes "as evening began" (Matthew) and "when the sun did set" (Luke) in the same sentence! He then, in the same paragraph, redundantly says that he healed all "having illness" (Matthew) of "various diseases" (Luke).

Table 6. The Healing of Peter's Mother-in-Law and The Sick Healed at Evening

Matthew	Mark	Luke
And coming into the house of Peter, he saw his mother-in-law laid out and enfevered and he touched her hand and the fever left her and she was raised up and she served them	And straightaway coming out of the synagogue they went into the house of Simon and Andrew with James and John. And the mother-in-law of Simon was lying abed enfevered and straightaway they speak to him about her. **And** approaching, taking her hand, he raised her up and straightaway the fever left her and she served them.	And rising from the synagogue, he went into the house of Simon. And the mother-in-law of Simon was taken with[7] a great fever and they asked him about her. And standing over her, he rebuked the fever and it immediately[8] left her and rising[9], she served them.
As evening began they brought to him many demon possessed and he cast out the spirits by word and he healed many having illness.	As evening began, when the sun did set, they brought to him all those having illness and those demon possessed and the whole city gathered at the door and he healed all of illness, having various diseases. And he cast out many demons and did not permit the demons to speak because they knew him.	And as the sun was setting, all that had illnesses of various diseases gathered to him and he laid his hands upon one and all and healed them. And also demons coming out of many crying out and saying: "you are the Christ the son of God" and he commanded them, not permitting[10] them to speak because they knew him to be the Christ.

Note that there is no orange color in the table above; that is, there is no Lukan alignment with Matthew that is not masked by three-way agreement. But as in the previous example of the Healing of the Paralytic, observe how much color there is in Mark's column. You'll not find this diversity anywhere in Matthew or Luke. Note also how the colors are equally distributed – as if *phraseology* is being intentionally blended. Now compare this with Luke's rendition. There is always considerably more unique (black) verbiage in his account, no matter who he is compared with. And much of this unique verbiage is embedded with words that are rarely used except by Luke. (There are three of them in the first three sentences.)

In this next short example of a fairly close three-way agreement (Table 7),[7] we have an example of Matthew and Luke simultaneously departing from Mark to use the vocative "Lord!" while omitting Mark's "but Jesus, moved with compassion..." Mark redundantly says, "[Jesus] says to him" (Matthew) "and saying" (Luke) that the leprosy "departed from him" (Luke) and that "he was cleansed" (Matthew).

7 A fragment from The Healing of a Leper, Throckmorton 31-32.

Table 7. The Healing of a Leper (Excerpt)

Matthew	Mark	Luke
και ιδου λεπρος ελθων προσεκυνει αυτω λεγων κυριε εαν θελης δυνασαι με καθαρισαι και εκτεινας την χειρα ηψατο αυτου ο ιησους λεγων θελω καθαρισθητι και ευθεως εκαθαρισθη αυτου η λεπρα	 και ερχεται προς αυτον λεπρος παρακαλων αυτον και γονυπετων αυτον και λεγων αυτω οτι εαν θελης δυνασαι με καθαρισαι ο δε ιησους σπλαγχνισθεις εκτεινας την χειρα ηψατο αυτου και λεγει αυτω θελω καθαρισθητι και ειποντος αυτου ευθεως απηλθεν απ αυτου η λεπρα και εκαθαρισθη	και ιδου ανηρ πληρης λεπρας και ιδων τον ιησουν πεσων επι προσωπον εδεηθη αυτου λεγων κυριε εαν θελης δυνασαι με καθαρισαι και εκτεινας την χειρα ηψατο αυτου ειπων θελω καθαρισθητι και ευθεως η λεπρα απηλθεν απ αυτου
And, behold, there came a leper and worshipped[11] him, saying, Lord, if you will, you can make me clean. And Jesus stretching out his hand, touched him, saying, I will; be clean. And immediately his leprosy was cleansed.	And there came a leper to him, beseeching him, and kneeling down to him, and saying unto him that, if you will, you can make me clean. And Jesus, moved with compassion,[12] stretching out his hand, touched him, and says to him, I will; be clean. And saying this, immediately the leprosy departed from him, and he was cleansed.	And behold a man full of leprosy: who seeing Jesus fell on his face, and besought[13] him, saying, Lord, if you will, you can make me clean. And stretching out his hand, touched him, saying, I will: be clean. And immediately the leprosy departed from him.

In this next example (Table 8), in which Mark greatly expands The Stilling of the Storm, we see examples of both OMO 2 (a longer account which adds many interesting details) and OMO 3 (a composite account that displays narrative difficulties).

Table 8. The Stilling of the Storm

Matthew	Mark	Luke
And when he entered into a boat, his disciples followed him. And behold, a great storm began[14] at sea so that the boat was hidden by the waves, but he slept.	And he says to them on that day as evening began: let us go to the other side. And after he dismissed the crowd, they took him as he was[17] into the boat. But there were also other small boats with him. And there began to be a great tempest of wind and the waves came into the boat so that it was already taking on water. But he was in the stern, on the cushion[18], sleeping. And	And it happened on one of those days[20] that he and his disciples entered into a boat. And he said to them[21] let us go to the other side of the lake.[22] So they launched.[23] But as they sailed[24] he fell asleep[25] But there came down a tempest of wind upon the lake and they were overcome[26] and were in jeopardy.[27]
Coming to him his disciples[15] roused him saying "Lord, save us! We perish!" And he says to them: "why do you of little faith[16] fear?" Then rising, he rebuked the wind and the sea and there began to be a great calm and the men were amazed saying what manner of man is this that also the wind and the sea obey him?	they rouse him and say to him: do you not care that we perish? And rising he rebuked the wind and says to the sea: "silence!, be still!" And the wind ceased and there began to be a great calm. And he said to them why do you fear? Why do you have no faith? And they were greatly afraid and said to one another: what manner[19] of man is this that also the wind and the sea obey him?	But coming to him, they rouse him saying Master! Master![28] We perish! But rising, he rebuked the wind and the raging of and water and they ceased.[29] And there began to be a calm. And he said to them where is your faith? But fearing, they were amazed saying to one another: what manner of man is this that also the winds and the waters he commands and they obey him?"

Matthew and Luke simultaneously depart from Mark's longer account at many points: they both omit that Jesus dismissed the crowds, that "he was taken into the boat as he was," that there were other small boats present,[8] and that Jesus was in the stern on a cushion. Matthew and Luke both have a similar, vocative interjectory expression: "Lord save us!" (Matthew) and "Master, Master, we perish!" (Luke). But Mark instead places an incongruent *rhetorical question* in the mouths of the disciples—in the middle of a storm! Simultaneously reversing narrative mood, both Matthew and Luke omit what Jesus actually said to the wind and the waves, but Mark inserts interjectory dialogue: "Silence! Be still!" Mark also redundantly repeats the essence of both Matthew's and Luke's account of Jesus' questioning of the disciples: "Why do you fear?" (Matthew) and "Why do you have no faith?" (Luke).

At first glance, all three accounts seem to display the same degree of color diversity. But though Mark has added many interesting details, there is nothing distinctive about Mark's language and expression. In contrast to this, Matthew and Luke plainly reflect their distinctive vocabulary, especially Luke. (See table footnotes. One can see this in virtually every comparison.) The sharing of words between Matthew and Luke are clearly, necessarily random cases of expression in accounts that cover the same narrative territory. But look carefully at Mark. His blending of Matthew and Luke is at the level of expression *and* content.

It is at this point in Mark's narrative that another kind of blending occurs. Mark has left the order of Matthew's Aramaic version, reflected in his order agreement with Luke against Matthew, at the point of Matthew's Plucking Ears of Corn on the Sabbath pericope and has adopted the basic order of Matthew's Greek version (against Luke) for the rest of his Gospel. Following the order of Luke's manuscript and manually finding the parallel account in the Aramaic and the Greek, Mark has now, presumably, reversed the manuscript positioning and will now, also, manually find the parallel account in Luke.

8 Strangely, these same small boats appear parenthetically also in Jn 6:23: "Howbeit there came other boats from Tiberius near to the place where they did eat bread, after that the Lord had given thanks."

Conveniently, Luke's block of pericopes realign upon the order of Matthew's Greek version at the point of The Parable of the Sower. Mark momentarily continues with Luke's order for the next block: The Stilling of the Storm, The Gadarene Demoniac, and Jairus' Daughter and a Woman's Faith. But in order to find this same block of pericopes in Matthew, he must scroll back four "chapters." Mark then backs up a few sentences in Matthew to pick up the flow, and in so doing, brushes up against Matthew's pericope about The Sick Healed at Evening. Remember the redundancy in Mark's account: "In the evening, when the sun did set"? Unlike Luke's account of The Sick Healed at Evening, Matthew's The Sick Healed at Evening (8:16–17) does not follow up with "[a]nd in the morning" (Mk 1:35) or "[a]nd when it was day" (as in Lk 4:42). Therefore, in picking up Matthew's splice between The Sick Healed at Evening and The Gadarene Demoniac, Mark loses the detail of the passing of night and the beginning of the next day. He therefore begins The Stilling of the Storm pericope with an out-of-place fragment from Matthew: "And he says to them on that day *as evening began* [emphasis added]." But when they get to the other side, the man from the tombs possessed by Legion sees him from a long way off. But how does he see if it is now dark?

Another narrative difficulty, again arising from the omission of an assumed detail, occurs in this very pericope. This time it is a detail from Luke. In setting up for this tremendously extended account of the Gadarene demoniac (5:1–20), Mark momentarily departs from Matthew, looks ahead in Luke, introduces the man not as demon-possessed but as one who possesses an "unclean spirit," and then adds a significant amount of unique material to develop context. But when Mark resumes his place in Luke's account to record the dialogue of a single demon, as opposed to Matthew's two, he omits Luke's sentence just before. Luke's detail that "he wore no clothes," therefore, drops out of Mark. Yet at the end of Mark's account, when the people come to the healed demoniac, they find him "clothed and in his right mind." But Mark has made no mention of the demoniac being naked, as Luke had done.

Another example of this kind of narrative difficulty occurs in The Sending out of the Twelve (Mt 9:35–10:16). Here Matthew, the controlling account, gives very clear instructions to the disciples: "When you enter a city or village, inquire who in that city is worthy and stay with him during the entire course of your visit in that city." Luke paraphrases Matthew and leaves out this explanation. Luke therefore has a sentence that momentarily dangles without meaning: "And whatsoever house you enter into, there abide, and thence depart." The reader must infer from Luke's next sentence that he means the same thing as Matthew: "And whosoever will not receive you, when you go *out of that city* [emphasis added]..." Then too, Luke's reduplicated, unique pericope concerning the sending out of the seventy very clearly repeats Matthew's missionary strategy and concludes with an even clearer statement: "Go not from house to house." As Mark follows Luke, omitting Matthew's explanation, he also picks up this dangling, Lukan sentence. But Mark does not amplify. Nor does he include Luke's pericope about the sending out of the seventy. The sentence therefore remains meaningless by itself unless the missing missionary strategy of Matthew's account is assumed.

So far, we have seen that subtle narrative difficulties normally result from synthesizing two similar accounts. But the Gadarene Demoniac pericope represents a case in which Mark synthesizes two accounts in which narrative difficulties are already present and obvious, even before the act of literary synthesis.

Luke says "Gadarene." Matthew says "Gergesene." There could easily have been two names for a specific geographic place, just as there is often two or three different names for the same individual. Mark chooses Gadarene.

Luke says that there was one demoniac. Matthew says that there were two. How does Mark resolve this? There are linguistic hints in Luke that he is simply ignoring Matthew's second man. For example, at the conclusion of this pericope, Luke repeats three times an adjectival phrase concerning the main character. Why is this necessary? Don't Luke's readers know whom he is talking about by now? Nevertheless, Luke twice reminds his readers whom he is talking about with the same lengthy, restrictive phrase: "the man from whom he had cast out the demons." Theoretically, this is necessary, at least in Luke's mind, because Luke must know that his audience is already familiar with

Matthew's account. Mark must know too. And Mark must also know that his audience is familiar with Luke's account. Mark also repeats an adjectival phrase three times at his conclusion, but they are very brief and subtle. These adjectival phrases are important because they (presumably) distinguish the demoniac from Matthew's second man.

At this point we must drastically interrupt the flow of this analysis, just as Mark has drastically interrupted the flow of his gospel by switching manuscripts. It is no longer so important to demonstrate that Mark has written a synthesis of Matthew and Luke which greatly abridges narrative and teaching material. Now it is important to understand *why* Mark has done this. If there is a place at which we might take a close look at what Mark is doing in his Gospel, this is the place. Not only has Mark switched manuscripts, but Mark will begin greatly expanding pericopes at this point. For example, Mark enlarges The Healing of Peter's Mother-in-Law and The Healing of the Leper by 15% and 4% respectively over Luke. Mark expands the pericope of The Healing of the Paralytic relative to Matthew, but perhaps because the pericope does not necessarily touch the very center of Mark's concern (which is the nature of the individual response of belief to Jesus' healing power), it is 6% shorter than Luke. This pericope is not about the faith of the paralytic. It is about the faith of the four who brought him.[9]

Matthew has been building conflict between Jesus and the religious establishment since the very beginning of his healing block, which begins with a leper. And the intensity of Matthew's conflict motive is clearly reflected in the pericope concerning the paralytic. Mark may have chosen not to expand this pericope because it too does not touch the center of his editorial motive, and because he does not want to detract from Matthew's conflict intensity, to which flow he joins himself at Matthew's Plucking Ears of Corn on the Sabbath pericope.[10] But the primary reason that Mark has not expanded this pericope may be be-

9 All three accounts are clear: "And when Jesus saw their faith he said to the paralytic..."

10 Mark therefore deletes the rationale for The Healing the Man with a Withered Hand (Mt 12:11–12) because it detracts from this intensity. This is partly due to the

cause its theological purpose already lumbers upon the surface of both Matthew and Luke: to proclaim in the clearest possible terms that Jesus' power and authority to heal is identical with his power and authority to forgive sin.

Likewise, Mark perhaps did not expand The Healing of the Man with a Withered Hand (Mk 3:1–6) because it was not primarily about healing. When Jesus healed the leper, he told him not to tell anyone but to go and offer the appropriate offering before the priest. Now Jesus walks directly into a synagogue and performs the healing of the man with a withered hand! This is not the way to stay out of trouble with the authorities. Jesus is deliberately entering into fatal controversy. This act provokes a secret council meeting of Pharisees (in consultation with the more politically powerful Herodians) in which it is decided to destroy him.[11] Matthew alone brings in a quote from Isaiah 42:1–3 explaining how Jesus will "bring forth judgment to the Gentiles" but will not allow public acclamation to unwittingly play him into violent hands until the right time. But in making this decision, Christ violates a principle that he gave to the disciples: that when persecuted, they should flee to another city.[12] And this is because no one decides on his own to be a martyr. He must be called of God for this purpose. [13] Christ was called of God to drink the cup of death. Mark does not alter this literary intensity.

Mark's expansion of The Gadarene Demoniac is only 10% longer than Luke, but this increase is proportionally much greater within a Gospel that is, overall, 38% shorter than Matthew and Luke. His expansion again works to put a human face upon the demoniac and colors the atmosphere in which he moves. He expands Luke's details about fetters and chains and Matthew's details about his fierceness, but adds excruciating details about the trapped and tortured soul within: "Night and day among the tombs he was continually crying out and bruising himself with stones." Mark follows Luke's addition concerning

fact that Matthew is conflating the dialogue of what was three pericopes in Matthew's Aramaic version, which can still be seen in Luke's account. In Luke we find the rationale (Lk 14:5) separated from the healing (Lk 6:6–11) by eight chapters.

11 Mk 3:6.

12 Mt 10:23.

13 Heb 5:4. "And no man takes this honor unto himself, but he that is called of God."

the final meeting between the healed demoniac and Jesus, but to Luke's "Return to your home and declare how much God has done for you," Mark adds, "and how he has had mercy on you."

Mark now has begun an expansion program that touches virtually every pericope from here to Bartimaeus. In the very next pericope, Jairus' Daughter and a Woman's Faith (Mk 5:21–43), Mark's expansion is unmistakable. In Matthew, Jairus says that his daughter has died. Mark and Luke say that she was "at the point of death." This is important later on as both Luke and Mark bring in a third party who tells the ruler not to trouble the Teacher any further since his daughter has just died. This narrative device greatly heightens the drama of this healing. Imagine if Christ were simply a magician who could alter the process of dying or an exorcist casting out demons by those same dark forces. What would he do with death itself? His magic would be powerless. His exorcism would be irrelevant. For no amount of magic or occultic power can restore life once it is lost. But Jesus shows no evidence that he doubted for a minute what he would do. Matthew is contracting this pericope to its minimum elements. Luke re-expands it. Mark expands it even further. Mark takes various details from Luke: Jairus' name, that he was the ruler of the synagogue, and that the girl was twelve years old. And he takes a key expression from Matthew: "...come and lay hands on her and she will live."

The first section, then, is a clear composite of both accounts, adding very little that is new except connective phraseology. In the introduction of the woman, Mark opts for Luke's more clinical term for hemorrhage, "an issue of blood," and all three agree that she has been suffering for twelve years. Luke says, "[S]he could not be healed by anyone." Mark elaborates and says that the woman has spent all her savings proving this to herself, and that all she had to show for such an investment was the small amount of wisdom that sometimes a doctor's cure is worse than the disease.

The next section is her approach to Jesus, her rationale for touching him, and the fact that she is made well. As we saw above, Matthew and Luke simultaneously deviate and say that she came "upon" him and touched the "**κρασπεδον**" (hem) of his garment. There is no reason why Mark has left this out. He uses the word seventy-two sentences later in his account in the same sense. But Mark does take up Matthew's detail of her inner rationale for touching him. As in the case of the demoniac, Mark brings the reader into direct contact with the suffering individual. And he further expands this to her inner knowledge that she was, in fact, healed in body. How does one know that a hemorrhage has stopped in one's body? Mark doesn't say. But he does draw a parallel with Jesus' inner knowledge that "power had gone out of himself."

And this is probably one of the most audacious claims ever made—to know what Christ was thinking when no one else did. Luke records that Jesus *said* that "he perceived that power had gone forth from him." Mark records that he *in fact* perceived it. Is Mark merely repeating something he heard from Peter? From Luke, one might think so, since he specifically mentions Peter expressing the puzzlement of what Jesus could mean by "who touched me?" But Mark does not mention Peter specifically, and expands the puzzlement to incredulity tinged with ridicule: "You see the crowds—yet you say who touched me?" But in Mark, Jesus didn't ask, "who touched me?" He asked, "Who touched *my garments* [emphasis added]?" For there were many who were mindlessly touching him because of the press. But there was suddenly one who *mindfully* touched him, confidently believing that his power would heal her. Jesus **περιεβλεπετο** (looks around; a Marcan word) to see who has done this. Mark is creating a context for this rhetorical question similar to another question that was asked long ago: "And the Lord God called unto Adam and said, Where are you?"[14] Jesus knew right well where she was.

We have seen this Marcan psychologizing before. And again and again it does not shrink back from the very threshold of the mind of Christ. After Jesus is baptized, Matthew and Luke have the Spirit lead Jesus into the desert for his fasting trial. Mark departs from their verb "led" and offers a more violent inner action, using a verb that he often uses to describe plucking out eyes or casting out devils— **εκβαλλω**.[15] In The Healing of a Leper (1:40–45), Mark departs from Matthew and Luke and adds that Jesus was "moved with compassion."

14 Ge 3:9.

15 Mk 1:12. "And immediately the Spirit *drives* him into the wilderness [emphasis added]."

In The Healing of the Paralytic (2:1–12), Mark again elaborates on Luke's simpler "when Jesus perceived" and says, "when Jesus knew in his spirit." In The Healing of the Man with the Withered Hand (3:1–6), Mark elaborates upon Luke's "And he looked around upon them…" to say, "And he looked around upon them with anger, grieved at the hardness of their heart…" In The Interpretation of the Parable of the Sower (4:13–20), Mark adds two rhetorical questions that illuminate Jesus inner psychological disposition: "Do you not understand this parable? How then will you understand any of the parables?" Likewise, in the very next parable, Mark strengthens Luke's direct statement ("No one after lighting a lamp, covers it with a vessel or puts it under a bed but puts it on a stand…") to a rhetorical question: "Is a lamp brought in to be put under a bushel?…or under a bed? And not upon a stand?" (Mk 4:21).

Recall that Mark departs from Matthew and Luke's vocative exclamation "Lord, we are perishing!" in The Stilling of the Storm (Mk 4:35–41). Though his usage of yet another rhetorical question seems to be incongruous with the pace of the action in Matthew and Luke, it is clearly consistent with his use of rhetorical questions to help us peer into the psychology of the disciples. And again we see something that is missing in Matthew and Luke. There is *angry* confrontation not only between Jesus and the disciples, but between the disciples and Jesus.

Luke says that the woman with a hemorrhage came, trembling, and fell down before Jesus (Lk 8:47). Characteristically Marcan, she also came with *fear* (Mk 5:33). What was the object of her fear and trembling? It was the same object of her belief (**πιστις**). First, she believed, based on everything that she had seen and heard, that he had the power and authority to heal her. This was not some superstitious woman thinking, "Maybe if I brush up against him, something will happen." No. Mark gives us too much information to make this mistake about her. She feared that she had taken something from the Lord that did not belong to her. And she was right.

In Luke and Mark, Jesus says to her, "…your belief in my power and authority to heal you is all that you need." Jesus then tells her to "be at peace." But why would Mark add, "be healed of your disease"? She has *already* been healed. This is an *ex post facto* assurance given to the woman that Christ has blessed the entire transaction between them—of her belief and his power. Mark has probably modified this account away from Luke because the narrative pace of this pericope is inconsistent with Luke's lengthy, explanatory confession of the woman. And it places strain on the "messianic secret." Luke says that the woman declared in the presence of all the people how she had been immediately healed. Why then wasn't there a rush of people to touch him? No one else stepped forward because no one else believed what that woman believed—that he was the Son of David, that he was the Messiah, and that he had the power and authority to heal her.

What did the rest of the people think about him? We will soon find out when he asks Peter, "Who do men say that I am?" Herod thought that he was John the Baptist risen from the dead. The religious establishment believed that he was merely a reed shaken by ordinary historical and psychological forces. Some thought that he was a political prophet-messiah. Some thought that he had tapped into the power of Satan himself. In Mark, these alternative theories about Christ are examples of unbelief. If anyone touched him with any of these beliefs, nothing happened. Mark will soon confirm this: "...and he could do there no mighty work...because of their unbelief (apistia)."[16] When a man comes from Jairus' house to let him know that "it's too late, the girl is dead," Mark changes the Lukan statement into a question: "Why trouble the Master any further?" By changing to a rhetorical question, Mark makes it clear that this man, through his presuppositions, has simply shut the door to the possibility that Jesus' power and authority would not stop at death.

And this heightens the irony of what is to follow. The Marcan Jesus has never broken eye contact with Jairus throughout. In the Epileptic Boy Healed pericope, the father will blurt out the substance of his inner struggle to believe. Here Jesus saves him the trouble. Without so much as a blink, he tells Jairus steadily, looking right past the envoy: "Do not fear, only believe." To the crowd of mourners Jesus says something quite silly: "Why do you make a tumult and weep? The child is not dead but sleeping." Why does Jesus say that the girl is sleeping? Perhaps Jesus caught a faint pulse which everyone missed. It *could* hap-

---

16 Mk 6:5–6.

pen. But this is not what is happening here. She's as dead as a brick. Jesus knows it. And they know it. But all it will take is a little confusion and Jesus will have safely escaped. Escaped from what? John adds an important piece of information at the very end of the Feeding of the Five Thousand pericope that all three of the Synoptics omit. John says, "When Jesus therefore perceived that they would come and take him by force, to make him a king, he departed again into a mountain himself alone." Later John explains, "You seek me, not because you saw the miracles, but because you did eat of the loaves, and were filled."

The Synoptics omit this material because they deal with this phenomenon in a way in which John himself largely ignores, by means of the messianic secret. In the midst of an overwhelming witness to his own messiahship, Christ gives the opportunity, however slight, for unbelief. They seize it. So Jesus forbids the parents to tell what *truly* happened. When the maiden and her parents finally emerged from that upper room, Jesus was safely off—at least in Mark—for a rendezvous with unbelief in his own hometown.

What was the reaction of the people to this event? They were "amazed." Mark's unique uses of **εκθαμβεω** (amazed), **εξιστημι** (amazed), and **εκστασις** (astonished) distinctly emphasizes the reaction of the people and the disciples to Jesus' healing miracles, his nature miracles, and the discovery at the tomb. But amazement is not belief. Jesus tells the man "do not fear," because fear is another kind of emotional reaction that inhibits cognitive belief. As long as these people remained dumbfounded, their belief could not receive his power. They were amazed. After the amazement cleared, what did they *think*? "Well I'll be damned, Jesus was right. She *was* sleeping!" There was no danger of mindless acclaim here. Just a bit of irony was all that was necessary to destabilize the crowd and preserve the messianic secret.

To review, we have begun our discussion about the specifics of *why* Mark has written at this point for two reasons. First, Mark has suddenly begun to greatly expand key healing pericopes. Second, he has suddenly switched manuscripts. Beginning with the pericope: *Herod Thinks John Is Risen* (6:14–16), Mark will invariably align with Matthew for sixteen pericopes. The blending of Matthew and Luke will be clear.

Marcan "interesting details," redundancies, and omissions will be scattered everywhere, as usual. But the question is not only why has Mark switched manuscripts; the question is, *why* has Mark made a transition to Matthew's Greek version as his primary source at such a difficult place?

There is an enormous editorial difficulty for Matthew at this very point in his own narrative. He must begin to realign himself with the chronological flow that he has disrupted in the creation of his Sermon on the Mount, his healing block, and his controversy-building section. So why *does* Mark join him here and not, perhaps, after he has resolved the problem? We must watch Mark shadow Matthew just as Matthew is making a chronological suture between the sending out of the twelve apostles, which occurred three chapters ago, and their return. Since then, there has been an extended commissioning sermon, John's envoy has come and gone, and the Plucking Ears of Grain on the Sabbath controversy and the incident of the Healing of the Man with a Withered Hand have significantly eroded the political tolerance of the Galileans. The religious establishment has decreed to explore ways in which Jesus of Nazareth might be disposed of. A considerable block of parables has been preached. But where have the disciples gone? Matthew must somehow get back to them.

We will see that Matthew is not following chronology; he is manipulating it. Matthew is writing a highly stylized play, not ordinary history. Structurally, Peter's confession is the linchpin of Matthew's play. Matthew must now quickly *become* chronological and place Jesus in fairly close chronological proximity to the triumphal entry into Jerusalem, since he has dispersed or deleted or contracted much of the old midsection of his Aramaic version. How does he do this?

Five times Matthew moves from a timeless teaching or dialogue section into the actual chronology of history with the editorial phrase "**εγενετο οτε**" ("at that time" or "at that point"). Matthew must move from the parables (of chapter 13) to the historical reality of The Return of the Twelve and The Feeding of the Five Thousand. We can see that the chronology of The Feeding of Five Thousand is historically linked to The Walking on the Water pericope, because this is one of the rare linkages to the more chronological account in John. The Sower is the central parable of Matthew's Gospel. And The Feeding of the Five Thousand and The Feeding of the Four Thousand are his central miracles.

Here Matthew repeats again his genre's key text: "No sign shall be given except the prophet Jonas" (16:4). And here Matthew contrives a crucial confrontation between Christ and Peter about how that sign should be interpreted. The intensity of Matthew is so unmistakable that John himself makes positive contact with the flow of Matthew at this very place. John, apparently, understands what Matthew has done. He takes what is implicit in Matthew's feeding of the five thousand and the Syro-Phonecian woman and makes it *explicit*. We must eat the flesh and drink the blood of Christ (Jn 6:53).

In Matthew, Herod hears of Jesus' fame and thinks it could be John the Baptist whom he beheaded (past tense). Herod must have something to hear of, so Matthew has already moved backwards to the pericope of *Jesus Is Rejected at Nazareth*, which happens very early on in Jesus ministry.[17] Then Matthew connects what Herod hears with a literary "flashback" to the whole affair of how John had come to be in prison[18] and how he met his end.

If Matthew is attempting to place Jesus at Caesarea Philippi, Matthew's start of Jesus' final march to Jerusalem, he appears to be moving in the wrong direction (from an editorial point of view). Matthew has contracted the sending out of the seventy, which Luke still preserves, with the sending out of the twelve. Just prior to the feeding of the five thousand in Luke, the returning disciples make their report to Jesus about what they have preached. Just prior to the feeding of the five thousand in Matthew, after John the Baptist's disciples bury the body, the disciples make their report to Jesus about what *Herod has done*. The disciples have finally returned, but in a different venue. Then Jesus retires to a desert place and the crowds follow him. All this is in the aorist (past) tense. When it is time to dismiss them, he tells his disciples to feed the crowd themselves. "And they say unto him: 'we have here but five loaves and two fishes'" (14:17). Here Matthew employs the historical present ("they say" instead of "they said"), imperceptibly shifts to the *actual* present, and the chronological suture dissolves into

17 Lk 4:16-30.

18 Which also happens much earlier in the ministry of Jesus (Lk 3:19–20).

the literary flow. And with this chronological contraction, Jesus is geographically moved to the wilderness of Bethsaida within easy, literary striking range of Matthew's editorial target: Caesarea Philippi, where a pivotal confession and denial occurs. Mark follows close behind.

Footnotes from Tables

1 Except for one occurrence in 1 Corinthians, the combination of "if…only" occurs only in Matthew.

2 Only Luke uses the phrase "not able" (3 times).

3 This is Luke's favorite word for "immediately," used 17 times (Matthew uses it twice in connection to the dried-up fig tree).

4 This is a Matthean phrase. He says a slight variant of it again during the controversy about Beelzebub in 12:25: "**ειδως δε ο ιησους τας ενθυμησεις αυτων ειπεν.**"

5 This is Matthew's favorite adverb; he uses it 87 times. Mark never uses it except 4 times in his version of Matthew's apocalyptic sermon about the last times. (Luke uses it 13 times.)

6 "Said to them." This is an almost exclusively Lukan expression (John uses it once). Luke uses it 26 times.

7 This is a Lukan preferential word; the specific form (present passive participle) occurs only here.

8 **παραχρημα**. A Lukan preferential word. Luke uses this word 15 times. Matthew uses it twice independently of Luke.

9 **ανιστημι**. A Lukan preferential word. Even though Matthew and Mark both use it 24 times combined, Luke uses it 72 times.

10 This is a Lukan preferential word; the specific form (present imperfect) occurs only here.

11 This is a preferential Matthean word. Only Matthew uses this form.

12 This emotional detail is typical of Mark. This particular elaboration is very similar to Mark's unique elaboration in The Rich Young Man pericope (Mk 10:17- 23): "And Jesus, beholding him, loved him."

13 This is a preferential Lukan word. He uses this word, **δεομαι**, 15 times. Matthew uses it once; Mark does not use it.

14 Matthew uses this same phrase at the rolling away of the rock from the tomb.

15 "[H]is disciples coming to…" is an exclusively Matthean phrase; he repeats it 6 times.

16 **ολιγοπιστοι**, "ones of little faith," is a Matthean word that Luke once imports in a synchronous verse.

17 This is an odd and somewhat awkward construction. Matthew and Luke simply have "he embarked." Mark has used this verb several times (**εμβαινω**). Why not now?

18 This word occurs only here.

19 This is the only time that Mark uses the phrase **τις αρα** (what manner).

20 **και εγενετο εν μια των ημερων** is a Lukan phrase that is repeated twice more.

21 "And he said to them" is a phrase that only Luke uses (8 times).

22 "Lake" is used only by Luke and by John in Revelation.

23 This verb is used once by Matthew, once in Romans, once in Hebrews, and 21 times in Luke/Acts.

24 Only Luke uses this word (5 times).

25 Only Luke uses this word (fall asleep).

26 Only Luke uses this word (3 times).

27 This Lukan word appears twice in Acts and in a similar context in 1 Corinthians, which shows a strong Lukan secretarial hand.

28 This is a term used only by Luke, always of Christ (6 times).

29 A preferential Lukan word.

7

The Structure of Matthew

In light of the circumstantial yet hypothetical scenario about why Matthew revised his original Aramaic Gospel (see Chapter 1), we must try to understand the structure of Matthew's two versions and the relationship of Mark and of Luke to these two structures. As we mentioned above, Papias indicates that Matthew wrote an early Aramaic Gospel, which we now assume, based on our "odd man out" deductions, was the source document not only for Matthew's Greek Gospel but also for Luke and Mark. This Aramaic original could have been memorized by many in the early community, thus providing a common template that could account for the Synoptics ' extensive literary synchronicity without extended passages of textual synchronicity.[1] In other words, passages and groups of passages in the Synoptics appear to be paraphrases of each other or some other controlling source, and the authors' extensive pericope manipulation

---

1 A rare, extended passage of textual synchronicity occurs in an important piece of dialogue between an unclean spirit and Jesus in the synagogue at Capernaum, which Matthew largely omits. Luke and Mark track for 28 words. One more exception is a 33-word synchronicity in Mt 10:21–22/Mk 13:12–13 and a 33-word synchronicity in Mt 16:24–28/Mk 8:34–9:1.

indicates considerable freedom in paraphrasing the presumed, memorized original source.

The standard model of biblical criticism holds that Matthew and Luke follow Mark's pericope order. We have implied that Matthew has significantly re-arranged the order of his Aramaic version not just to achieve a pleasing structure, but to create a unique literary genre. That the general characteristics of this genre are variously mirrored in Mark and Luke is strong evidence that both Mark and Luke had access not only to Matthew's Aramaic version, but also to Matthew's Greek edition as well.

The thesis of an extensively revised Matthean Greek version could also explain why Matthew's commonly recognized five discourses (suggestive of the Pentateuch) vary so significantly in length. What if the original Aramaic version indeed had five relatively balanced discourses, and it was Matthew's later revisions in his Greek version that made them uneven? This would comport well with the assumption above—that Matthew's Aramaic version was indeed a New Torah—and we will have stumbled upon its primary literary structure. If Mark and Luke have followed Matthew's Aramaic version to any extent, their general order agreement may be used to help reconstruct Matthew's original order. If our assumptions are so far true, then Matthew's divergences from the majority order should not be entirely random; that is, some rationale for his departures from the original Aramaic version's presumed order should appear that comports logically with the editorial emphasis of the *structure* of the Greek version.

Therefore, before we attempt to reconstruct something that may no longer be examined directly, we must be sure that we observe a definite structure in the version of Matthew that we can examine directly. The extant version of Matthew, with which we are all familiar, seems to consist of fourteen distinct sections, shown in the table below.

Table 9. The Structure of Matthew

S-1 Prophetic Prologue

- Genealogy
- Annunciation to Joseph
- The three wise men
- Flight into Egypt
- Slaughter of innocents
- Joseph arrives in Nazareth

S-2 Jesus' Baptism

- John the Baptist's message and manner
- John the Baptist's preparation
- Baptism of Christ
- Satan tempts Jesus

S-3 Jesus Begins Galilean Ministry

- Zebulon
- Calling of the four fishermen
- Jesus' healing fame

S-4 Jesus Delivers the Sermon on the Mount

- Who is blessed
- Spiritual Israel is the light of the world
- A righteousness that exceeds the Pharisees
- New laws tightening the interpretation of the old laws
- A secret (private) relationship with the Father
- How to pray
- Put our heart in Heaven
- Our eyes clear
- Do not worry
- Do not judge or compromise
- Persevere cheerfully through the narrow gate
- Do Christ's commands, not our own

S-5 Jesus' Healing Ministry

- Cleanses a leper
- Heals a centurion's servant (no faith in Israel like this)
- Heals the demon-possessed and sick
- Discipleship means wandering and leaving the dead world behind
- Stills the storm
- Heals the demoniac and is asked to leave Gergesene
- Forgives paralytic
- Heals paralytic
- Christ's purpose is to heal the sick through repentance
- New wineskins are needed to have Christ enter within
- Heals the ruler's daughter and the hemorrhaging woman
- Heals the blind
- Heals the mute
- Pharisees accuse Jesus of exorcism through demons

S-6 Jesus Commissions Laborers to Gather his Church

- Jesus is moved with compassion for the sheep of Israel
- Twelve apostles chosen and sent out on a missionary journey
- Commissioning sermon
- Ordains twelve apostles
- Sent to the Jews
- As sheep among wolves
- Hated of all
- Emulate the Master
- God will protect
- Gospel sows division
- Who is worthy

S-7 Jesus' Judgment of Israel

- Israel has rejected John the Baptist
- Israel rejects John and Christ for equal and opposite reasons
- Jesus' judgment on Chorazin, Bethsaida, and Capernaum
- The kingdom is hidden from the wise; revealed to the simple

- Christ is Lord of the Sabbath
- Jesus quotes Hosea: "mercy not sacrifice"
- Healing incident on the Sabbath
- The Jews hold a council to destroy Jesus
- Isaiah 42:1: Christ will show judgment to the Gentiles
- Pharisees accuse Jesus of demon possession
- The religious establishment is a "generation of vipers"
- They will be given no sign but the sign of Jonas the Prophet
- Judgment on the Judaizers is complete
- Bloodlines mean nothing in the heavenly family

S-8 Jesus Parabolically Teaches his Sheep in a Hostile World

- Parable of the sower
- Reason for parables
- Interpretation of sower
- Parable of the weeds
- Jesus' use of parables
- Interpretation of the weeds
- Parables of hidden treasure
- Parable of the net
- Parable of the householder

S-9 Jesus Feeds and Sustains his Sheep in a Hostile World

- Rejection at Nazareth
- The beheading of John
- Feeding of the five thousand
- Walking on the water
- What defiles man
- Syro-Phoenician woman
- Feeding of the four thousand
- No sign but Jonas
- Beware the doctrine of the Jews

S-10 Jesus Ordains his Church upon the Faith of Peter

- The confession

- The rebuke of Peter
- The transfiguration
- Cure of the epileptic
- Taxes are for strangers
- Be humble as a child
- Despise not children
- Two or three make a church
- The unforgiving servant
- Divorce is adultery
- Rich young ruler
- First last; last first
- Prediction of death
- The Son a ransom for many
- Heals two blind men

S-11 The Son of David Enters Jerusalem

- The disciples obtain the ass
- Tell Zion that the king is coming
- The crowds say, Hosanna
- Jesus expels the money changers
- Heals the blind and the lame
- Praise from the mouth of babes
- Cursing of the fig tree
- By what authority do you do these things?
- Parable of two sons
- Parable of the vineyard
- Parable of the wedding feast
- Is it lawful to give tribute to Caesar?
- In the resurrection, whose wife shall she be of the seven?
- Which is the great commandment in the law?
- If David then calls him Lord, how is he his son?

S-12 Jesus Condemns the Scribes and Pharisees

- Obey the Pharisees, but do not imitate them
- Eight-fold woes upon the scribes and Pharisees
- O Jerusalem, Jerusalem…

S-13 Jesus Issues his Apocalypse

- No stone left upon another
- Many shall come in my name
- You shall be hated of all nations
- False Christs will arise
- The coming of the Son of Man will be unmistakable
- No one knows when the Son will come
- The Son's coming will be like the flood of Noah
- Be on careful watch for the coming of the Son
- The parable of the talents
- Christ will judge all nations

S-14 Passion Week

- Jesus is anointed for burial
- Judas Iscariot goes to the chief priests
- The procurement of the place to eat the Passover
- One of you will betray me
- This is my body; this is my blood
- Exit to the Mount of Olives
- Prophecy of Peter's denial
- Jesus prays in Gethsemane
- He that betrays is near
- Jesus is confronted by swords and staves
- Judas betrays Jesus with a kiss
- Peter cuts off the ear of an assailant
- His disciples flee
- Jesus led to Caiaphas the high priest
- Peter follows at a distance
- Jesus is questioned and struck
- Peter denies Christ three times
- Early in the morning Jesus led before Pilate
- Judas' remorse; potter's field
- Are you the king of the Jews?
- The Jews accuse Jesus
- The people call for Barabbas
- Pilate trapped as a pawn

- Jesus scourged
- Soldiers mock Jesus with a crown of thorns, etc.
- Crucified at Golgotha
- He would not drink vinegar and gall
- Cast lots for his vesture
- "This is Jesus, King of the Jews"
- Crucified between two thieves
- Jesus is mocked
- Darkness from the 6th to the 9th hour
- *Eli, Eli, lama sabachthani?*
- A drink of vinegar
- Gives up the spirit
- Veil of the temple torn in two
- Earthquake
- Bodies of dead saints appear in the holy city
- Centurion: "Truly this was the Son of God"
- Mary Magdalene and others look on
- Joseph of Arimathaea asks Pilate for the body
- Joseph prepares the body; buries it in his own tomb
- A watch is set over the body
- Mary meets the resurrected Christ
- Tell my brothers to meet me in Galilee
- The priests make a conspiracy with the guards
- Jesus meets the eleven disciples in Galilee
- The Great Commission

If we compare the pericope order of Mark/Luke with the pericope order of Matthew in the places where movement is most evident (Figure 2), we will immediately see that pericopes do not randomly migrate throughout Matthew. They move in groups, and sometimes in blocks. Teaching pericopes have been moved backward and have been *grouped together* to form the Sermon on the Mount in Section 4. Healings have been advanced, forming a major healing block in Section 5. Parables have been grouped together in Section 8. Finally, various teachings prior to the entry of Jerusalem have been moved to a post-entry Section 12. And the movement displayed below achieves the fourteen-part structure we now see in Matthew. Green represents teaching pericopes, purple represents healing pericopes, brown represents parables, and red represents special speech/act pericopes – that is, they are crucial teaching pericopes bound up in the flow of action. Black is a key editorial comment concerning Jesus' rejection in Galilee.

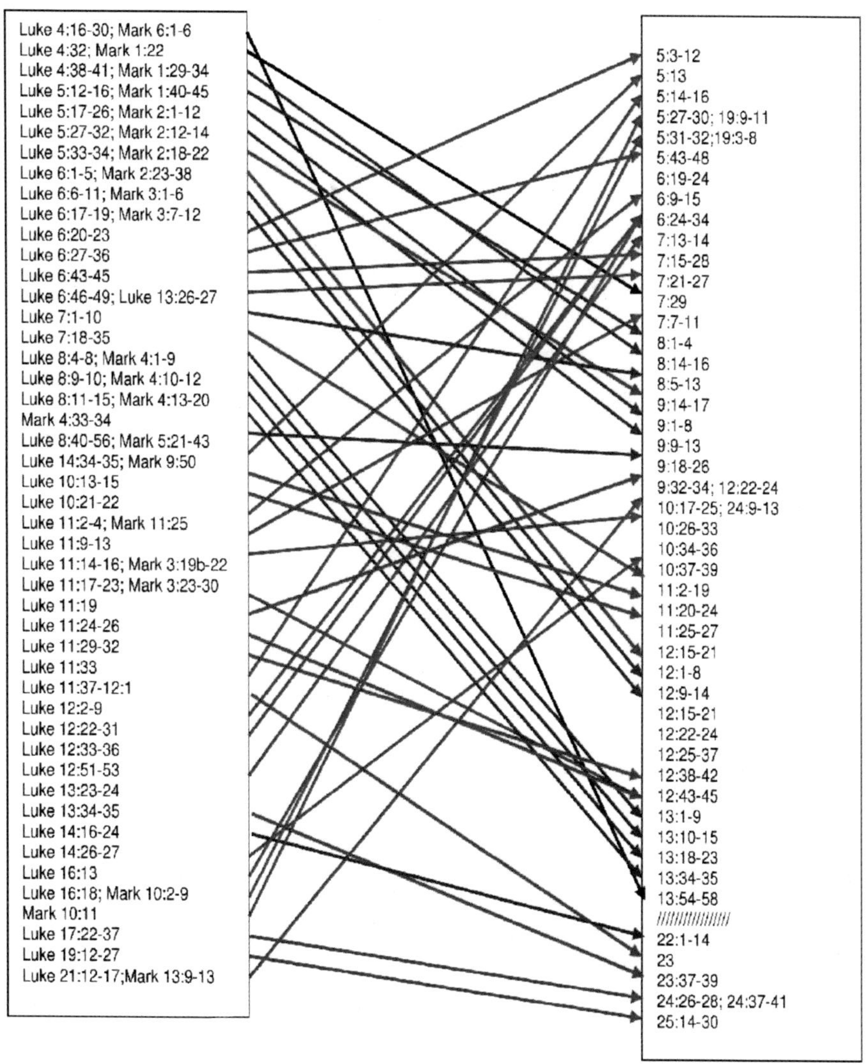

Figure 2. Pericope Order Comparison between Mark/Luke and Matthew

This structure now clearly reveals something stable about Matthew's perspective and editorial intent. The order of Mark and of Luke appear stable relative to the first half of Matthew. And since it is extremely unlikely that *two* authors have independently looked at the order of Matthew as a template and have distributed its parts in the same relative rearrangement, Matthew must be doing the editorial movement. The preservation of ordered blocks of pericopes from Luke/Mark's basic order (represented by roughly parallel lines) is an indicator that Matthew is aware of this basic, global order.[2] If we did not know about an earlier Aramaic version of Matthew, we would helplessly wonder where this basic order was coming from. Mark? Luke? It is much more logical that the basic order which lay upstream from all three of these authors, which Matthew has modified more radically than either Luke or Mark, is Matthew's Aramaic version.

Let's review what we have so far. We have discussed at length the circumstantial evidence that 1) there does indeed appear to be a source lying just upstream of the Synoptic tradition which accounts for much of the unity and diversity of the Synoptic account, which appears to be Matthew's earlier Aramaic Gospel; 2) structural evidence of the original basic order of this Aramaic version can still be seen in Luke and Mark's order agreement against Matthew, particularly in the first half of the Synoptic Gospels; and 3) even if the upstream document is *not* the Aramaic version, the fact that Matthew's movements against this basic order are not random but occur in pericope blocks and also achieve a coherent structure (Table 9 above) are clear indicators that Matthew is aware of this upstream document.

Yet the strangest part is this: 4) Matthew's literary architecture—part Greek play, part prophetic parable—is *also* oddly mirrored in both Luke and Mark in terms of structure, content, plot, and overall pericope organization.[3] Yet Matthew has seemingly achieved a literary effect of

2 The pericope is contextless. The meaning of *pericope* is "to cut around." The pericope, by definition, then, is something which stands by itself as a very short story. Therefore it is extremely unlikely that Matthew could have accidently achieved these partial pericope order agreements relative to Luke/Mark if he were working from an entirely different template.

3 For example, there is a teaching series; a healing series; a sharply rising conflict between Jesus and the religious establishment; a period of considerable tension in

much greater intensity than Luke or Mark. The strong, primary Matthean currents of an impossible righteousness, a terrible divorce between God and Israel, a sharp conflict between Jesus and the religious establishment, and Peter's fall from grace and betrayal of Christ are good thematic examples of this heightened intensity.

5) Phraseological evidence presented above very strongly indicates that Mark is conservatively synthesizing the phraseology of Matthew's Greek version and Luke. And even though Mark initially follows Luke's more primary reliance on Matthew's Aramaic version, beginning in Matthew's central section, at the pivotal point of Peter's confession and denial, Mark suddenly and decisively begins to follow the structure of Matthew's Greek version. Having looked at these phraseological and structural variations, we have made significant progress in understanding what Mark is attempting to do. But we must narrow our focus even further. If Mark is indeed a variation upon a theme, we must take a closer look at some of the Matthean themes he might be varying.

---

which Jesus teaches his sheep in a hostile political environment; a climatic confession by Peter concerning the identity of Jesus; an inexorable, final march to Jerusalem; a triumphal entry into Jerusalem which includes a dramatic cleansing of the temple; the issuance of an apocalyptic judgment; a catastrophic betrayal by Judas, Peter, the apostles, and the crowds; and the passion week.

8

The Themes of Matthew

Compared with Luke and Mark as they now stand, the Gospel of Matthew radically challenges the religious establishment of Israel in the same way that Paul's apocalyptic gospel revelation has challenged the religious establishment of the "sect of the Nazarenes," which produced tremendous stresses within the early church. And in Matthew we see the same kind of literary tragedy that we see in the historical tragedy of Paul, who is eventually betrayed into the hands of the Jews and the Romans through the negligence of the Christian Judaizers centered at Jerusalem.

These parallels strongly suggest that Paul's betrayal finally provoked a catastrophic spiritual catharsis in Matthew which resulted in a radicalized rewrite of his Aramaic New Torah document. This rewrite has yielded the contours of the Jonas Genre, strongly echoed in Mark and Luke. In our consideration of key theological terms, storyline, linguistic structure, mood, and authorial intent, we have seen that the Synoptic Gospels are a kind of prologue which forces the reader to look elsewhere for its conclusion. A theological analysis of the Synoptic Gospels demonstrates that it is a drama primarily and intentionally about the *death* of Christ, which would seem to have no fitting conclusion apart from Paul's crucifixion theology. In both Matthew and Paul's writings there are strong thematic currents of an impossible righteousness, a terrible divorce between God and Israel, and a baptism of death in Christ required of all his followers.

We have belabored the structure of Matthew because the relationship between Matthew and Paul will not be found in a shared vocabulary. And it will not be found in stand-alone religious ideas. It will be found in comparing the thematic structure of Matthew with the basic theological program of Paul. This is also why we have belabored the editorial intent of Matthew. If the relationship between Matthew and Paul turns almost entirely on the thematic structure and editorial intent of Matthew, we had better be sure about these things or we will never have confidence in such a connection. Unless we are sure that Matthew has *intentionally* contrived the Sermon on the Mount, for example, any themes that we find there will become a mirage of our own imagination. And it will be futile to attempt to find a resolution to the difficult enigmas of Matthew in Pauline theology.

Righteousness in the Sermon on the Mount

We have already noted that key theological terms such as *belief, hope, righteousness, peace, joy,* and *salvation,* so common to Paul, are rarely mentioned or otherwise vaguely defined in the Synoptic Gospels. We might also add to this list more developed Pauline theological terms like *reconciliation, justification,* and *grace.* But there is one significant exception to this in Matthew. Though no explicit Pauline definition is given when used, "righteousness" (and words associated with righteousness) represents a significant emphasis in Matthew. Righteousness (**δικαιοσυνη**) occurs twice in John, once in Luke, and not at all in Mark. Matthew alone represents sins as "debts" (**οφειλημα**) in the Lord's Prayer, illustrated graphically in the debtor who "owed" his master 10,000 talents.

But an enormous enigma lies behind Matthew's conception of righteousness. Matthew says that though our righteousness must exceed that of the Pharisees, "the publicans and the harlots go into the kingdom of God before them."[1] How can this be? How can the publicans and the harlots find a righteousness which exceeds the pharisaical commitment to keep the whole law? Will it be an antinomian righteousness, derived from a Pauline theology of good intentions divorced from good actions? Paul, for one, emphatically closes this door: "God forbid. How shall we, that are dead to sin, live any longer therein?"[2] The entire structure of Matthew is built upon the footings of the Sermon on the Mount. Its underlying theme is righteousness: "For I say to you, That except your righteousness shall exceed the righteousness of the scribes and Pharisees, you shall in no case enter into the kingdom of heaven." [3] "But seek first the kingdom of God, and his righteousness; and all these things shall be added unto you."[4]

As in the Pauline epistles, the idea is simply stated but difficult to fully understand. In Matthew, the truly blessed are constantly being contrasted with a legalistic, hypocritical religious establishment. We see a parallel contrast between those who cling to their own righteousness and those who have abandoned everything to embrace the righteousness of God. At the end of Paul's dissertation in Romans, we find the answer to the dilemma which Matthew begins in the Sermon on the Mount but never fully resolves: why don't the Pharisees find righteousness, but the publicans and harlots do? "Wherefore? Because they [the Pharisees] sought it [righteousness] not by faith, but as it were by the works of the law." [5] Hence they arrived at the belief that righteousness was something that could be generated within the human soul instead of something that was given as a gift from above. Matthew poses the dilemma; Paul solves it by showing how that God himself has chosen the sacrifice of Christ to be the means whereby our past sins might be forgiven. Not only are we justified, as Abraham was, but now we know *why* we are justified. We are justified by our belief in God's redemptive act in Christ. And we also now know how God himself can justify sinners and yet still be just.[6]

---

1 Mt 21:31c "Jesus said to them, Verily I say unto you, That the publicans and the harlots go into the kingdom of God before you."

2 Ro 6:2.

3 Mt 5:20.

4 Mt 6:33.

5 Ro 9:32.

6 Ro 3:26

This is why Matthew so ruthlessly juxtaposes the publican and harlot together with the Pharisee. In the tradition of Isaiah, Matthew implies that our own righteousness is a filthy rag.[7] God's righteousness is a gown for a god.[8] The righteousness God seeks in us is *his* righteousness and not *our* righteousness. God desires the righteousness that he works in us through Christ and not what we work in ourselves apart from him.

Though in Matthew the soul dies for Christ's sake, Christ does not destroy the law. "Whosoever therefore shall break one of these least commandments, and shall teach men so, he shall be called the least in the kingdom of heaven."[9] Though Paul dies to the law,[10] he does not destroy it.[11] Antinomianism destroys the law. In Paul's gospel, Christ's gift of a righteousness-of-the-law, entirely fulfilled in his own body for our sakes, destroys not the law but sin's power over us through its agency.[12] Whether we be Pharisee or publican, Paul says that "all have sinned." [13] We have all failed the standards of the law,[14] not as it applies to someone else, but as it applies to us.[15] We have all failed the moral

---

7 Is 64:6. "But we are all as an unclean thing, and all our righteousnesses are as filthy rags; and we all do fade as a leaf; and our iniquities, like the wind, have taken us away."
8 Mt 22:11–12. "And when the king came in to see the guests, he saw there a man which had not on a wedding garment: And he saith unto him, Friend, how camest thou in hither not having a wedding garment? And he was speechless."
9 5:19. This is also illustrated in Matthew's exclusive use of the word **ανομια**, which means "without law" or lawlessness. He does not use **πονηρος** or **κακος.**
10 Ro 7:4. "Wherefore, my brethren, ye also are become dead to the law by the body of Christ."
11 3:31. "Do we then make void the law through faith? God forbid: yea, we establish the law."
12 "But sin, taking occasion by the commandment, wrought in me all manner of concupiscence" (Ro 7:8). "Therefore Christ was crucified and we in him in order that the body of sin might be destroyed, that henceforth we should not serve sin" (Ro 6:6).
13 Ro 3:23.
14 3:20.

standards we expect of others.[16] Though the law requires death for sin,[17] Christ annulled the judgment against us through his own death.[18] Therefore, in dying, Paul argues, and Matthew's Sermon on the Mount graphically illustrates, Christ "establishes" the law.

Matthew has intentionally edited a great deal of raw teaching material into a single Sermon on the Mount which brings the Jew into hopeless conflict with law—from which there is no escape except for the escape of Paul: "O wretched man that I am! who shall deliver me from the body of this death? I thank God through Jesus Christ our Lord....Being justified freely by his grace through the redemption that is in Christ Jesus: Whom God hath set forth to be a propitiation through faith in his blood, to declare his righteousness for the remission of sins that are past, through the forbearance of God; To declare, I say, at this time his righteousness: that he might be just, and the justifier of him which believes in Jesus."[19]

The delivery of the Sermon on the Mount is very much like the delivery of the law of Moses itself.[20] But here Matthew tells us of a triply excessive law. First, it interprets the Mosaic law with a rigor that goes far beyond the shallow rationalizations of the religious establishment.[21] Second, Christ adds another dimension of unachievable rigor by great-

---

15 7:15. "For that which I do I allow not: for what I would, that do I not; but what I hate, that do I."

16 2:1. "Therefore you are inexcusable, O man, whosoever you are that judge: for wherein you judge another, you condemn yourself; for you that judge do the same things."

17 6:23. "For the wages of sin is death; but the gift of God is eternal life through Jesus Christ our Lord."

18 5:8-9. "But God commended his love toward us, in that, while we were yet sinners, Christ died for us. Much more then, being now justified by his blood, we shall be saved from wrath through him."

19 7:24; 3:24–26.

20 For example, consider how Matthew sets it up: Jesus goes up into the mountain and the disciples come to him. Then "he opens his mouth and taught them saying..." The "opening of the mouth" is a clear indication that something momentous is about to happen. At the introduction to the parables in chapter 13, Matthew quotes Ps 78:2, which includes this same phrase, thereby linking Christ to David the psalmist.

21 This is illustrated in summary fashion in the matter of "*corban*" (Mt 15:5; Mk 7:11).

ly increasing the demands of the law with his "You have heard it said [by the Law of Moses] that…but I say to you…" formula, recorded only in Matthew. In chapter 19, Matthew records the pharisaical objection to this new way of interpreting the law by invoking the Mosaic divorce law exceptions, to which Christ responds not in terms of the brittleness of the law, but of its softness and superficiality. It was the hardness of the hearts of the fathers of the establishment that caused Moses to soften the message and permit divorce.[22] Faced with the unrelenting severity of the *spirit* of the law, even the disciples become exasperated. They are brought to the same position as the servant who buried his talent because of the severity of his Lord.[23] The disciples say, "If the case of the man be so with his wife, it is not good to marry."[24] The disciples reason that if the demands of the law are this severe, then they are forced into a position of not entering into situations in which its exactitude guarantees their failure.

But Christ then adds a third element of excessiveness to the law. The standard he sets for us is an impossible one. It is *perfection*: "Be perfect even as the Father in heaven is perfect."[25] This is not a perfection of good intentions or a program of psychological authenticity. And it is not just an improved system that avoids the rationalizations of the religious establishment. This super-law requires an *impossible* level of righteousness. Jesus said, "It is easier for a camel to go through the eye of a needle, than for a rich man to enter into the kingdom of God."[26] The disciples were incredulous that this could be so. Surely this teaching violated not only the Wisdom literature of the Jews, but also common sense? For if a man is practicing righteousness (or "right living"), will he not be rewarded in this life with children and houses and lands?[27] Was Christ merely teaching, indirectly that the idol of wealth corrupts

---

22 Mt 19:7–8. "They say to him, Why did Moses then command to give a writing of divorcement, and to put her away? He says to them, Moses because of the hardness of your hearts suffered you to put away your wives: but from the beginning it was not so."

23 25:24–30.

24 19:10.

25 5:48.

26 19:24.

27 Mk 10:30.

and that absolute wealth corrupts absolutely?[28]

No. Christ says that heaven is about wealth.[29] The problem, Christ says, is that the rich man has trusted in his earthly wealth that he has earned and cannot let it go for the true riches in heaven that he has not. John reiterates this: "You say, I am rich, and increased with goods, and have need of nothing; but do not know that you are wretched, and miserable, and poor, and blind, and naked."[30] In the Sermon on the Mount, those who know that they are righteousness-poor, but nevertheless crave for the *substance* of God's righteousness instead of some manufactured hypocritical illusion, are those who will be blessed with the righteousness of the kingdom of heaven. Paul says that the whole project of a child of heaven is to be "… found in him, not having my own righteousness, which is of the law, but that which is through the faith of Christ, the righteousness which is of God by faith."[31]

The publicans and the harlots knew very well why they could not achieve righteousness. They had no power in themselves to do so. As Paul earlier had said, "For the good that I would, I do not: but the evil which I would not, that I do."[32] The Pharisees, on the other hand, were convinced that they could achieve righteousness *without* the help of

---

28 Jas 2:6.

29 "Rejoice, and be exceeding glad: for great is your reward in heaven" (Mt 5:12). "Jesus said to him, If you will be perfect, go and sell what you have, and give to the poor, and you shall have treasure in heaven" (Mt 19:21).

30 Re 3:17. John has the same idea of righteousness—not primarily as a religious idea, but as "life." He is saying that we must constantly abide in him as the branch abides in the root: "Abide in me, and I in you. As the branch cannot bear fruit of itself, except it abide in the vine; no more can you, except you abide in me" (Jn 15:4). Paul has already used this metaphor: "Boast not against the branches. But if you boast, you don't bear the root, but the root, you" (Ro 11:18). And Paul has already developed the argument of being *in* Christ: "Therefore if any man be in Christ, he is a new creature: old things are passed away; behold, all things are become new" (2 Cor 5:17). Paul and John, with different approaches, make the case that our righteousness must be *continually* drawn from Christ. Once we attempt to manufacture our own righteousness by setting up on our own, it lives for a while, but then dies from lack of nutrients and through the increasing toxicity of sin working through our own powerlessness.

31 Phil 3:9.

32 Ro 7:19.

God, though it resulted in a religious system which created as many loopholes as it did laws. And it also created insurmountable pressures of inner deceit. This deceit flowed into the outward world as blatant hypocrisy. To relieve these tremendous pressures, this hypocrisy projected a complex system of religious tradition upon the backs of others which only professional Pharisees were in a position to keep. To escape a reckoning with their own conscience, they condemned the laity as utterly ignorant and vulgar.

The Sermon on the Mount is not an unintelligible, random patchwork of moral teachings. It is a focused preparation for the Pauline gospel of the righteousness of God. Thus it is not merely an argument against rationalizing away the demands of the law. It is not merely an argument against a hypocritical keeping of that law, however exacting that hypocrisy might be. And it is not merely an argument about mediocrity and about our tendency to impress God with superficial, pious confessions acknowledging the "ideal" of perfection and of how far short we fall from it. The Sermon on the Mount presents the impossible demand to *be* perfect.

The Sermon on the Mount argues that if we are not perfect, *we will not see God*. What keeps us from God is not rationalization or hypocrisy or mediocrity. It is our unshakeable belief that a self-righteousness good enough for us should be good enough for God. The Sermon on the Mount leaves us hungering and thirsting after righteousness. This hunger and thirst leads us to the Pauline doctrine of justification by belief in Christ apart from the works of the law.

The Pharisees were adamantly convinced that they had "arrived" at the throne of God with their relative self-righteousness. Christ told them that their righteousness was, essentially, a filthy rag before the Father. Though the outside appeared dry, the inside was soaked with sin.[33] Christ saw the hungering and thirsting after true righteousness in the publicans and the harlots. He knew that they knew of their own spiritual poverty. This is why they received the baptism of utter repentance from John the Baptist. John's baptism lead eventually to a repentance so complete that Paul described it as a baptism into the death of Christ—a crucifixion of the soul. Only then could true life begin. Christ did not come to call those who were righteous in their own

33 Mt 23:25, 27.

eyes and so could not brook the need for repentance. Christ came to call to life those who were already dead with guilt. He came to call those who knew that they were wretched, miserable, poor, blind, and naked—yet hungered, nevertheless, for glory, honor, immortality, and eternal life.[34]

The Great Divorce

Matthew records that many will come to the kingdom of Heaven from the east and from the west (such as the Magi). Those who do not come will be visited by Christ in judgment, and "all the tribes of the earth will mourn" at his appearing. When Jesus *commissions his laborers to gather his church* (Section 6), Jesus instructs them not to go into Samaria. But he foretells that this will not always be the missionary strategy of the church: "Therefore say I unto you, The kingdom of God shall be taken from you, and given to a nation bringing forth the fruits thereof."[35] But what of the common expectation that the Messiah would deliver the people from their oppressors? Matthew says that an angel told Joseph that Mary's baby would save his people from their sins. The angel made no reference to the salvation of the people from their *enemies* (i.e., the Romans).[36]

The storm clouds build early in Matthew. A crisis is coming for Israel: "And I say to you, That many shall come from the east and west, and shall sit down with Abraham, and Isaac, and Jacob, in the kingdom of heaven. But the children of the kingdom shall be cast out into outer darkness: there shall be weeping and gnashing of teeth."[37]

Within the catalog of teachings, healings, divine claims, and acts of power, the reader of Matthew is everywhere confronted with the theme that though Christ is sent to the house of Israel, he is categorically rejected by them. He is judged to be a blasphemer and a deceiver of the people because he forgives sins, casts out demons, eats with publicans and sinners, touches the leprous, heals Gentiles and Jews on the Sabbath, and speaks against the temple and the hypocrisy of the religious establishment.

---

34 Ro 2:7.

35 Mt 21:43.

36 As Luke does in 1:71.

37 Mt 8:11–12.

Simultaneously, Jesus *himself* categorically rejects "this generation" of incompetent and malicious religious leaders, presaging God's rejection of Jerusalem and her destruction. He tells the twelve apostles to preach only to Israel, not to the Samaritans or the Gentiles, so that every word of judgment would not be misconstrued: they were not generalizations. They were all intended for Israel. Christ sends the apostles out, not as co-laborers with those who sit in Moses' seat, but as sheep among wolves, to fellow sheep without shepherds, as laborers among unharvested fields.[38] "Whoever is not offended by me," Christ says, "this man is blessed." Immediately following is a prayer very reminiscent of John, saying in effect: I am rejected by "prudent" Israel, who has "condemned the guiltless"; nevertheless, I am the man who will gather the remnant sheep.[39]

This is talk of divorce, not of deliverance from political enemies. One can see Matthew's emphasis and linkage with Paul here by examining his use of **εκκοπτω** or "cut out." He records John the Baptist as saying, "It doesn't matter if you are children of Abraham; if you do not produce the fruit of his faith, you will be **εκκοπτω** and thrown into the fire." Christ repeats this late in the Sermon on the Mount. Twice Matthew, in separate pericopes, repeats the saying that if even our own members "offend" us—that is, cause us to shrink back from obedience to Christ—then we must irrevocably cut them off. Paul very graphically emphasizes the amputational nature of divorce with Judaism, if not the Jewish Christian church: "I would that they [the circumcision party] were even cut off (**αποκοπτω**) which trouble you."[40] He too saw that Judaism would be intransigent concerning the offense (**σκανδαλον**) of the cross of Christ (1 Cor 15:23).

38 Mt 9:36–38.

39 11:25. "O Father, Lord of heaven and earth, because thou hast hid these things from the wise and prudent, and hast revealed them unto babes." The prayer also bears a very strong affinity to Paul's position in 1 Cor 1:19: "For it is written, I will destroy the wisdom of the wise, and will bring to nothing the understanding of the prudent."

40 Paul here is making an earthy wordplay about circumcision: "And I, brethren, if I yet preach circumcision, why do I yet suffer persecution? then is the offence of the cross ceased. I would they were even cut off which trouble you" (Gal 5:11– 12).

In Matthew, Christ colors his entire project in the color of offensiveness (**σκανδαλον**). In response to John the Baptist's prison envoy, Jesus is gently encouraging: "Blessed is he that is not offended in me."[41] He is far less tolerant of those who hear the gospel but immediately fall away when tested.[42] His own people of Nazareth were offended at the mere ordinariness of their familiarity with him. Upon hearing of the Pharisees' offense at his response to his "unwashed hands" challenge,[43] Jesus is severe: they will be "rooted up" by the Father himself. Jesus is even more severe towards those who offend the little children of his kingdom.[44] Peter claimed that he would never be offended at Christ[45] but instantly betrayed him at the threat of being recognized by a young woman's having recognized him as being with the Galilean now on trial.[46]

Matthew's editorial intent is clearly, radically Pauline: if we do not embrace the offense of Christ, we will be cut off. This is why the betrayal of Peter is so central to the flow of the Synoptic template: "Get behind me, Satan: you are an offence to me: for you savor not the things that be of God, but those that be of men."[47] Matthew's Gospel is addressed to all those who will come into Christ's "church" on the basis of Peter's confession: "And I say also to you, That you are Peter, and upon this rock I will build my church; and the gates of hell shall not prevail against it."[48] The implicit claim here is that Christ is building a new house. He is ignoring the "house of Israel." He is reconstituting the assembly. And God will bind and loose in heaven whatever this reconstituted church binds and looses. The members of this church will no longer seek judgment from secular rulers or the Sanhedrin but from this new church herself. Both John the Baptist and Jesus deliver their fateful decree: The religious establishment of Israel is a "generation of vipers." They are an "evil and adulterous generation" who could not

41 Mt 11:16.
42 13:20–21.
43 15:1–20.
44 18:6.
45 26:33.
46 26:69.
47 16:23.
48 16:18.

recognize its own messiah and was worthy of no other sign beyond the sign of Jonah the prophet.

The editorial intent of Matthew is to deliver a divorce decree. And the grounds are as follows: "The men of Nineveh shall rise in judgment with this generation, and shall condemn it: because they repented at the preaching of Jonas; and, behold, a greater than Jonas is here."[49] Jesus says that Israel will be worse off *after* Jesus performs his exorcism than before.[50] Except as a prelude to judgment, all the good that he did in Israel will be for naught. All the healings and signs of power and cures will come to nothing. The nation of Israel will relapse into darkness and become spiritually sicker than ever. Matthew does not shrink from recording that the morally depraved Ninevites will rise from the grave during the great Judgment to condemn great Israel. The Queen of the South will come not to bow before the High Priest, but to judge him.

Even ties of blood will not stop this divorce, unless they reappear as children of the new kingdom of heaven, which is not based on law or blood, but on true love and joyful obedience to God.[51] God will make for himself new children from among the Gentiles. In his exodus from Israel, Jesus will be taking the lost sheep of Israel with him[52] and none will snatch them out of his hand.[53] This same thesis appears in Mark, where he picks up the tough talk of Matthew to level it against his own church, which stands on the threshold of denying Christ before the Neronian persecutions. The author of Hebrews does the same thing: Jewish Christians are beginning to forsake the assembling of themselves

49 Mt 12:41.

50 12:43–45.

51 12:46–50.

52 Jn 10:16. "And other sheep I have, which are not of this fold: them also I must bring, and they shall hear my voice; and there shall be one fold, and one shepherd." Paul neatly summarizes this phenomenon in Eph 2:11-22. In fact, Paul states flatly that in Christ's body, which is the church, there is no longer Jew nor Greek (Gal 3:28).

53 Mt 21:43. "Therefore say I unto you, The kingdom of God shall be taken from you, and given to a nation bringing forth the fruits thereof." Also Jn 10:28–29: "My sheep hear my voice, and I know them, and they follow me: And I give unto them eternal life; and they shall never perish, neither shall any man pluck them out of my hand."

together[54] as a stand-alone church for fear of the Judaizers, just like Peter had done at Antioch.[55] But if anyone draws back from the exodus of Christ, he will be left behind by divorce: "Now the just shall live by faith: but if any man draw back, my soul shall have no pleasure in him."[56]

The uniquely Matthean story of Herod massacring the innocents graphically illustrates what the religious establishment of Israel was doing to its own children. Similarly, the distinctly Matthean story of Christ's flight into Egypt and his subsequent call from there is unmistakably typological of Moses' flight to Midian.[5] In the very body of Christ was the new Israel. They have been called out of the bondage of the Egypt of sin to inherit the kingdom of God. Likewise, God's divorced wife is a new kind of Egypt from which Christ calls his abused and neglected lost sheep into the New Israel: his new "church" and his New Covenant.[58] Only Matthew refers to these "lost sheep."

Christ's mission is not to go *only* to the Jews, but to go *first* to the lost sheep within the Jewish nation. That is his priority. Yet in Matthew, Jesus constantly interacts with those who "in every nation…fear him, and work righteousness": he cures the leper, the centurion's servant, and the daughter of the Syro-Phoenician woman.[59] In the parable of the tares in the field, Matthew argues that Christ sees his mission field as the world and not just the Jews.[6] This, itself, is heretical. The Jews saw their nation as chosen by the sovereign will of God. And according to the Jewish sense of limited salvation, all other nations and the people within them were, as a consequence, chosen to damnation by that same sovereign will. Christ's emphasis on the individual's response to his

54 Heb 10:25.

55 Gal 2:14.

56 Heb 10:38.

57 Ex 2:11–15.

58 There are many references which support this analysis. In chapter 23, he more explicitly states that it is the "scribes and the Pharisees [who] sit in Moses' seat" who "bind heavy burdens and grievous to be borne, and lay them on men's shoulders." It is like making bricks without straw. Only in Matthew do we find this analysis of the religious establishment of Israel: "Woe unto you, scribes and Pharisees, hypocrites! for ye compass sea and land to make one proselyte, and when he is made, ye make him twofold more the child of hell than yourselves" (Mt 23:15). 59 Acts 10:35. It takes Peter a long time to realize this.

60 Mt 13:38.

word in the parable of the sower would also violate the Jewish doctrine of a kind of mechanical grace, in which all those who were racially Jews were, by definition, chosen.[61] There was no "cooperating" with this fate to make it a reality. It was just so. So the varied individual responses of the soils in this parable overturned the whole idea of the dualism between Israel and the rest of the world – between the chosen Jew and the total depravity of the Gentile soul. In the parable of the wicked tenants, the conclusion that Jesus forces his audience to utter is that "he will miserably destroy those wicked men, and will let out his vineyard unto other husbandmen, which shall render him the fruits in their seasons."[62]

Then he quotes Psalm 118:22-23 as precedent and commentary for divorce: "Jesus says unto them, Did ye never read in the scriptures, The stone which the builders rejected, the same is become the head of the corner: this is the Lord's doing, and it is marvelous in our eyes? Therefore say I unto you, The kingdom of God shall be taken from you, and given to a nation bringing forth the fruits thereof. And whosoever shall fall on this stone shall be broken: but on whomsoever it shall fall, it will grind him to powder. And when the chief priests and Pharisees had heard his parables, they perceived that he spoke of them."

Matthew has Jesus make a definite transition to parabolic discourse in chapter 13 (Section 8). Jesus' teachings now go far beyond the Sermon of the Mount. No longer merely pressing the limit of morally interpreting the law, Jesus is now pressing the outer limits of the entire idea of his identity as Christ and of the kingdom which he is inaugurating in the context of a hostile religious establishment. Now his teaching is *subversive*. The Sanhedrin realizes that if Jesus is taken "literally," the Romans will soon come "to take away our place and our nation."[63] Parables now mediate all Jesus' public words since he is now in the presence of his estranged wife, against whom divorce proceedings have already begun. Jesus must speak in messianic secrets

61 John the Baptist has already repudiated this idea of divine grace working merely mechanically through a biological generation: "And think not to say within yourselves, We have Abraham to our father: for I say to you, that God is able of these stones to raise up children unto Abraham" (Mt 3:9).

62 Mt 21:41.

63 Jn 11:48.

to his children, helpless and unmothered, while unfaithful Israel looks on, lest he be formally indicted for "corrupting her youth"[64] as a deceiver before the time appointed.

The First Will Be Last; the Last Will Be First

Matthew's literary structure folds almost exactly in half upon the enigmatic confession sequence of Peter; it is, indeed, the hinge upon which his Gospel pivots. Matthew not only has a more elaborate presentation of Peter's confession than Luke and Mark, he is more intent on presenting the irony of Peter's impending moral collapse. In Satan's testing of Christ, Satan offers Christ the keys of the world if he would change stone to bread; in Christ's testing of Peter, Christ offers Peter the keys to the Church if only Peter would allow Christ to change his heart of stone to feed bread to his church. And immediately after the confession we encounter verbiage strangely reminiscent of Christ's testing in the wilderness: "For what is a man profited, if he shall gain the whole world, and lose his own soul? or what shall a man give in exchange for his soul?"[65] Matthew is using Peter as an antitype of Christ.

> [Jesus] saith unto them, But whom say ye that I am? And Simon Peter answered and said, Thou art the Christ, the Son of the living God. And Jesus answered and said unto him, Blessed art thou, Simon Barjona: for flesh and blood hath not revealed it unto thee, but my Father which is in heaven. And I say also unto thee, That thou art Peter, and upon this rock I will build my church; and the gates of hell shall not prevail against it. And I will give unto thee the keys of the kingdom of heaven: and whatsoever thou shalt bind on earth shall be bound in heaven: and whatsoever thou shalt loose on earth shall be loosed in heaven. Then charged he his disciples that they should tell no man that he was Jesus the Christ. From that time forth began Jesus to shew unto his disciples, how that he must go unto Jerusalem, and suffer many things of the elders and chief priests and scribes, and be killed, and be raised again the third day. Then Peter took him, and began to rebuke him, saying, Be it far from thee, Lord: this shall not be unto thee. But he turned, and said unto Peter, Get thee behind me, Satan: thou are an offence unto me

64 This is the charge ultimately brought against Socrates.
65 Mt 16:26.

for thou savourest not the things that be of God, but those that be of men.[66]

In the testing of Christ, Satan offers Christ the keys of the world in exchange for Christ's respect. In Matthew, Peter exchanges the keys of Christ for the respect of men. In Matthew, Jesus says that it is upon the simple, unguarded utterance of belief of Simon, son of Jonah, that he will build his church, not upon the humanistic authority and worldly theology of Simon the Rock. In the Greek it is much easier to see this. When Christ says, "Upon this *petras* [rock] I will build my church," we cannot see that both "this" and "*petras*" are feminine. These words therefore do not easily agree with "Petros" (Peter), which is masculine. Matthew should therefore be read: "You are Peter, but upon *this* rock (feminine "this" and feminine "rock") I will build my church, and the gates of hell will not prevail against her." The nearest feminine noun with which "this" can agree is "faith" (16:8), which makes perfect sense. "It is upon this [faith] that I will build my church."

Though Mark closely follows Matthew by including Jesus' repudiation of Peter, which Luke omits,[67] the concise structure of Mark seemingly cannot bear the complex irony of this pericope. Therefore

---

66 Mt 16:15–23.

67 Gracious Luke inserts verbiage at the Last Supper that assures the church that the "first" apostle will indeed be last. Luke, too, refers to the faith of Simon and not to the worldly theology of Peter: "And the Lord said, Simon, Simon, behold, Satan has desired to have you, that he may sift you as wheat: But I have prayed for you, that your faith fail not: and when you are converted, strengthen your brethren" (Lk 22:31–32). John is also very forgiving of Peter's moral collapse. In the exchange between Jesus and Peter at John's unique footwashing, we see John pushing the explanation for Peter's moral collapse upon mere ignorance. And in John's epilogue (21:15–17), he pushes the explanation in the direction of a leadership failure which, in turn, is due to Peter's lack of love for Christ. In a passage seemingly designed to achieve the prophetic restoration of Peter found in Luke, Jn 21:18–19a reads: "When you were young, you girded yourself, and walked where you wanted: but when you are old, you will stretch forth your hands, and another shall gird you, and carry you whither you would not. This he spoke, signifying by what death he should glorify God." Note that John uses the same name as Matthew at Peter's confession/denial scene and as Luke at his Last Supper scene: "Simon Barjonah." "Simon, son of Jonah, do you love me more than these?" (Jn 21:15a). Perhaps through Matthew, John has understood that Peter has become an

Mark, presumably, abbreviates Peter's confession, deletes all of Matthew's "rock"- oriented dialogue, deletes Matthew's account of Peter's fledging faith in the walking on the water pericope, inserts the unique Marcan verbiage in the forgotten bread pericope ("Having eyes, do you not see? and having ears, do you not hear? and do you not remember?"),[68] and inserts a rare Marcan pericope about the gradual healing of a blind man of Bethsaida[69] to link this verbiage to Peter's confession. Mark also moves the phrase "he that has ears to hear, let him hear" to a position *after* Matthew's sower parable and immediately inserts another unique pericope about how Peter's hearing will improve at some point in the distant future:

> And he said, So is the kingdom of God, as if a man should cast seed into the ground; And should sleep, and rise night and day, and the seed should spring and grow up, he knows not how. For the earth brings forth fruit of herself; first the blade, then the ear, after that the full corn in the ear.[70]

Matthew portrays Peter as having become a rock of offense to Christ, just as Christ has become a rock of offense to Israel. Matthew very adroitly presents the irony of Peter callously rejecting what Paul unreservedly embraced: Christ crucified.[71] And this may be because Matthew himself now believes that the ironic contrast of Peter and Paul has been divinely contrived. Matthew says, "Now the names of the twelve apostles are these: The first, Simon, who is called Peter..."[72] Peter had gravitated to a leading position within the early church, but now Matthew is suggesting something more. He is suggesting that Peter is somehow the chief apostle. Matthew exploits the fact that Jesus called Peter's name out first when he sent out the twelve. And when it was time to begin the final tour before heading to Jerusalem, Jesus began by recalling his disciples, beginning with Peter. Matthew, perhaps, has

---

example of Israel, especially as Paul has portrayed her in Ro 9–11: she has fallen through unbelief, but in the end, Paul believes, she will be restored.

68 Mk 8:18.

69 8:22–26.

70 4:26–28.

71 1 Cor 1:23. "But we preach Christ crucified, unto the Jews a stumblingblock, and unto the Greeks foolishness."

72 Mt 10:2.

lately understood how Saul of Tarsus came to be called Saul "the least" or Saul "the last" (or simply Paul).[73]

Matthew has broken off the aphoristic pericope conclusion, "But many that are first shall be last; and the last shall be first," from the curing of the centurion's servant (where it remains in Luke). He reinserts it to a much less logical place: as a response to Peter's assertion, "Lo, we have left all to follow you."[74] This alters Christ's response considerably. Christ seems to be saying to Peter, "But you *haven't* left all to follow me." Peter, indeed, did not leave all to follow Christ. He merely left his trade, temporarily.[75]

The Synoptic Gospels make it painfully clear that Peter left Christ to follow his own interests. As Peter's betrayal becomes better known within the early community, some even begin to contrast Peter with the *rest* of the disciples. The Synoptic Gospels focus on Peter's denial of the person of Jesus Christ and that he was a Galilean. John, however, records a much more logical and categorical denial: "Then the damsel that kept the door says to Peter, are you not also one of this man's disciples? He says, I am not."[76] This may be why Mark records a *distinction* between Peter and the disciples: "But go your way, tell his disciples *and Peter* that he goes before you into Galilee: there shall you see him, as he said to you [emphasis added]." [77]

Here again, if it were not for John, we could not be so fully aware of what Matthew might be doing concerning the seeming primacy of Peter. In contrast to Matthew, for example, John places Philip in a much more central role. Peter is brought to Christ by his brother Andrew, but Philip is sought out personally by Jesus.[78] Andrew *tells* Peter early on that he had found the Messiah. But when Philip brings Nathaniel to Christ, Philip makes an aggressive confession: "We have found him, of whom Moses in the law, and the prophets, did write, Jesus of Nazareth, the son of Joseph." At a pivotal event of all four gospels, the feeding of

73 *Paulus,* which means "small" or "least."

74 Mt 19:27–30. Note that Mark follows Matthew here (Mk 10:28–31).

75 Mt 4:20.

76 18:17.

77 Mk 16:7.

78 Jn 1:43.

the five thousand,[79] John has Jesus singling out *Philip* in order to test him. During this test, Peter speaks out as but "one of the disciples." At the last Passover feast,[80] the Greeks who came to the feast desiring to see Jesus came to *Philip* in order to arrange an interview, addressing him as "Lord" (κυριος), a title elsewhere reserved for Christ.

John also helps us to understand what appears to be an elaborate word-play in Matthew concerning the naming of Peter. If we had only Matthew, we might assume that Petros (Peter) was also some sort of title. But there is no further evidence of this in the rest of the New Testament. In John, "rock" begins as a *characteristic* which Jesus saw in Peter. Just as there is a big difference in English between Arthur King and King Arthur, so there is also in the Greek. Christ is a title, not a characteristic—or even a name. Therefore we find Paul referring to him as Christ Jesus.[81] But John is clear that a *character* name was assigned to Peter from the very beginning and not as a result of a later confession. Unlike the "Christ Jesus" construction, Peter is never referred to as "Rock Simon" as if it were a title.

In Matthew, the naming of Peter is foundational because Peter is a rocky obstruction that lies directly in the path of Christ. And in Peter's pivotal confession, we do not come upon bedrock, we come upon an obstruction of sandstone. We confront a double-minded man, unstable in all his ways.[82] And this instability is achieved when Matthew juxtaposes the confessor, Simon, son of Jonah, with Peter, the "rock of my offense." Peter the coward. Peter the betrayer. For all Peter knew, he had fallen asleep on watch and had allowed Jesus' band to be taken by surprise by the temple contingent sent to arrest Jesus at Gethsemane. Peter therefore makes a confused attempt to "save" Jesus from circumstances that he believes are beyond Jesus' control.

The account is moving too quickly for Matthew to have Jesus stop and explain the "unfaith" that Peter's desperate violence betrays. But Matthew does consummate the thematic irony that he has been work-

---

79 6:5–14.

80 12:20–22.

81 He employs this usage 56 of 58 times.

82 Jas 1:8.

ing to achieve since the beginning of his Gospel. Jesus stops and chides Peter with an idea still beyond Peter's unconverted comprehension: "Don't you think that I cannot even now pray to my Father, and he shall immediately give me more than twelve legions of angels?"[83] In Matthew's testing in the wilderness pericope, he places Psalm 91 in the unwitting mouth of Satan: "And he says to him, If you are the Son of God, throw yourself down: for it is written, 'He shall give his angels charge concerning you: and in their hands they shall bear you up, lest at any time you dash your foot against a stone.'"[84] The angels were the ministers of Christ during the temptation, and they were the ministers of Christ at Gethsemane. Jesus was never in any danger. He deliberately chose to let Judas' betraying sword stand that his purpose might be fulfilled. Just as the angels strengthened Jesus in the desert, so they strengthened him now at Gethsemane—to steadfastly reject the betraying sword of Peter. If there were any "temptation" that struck more forcefully at the very heart of Jesus, it was not mere hunger for bread. It was the dread of a humiliating separation—even for a moment—from his own father. Peter, the rock of offense, did not, after all, deter Jesus from fulfilling that which must be.[85] Jesus would not stumble over this stone. He was determined to drink the cup of crucifixion.

It is true that in Acts Peter seems to occupy a position of preeminence in the early church, but as the structure of Acts is considered in its entirety, we realize that much of this is an editorial effect that Luke has achieved by creating a definite *transition* between the ministry of Peter and the ministry of Paul. When Paul goes before the Jerusalem church to lay before them his gospel to the Gentiles, he knows nothing of the primacy of Peter: "And when James, Cephas, and John, who seemed to be pillars, perceived the grace that was given unto me, they gave to me and Barnabas the right hands of fellowship; that we should go unto the heathen, and they unto the circumcision."[86] Peter drops out of Luke's account in Acts 13, only to appear once more giving a speech at the Jerusalem council concerning what to do about Gentiles

83 Mt 26:53.

84 4:6.

85 26:54.

86 Gal 2:9.

who have believed, seemingly in support of Paul. Peter boasts that God chose him to go to Cornelius' house to preach the gospel. Therefore, Peter reasons, what's wrong with Paul doing it? What Peter apparently did not understand was that God had given him a general *command* to go to the Gentiles. Peter, like Jonah, initially responds in effect, "No, Lord, I have never had intercourse with peoples that are common and unclean." As far as Peter is concerned, God was merely telling him that it was *acceptable* that the Gentiles believe. Hence this apartheid attitude towards the Gentiles determines the tenor of the epistle of the Jerusalem church to the Gentile church at Antioch. But it is *James* who arbitrates the final judgment of the Jerusalem Council.[8] And it is the verbiage of James' judgment, not Peter's, that is incorporated into the letter.[88]

The parable of the two sons,[89] added by Matthew, illustrates the transition between Peter and Paul in Acts. Just as the publicans and harlots illuminated the righteousness of God through their repentance and baptism by John, so did the Gentiles through their acceptance of Paul's preaching. Paul asks, "But if our unrighteousness commend the righteousness of God, what shall we say?"[90] Later Paul asks, "But if, while we seek to be justified by Christ, we ourselves also are found sinners, is therefore Christ the minister of sin?"[91] In the parable of the two sons, Matthew argues that the blame remains upon the unrepentant, despite this jealousy towards those who repent: "For John came to you in the way of righteousness, and you believed him not: but the publicans and the harlots believed him: and you, when you had seen it, repented not afterward, that you might believe him."[92] Matthew appears to be lecturing the Jerusalem church herself in his gospel: "Paul has found the righteousness of Christ which you have denied, but now that the Gentiles have been reconciled to God apart from the law of Moses, will you not repent of your synthesis with Judaism and believe Paul?"

87 Acts 15:19.
88 15:13–31.
89 Mt 21:28–32.
90 Ro 3:5.
91 Gal 2:17.
92 Mt 21:32.

The parable of the laborers in the vineyard,[93] also added by Matthew, directly supports the Pauline defense of God's poetic license in manipulating the spiritual destiny of Israel in Romans 9–11. When the Jews complain against the propriety of God for giving to the Gentiles the very thing that the Jews have presumably sought for so much of their history, Matthew says of God's poetic license, "Is it not lawful for me to do what I will with that which is mine? Isn't your judgment wrong, because I am right?"[94]

Paul explains in his Romans argument that even Moses himself had predicted this reversal: "But I say, Did not Israel know? First Moses says, I will provoke you to jealousy by them that are no people, and by a foolish nation I will anger you."[95] Paul reasons that this provocation is a final, divine gambit to save Israel: "...salvation is come to the Gentiles, for to provoke them to jealousy."[96] In the parable of the two sons, the final emphasis is on the unrepentant son. In the parable of the laborers it is that "the last shall be first and the first last."

And in Matthew's addition to the parable of the marriage feast, Matthew is again warning the apostolic community: "We were all called, but Paul was chosen,[97] because he has conformed his preaching to the righteousness of Christ and we have not. Peter was the first to be called an apostle, but he will be last in the kingdom of God. Paul was the least of all of us, but God has chosen him to be first." Matthew concludes the parable of the marriage feast ominously:

---

93 Mt 20:1-16.

94 20:15.

95 Ro 10:19; Dt 32:21. 96 Ro 11:11.

97 Acts 9:15. "But the Lord said unto him, Go your way: for he is a chosen vessel unto me, to bear my name before the Gentiles, and kings, and the children of Israel." Luke nonchalantly does not observe this distinction in Lk 6:13: "And when it was day, he called unto him his disciples: and of them he chose twelve, whom also he named apostles." John also does not observe Matthew's distinction between "called" and "chosen," but then has difficulty, knowing that some distinction must be made. Compare, for example, Jn 6:70 ("Jesus answered them, Have not I chosen you twelve, and one of you is a devil?") and Jn 13:18 ("I speak not of you all: I know whom I have chosen: but that the scripture may be fulfilled, He that eats bread with me hath lifted up his heel against me").

"There will be many who are called, but few chosen."[98] In one final, ironic twist, Matthew has Jesus quote a conflation of Ps 118:22 and Is 8:13–14: "The stone which the builders rejected, the same is become the head of the corner: this is the Lord's doing, and it is marvelous in our eyes. Therefore I say to you, The kingdom of God shall be taken from you, and given to a nation bringing forth the fruits thereof. And whosoever shall fall on this stone shall be broken: but on whomsoever it shall fall, it will grind him to powder."

The themes of wedding garments, good and bad sons, and the righteousness of God's poetic justice all reappear in Luke's prodigal son parable, but Luke's positioning and context mutes Matthew's main reason for including them. Matthew forcibly affixes a judgment upon Israel and thus Peter in all three. This was the experience of Israel. This was the experience of Peter. In Matthew, Jesus illustrates what Jonah the prophet should have done; Peter illustrates what Jonah did. In contrast to John, who places Philip in a primary position, Matthew intentionally elevates Peter to the position of chief apostle, precisely because he had become the *anti*-type of Christ. At last, like Israel herself, the first apostle eventually tumbles to a position of disgrace and powerlessness; the last apostle, Paul, ascends to primacy through humiliation, suffering, and faithfulness. It is a messianic drama that begins in Matthew and continues until the Revelation of John.

---

98 Mt 22:14. Matthew concludes his laborers in the vineyard parable by repeating again, "The last shall be first and the first last." This fits. And in some minority manuscripts, Matthew adds, "For many are called, but few chosen." It could be that Matthew was so aggressive in making this point that future scribal activity deleted it because it was thought to be a mistake.

9

The Intent of Mark

We have now seen considerable literary evidence that Mark is blending both the orders and the phraseology of Matthew and Luke upon the canvas of the Synoptic template that Matthew has created, and that this blending is not to resolve theological controversy. At times his blending is so close that his account becomes redundant. This blending partially accounts for the density of Mark—his words are longer and his sentences are filled with more significant words than either Matthew or Luke.

This increased density, the occasional use of clumsier, coarser language, the excessive use of the historical present, and the repeated use of "immediately" as a one-word editorial stitch all create the illusion of narrative speed. But this is not because Mark is in a hurry. This sense of time compression in Mark is greatly increased by the simple fact that he has omitted thirty-eight Synoptic sections, most of which are teaching pericopes. Mark's omission of so much teaching material is not for the purpose of giving more information about the "what," "when," "where," and "why" of Jesus' ministry, because Mark has also deleted many narrative pericopes and rarely adds completely new material. Instead, he very visibly and very greatly expands a few key healing pericopes.

But even in these expansions, Mark adds nothing of any *narrative* substance beyond the inclusion of many "interesting details." Despite Mark's alignment with Luke throughout Matthew's lengthy Sermon on the Mount and Matthew's healing block (8:1–12:50), Mark seems determined to follow Matthew, beginning with the pericope Herod Thinks John is Risen, no matter what the literary difficulty. And except for a few departures, Mark never leaves the structure and flow of Matthew for the rest of his Gospel. Mark has chosen to align with Matthew despite the difficulties because it is at this very place that Matthew begins to build up to his climatic confession of Peter. Mark is importing not only the confession but the climatic positioning of this confession. But if we examine Mark closely, we will see that Peter's confession is not Mark's linchpin, linguistically or structurally. Peter's confession is *near* the center of Mark. But Peter's confession is not at the center. Matthew puts us in the place of apostolic incomprehension. Mark pulls us deeper within this incomprehension to a place of astonishment. Fear. Anger. Unbelief. Paralysis. We must allow Mark to draw us into these psychological depths. Then we will see the central intent of Mark.

In John's raising of Lazarus (11:1–44), John departs from his sign and soliloquy presentation pattern of Christ to delve deeply into the psychology of belief. Luke's Jesus sweats drops of blood in divine agony at Gethsemane. But in John, the Son of God cries human tears of human anguish:

> Then said Martha to Jesus—Lord, if you would have been here, my brother would not have died. But I know, that even now, whatsoever you will ask of God, God will give you. Jesus said to her, Your brother shall rise again. Martha says unto him, I know that he shall rise again in the resurrection at the last day. Jesus said to her, I am the resurrection, and the life: he that believes in me, though he were dead, yet shall he live: And whosoever lives and believes in me shall never die. Do you believe this? She says to him, Yes, Lord: I believe that you are the Christ, the Son of God, which should come into the world.

The reader must use some imagination to understand what is happening between Martha and Jesus. Jesus is trying to draw Martha over the brink of her own unbelief. Jesus is trying to induce Martha to say, "I believe that you have the power to call Lazarus out of the grave right at this very moment." But she says everything she can short of this. When Jesus knows that Martha will go no further, he tells her to call her "more faithful" sister. But Mary does not fully believe either: "Then when Mary came to where Jesus was, and saw him, she fell down at his feet, saying to him, Lord, if you had been here, my brother would not have died." In the raising of Lazarus, John's irony achieves such a pathos of extraordinary intensity in Jesus' dialogue with Martha that even Jesus cannot bear to recreate it in dialogue with Mary. Jesus weeps to relieve the pressure for our own tears. Pathos is merely implicit in the Matthew's Gospel, but at this moment in John, pathos is explicit. Yet even here, if the reader is not paying attention, it is possible to miss it.

Mark's whole Gospel is pathos. You cannot miss it. It appears that Mark has deleted so much teaching material in order to keep the atmosphere of Christ's presence from dissipating in the mind of the reader. In John, the woman at the well escapes the pressure of Christ's presence by means of a theological abstraction:

> Jesus says to her, Go, call your husband, and come here. The woman answered and said, I have no husband. Jesus said unto her, You have well said, I have no husband: For you have had five husbands; and he whom you now have is not your husband: in that you said truly. The woman says to him, Sir, I perceive that you are a prophet. Our fathers worshipped in this mountain; but you say, that in Jerusalem is the place where men ought to worship…[1]

Mark has no banter about theological abstractions. Mark allows for no escape. In pericopes with three-way synchronicity, all Marcan expansions of Matthew and Luke elaborate on the complex nature of belief. Mark supplies the missing psychological analysis of Martha's excruciating inner conflict in the mouth of the father of the epileptic boy: "Lord, I believe—help my unbelief!"[2]

---

1 Jn 4:16–20.

2 Mk 9:24.

Matthew's intent was to show us how the first, Peter, became last, and how the last, Paul, became the chief apostle by contrasting the Pauline belief of Simon, son of Jonah, with the unbelief of Peter "the rockheart." James was quite content to let this psychological dualism stand: "...He that wavers is like a wave of the sea driven with the wind and tossed... A double-minded man is unstable in all his ways."[3] Paul had attempted to resolve the inner conflict by absolving the soul and condemning sin in the flesh: "For I delight in the law of God after the inward man: But I see another law in my members, warring against the law of my mind, and bringing me into captivity to the law of sin which is in my members. O wretched man that I am! who shall deliver me from the body of this death? I thank God through Jesus Christ our Lord. So then with the mind I myself serve the law of God; but with the flesh the law of sin."[4]

In Mark, we peer into the very essence of that Pauline law. Mark says, "I will tell you what that law (or principle) is which has brought us into captivity to sin. That psychological, spiritual principle is *unbelief*." When we look at the characters in Mark's expanded pericopes, we are looking into the psychology of Peter. And we look straight into the face of Peter as he denies Christ. But Mark is not content to leave Peter as typological of Israel's rejection of her own messiah, as Matthew has done, because Mark's intent is to show us that Peter's unbelief is typological of our *own* unbelief. When we peer into the face of Peter, we see our own face. It was Elijah who had set the standard for the essentially *psychological* question that Mark assays to answer: "And Elijah came unto all the people, and said, How long will you go on halting between two opinions? if Yahweh be God, follow him: but if Baal, then follow him. And the people answered him not a word."[5]

Matthew shows us how Peter's denial of Christ was an unavoidable consequence of Peter's enslavement to his lust for the praise of other men. In Luke, Christ predicts that Peter will be tested by Satan for a considerable period, and then Peter would ultimately be converted.[6]

3 Jas 1:6b, 8.

4 Ro 7:22–25.

5 I Kgs 18:21.

Although John, too, saw exactly what Matthew saw, he nevertheless agrees with Luke and claims that there is hope for Peter. John asserts that Christ himself predicted that Peter would be fully converted in old age: "Truly, truly I say to you, When you were young, you clothed yourself, and walked wherever you wanted: but when you shall be old, you shall stretch forth your hands, and another shall clothe you and carry you where you would not. This he spoke, signifying by what death he should glorify God."[7]

Matthew has made a powerful case against Peter. His was an empty confession. But Mark is showing us that even in the midst of unbelief, Peter believed. In the midst of denial, he never fully released his hope in Christ. In Matthew's primary parable of the sower, there are only four options.[8] The seed of the *logos* is plucked away in the midst of unbelieving ignorance,[9] it becomes uprooted during times of trial, it is choked out by weeds of worldly cares and lusts, or it produces a healthy crop.

In a rare addition of material, Mark gives one more option: the seed of belief lies dormant for a time, but then, when the time is right—we do not know when—the seed bears fruit. And even then, the development of belief is a gradual process. First there is a tiny blade. Then the ear. Then the fruit fully develops over time within the ear. [10] Just before the confession of Peter, Mark inserts material about a deaf mute whom Jesus takes aside privately and heals,[11] and he inserts another rare pericope about a blind man who is also taken aside and healed by a two-stage process.[12] Like Peter, the deaf mute speaks, but not very well. The blind man at first sees, but not very well.

In Luke's account, Paul's blindness was cured instantaneously and, seemingly, completely. "And immediately there fell from his eyes as it had been scales: and he received sight forthwith, and arose, and was

6 Lk 22:31–32.

7 Jn 21:18–19.

8 Mt 13:19–23.

9 13:19. "When any one hears the word of the kingdom, and does not understand it, then comes the wicked one, and steals away that which was sown in his heart."

10 Mk 4:26–29.

11 7:31–37.

12 8:22–26.

baptized."[13] But Mark says that the process of conversion is not so simple. In the cure of the epileptic boy, Mark's added material makes it clear that Jesus' cure for the soul is sometimes so convulsive that a death-like trance ensues, from which it seems that the patient might not ever recover: "And after crying out and convulsing him terribly, [the spirit] came out, and the boy was like a corpse; so that most of them said, 'He is dead.'" But in another two-stage healing process, "Jesus took him by the hand, and he arose."[14]

There is another detail in Mark's commentary about this epileptic boy that we must not miss. Is this a simple case of epilepsy? We assume so. From the Synoptic accounts it certainly appears so. Matthew says that the boy is "moonstruck" (**σεληνιαζεται**), sometimes falling into both fire and water. Dr. Luke's description is more technical: "a spirit seizes him, and he suddenly cries out; it convulses him till he foams, and shatters him, and will hardly leave him." [15] Mark closely follows Luke: "…it seizes him, dashing him down, and he foams and grinds his teeth and becomes rigid."[16] When the boy is brought to Jesus, Mark again expands: "and when the spirit saw him, immediately it convulsed the boy, and he fell on the ground and rolled about, foaming at the mouth." It does seem clear that these men are all describing what we would call today a grand mal seizure. And yet Mark says that it was merely a dumb and deaf spirit: "And Jesus … rebuked the unclean spirit, saying to it, you dumb and deaf spirit, I command you, come out of him…"[17]

Peter at first preached powerful sermons about the reality of Jesus' resurrection such that even those who basked in the shadow of Peter were healed of disease.[18] But as time wore on, people began to realize that Peter had nothing to say about the *significance* of Jesus' resurrection or his death. Matthew is quick to point out that there will be many who will say, "Lord, Lord, have we not prophesied in your name? and in your name have cast out devils? and in your name done many wonderful works?" —but will nevertheless be rejected by Christ in the

13 Acts 9:18.
14 Mk 9:26–27.
15 Lk 9:39.
16 Mk 9:18.
17 9:25.
18 Acts 5:15.

end. Peter both saw and heard the vision atop Simon the Tanner's house in Joppa that the Gentiles were no longer common or unclean.

Yet in Paul's letter to the Galatians, we learn that Peter shamefully withdrew from the Antiochian (Gentile) Christians upon hearing that James' spiritually apartheid envoy was enroute,[19] shortly before Paul's own betrayal into the hands of the Romans by a negligent Jerusalem church. Through this despicable behavior, Peter tramples underfoot the very blood of Christ that made the Gentiles clean.[20] The Synoptic template, which is a shattering exposé of Peter's denial of Christ, is published at about the same time as Paul's imprisonment and is faithfully reproduced in the accounts of both Luke and John.

But Mark is not content to accept an epileptic psychological diagnosis for Peter, continually convulsing between the belief of Simon, son of Jonah, and the unbelief of Peter the rockheart, between defense of Christ by violence and denial of Christ in the dark of night. Mark knows that the church should not give up on Peter, because Jesus has prayed and fasted for his soul. If the church gives up on Peter, it must give up on itself, because Peter is typological of every human soul. If Jesus cannot save Peter, then Jesus cannot save anyone. Jesus claimed that he could raise up children of Abraham from the rock.[21] Peter was just such a rock. So Mark continues to attack the criticism against Peter, that his spiritual epilepsy is worse than it ever was. Mark adds even more detail to the healing of the epileptic boy: "I command you, come

---

19 Gal 2:11–13a. "...When Peter was come to Antioch, I withstood him to the face, because he was to be blamed. For before that certain came from James, he did eat with the Gentiles: but when they were come, he withdrew and separated himself, fearing them which were of the circumcision. And the other Jews dissembled likewise with him..."

20 The allusion here is to Heb 10:29. "Of how much sorer punishment, do you suppose, shall he be thought worthy, who has trodden underfoot the Son of God, and has counted the blood of the covenant, wherewith he was sanctified, common thing, and has done despite unto the Spirit of grace?"

21 Mt 3:9. "And think not to say within yourselves, We have Abraham to our father: for I say unto you, that God is able of these stones to raise up children unto Abraham."

out of him—and never enter him again."[22] This is a detail we must not miss.

Papias was right, after all. Mark had become the interpreter of Peter. As Matthew resumes a more chronological flow, beginning his structural preparations for the confession of Peter, Mark continues to shadow Matthew very closely in order to construct his own comprehensive Petrine commentary. Herod hears of the fame of Jesus and begins to question who he is. However difficult, Matthew will use Peter to supply an answer. At one end of the continuum stands brutal Herod. At the other end is the blind belief of Bartimaeus. Somewhere, somehow, caught between the two, is Peter's equivocal belief. Mark has moved so briskly that the mind has never gotten bogged down with theological abstraction. Now, suddenly, there is no blur. Suddenly there is enormous interpersonal detail, emotional color, and psychological depth that touches every pericope from here to Bartimaeus.

The rationale for significant Marcan deviations from Matthew's pericopes in this section, which includes the pericopes of Jesus Is Rejected at Nazareth through The Healing of Bartimaeus, is the psychological *process* of apostolic conversion to what Jesus taught. James implies that the **διψυχος** (double-souled) man is a freakish anomaly.

Paul says that *all* men constantly find that they are powerless to do that which they know to be the right thing and instead do the wrong thing because of sin which dwells in their flesh. Mark combines a part of what James says with a part of what Paul says. Mark implies that *all* men are double-souled, changing one word in the Pauline formula[23] to help us to understand why Peter denied Christ: "Now if I do that which I would not, it is no more I that do it, but *unbelief* that dwells in me."

Taken together, Paul, John, and Mark have made an enormous effort to elaborate on the essence of what it means to believe. As long as I am in dialogue with Christ, I become the "me" that he has intended me to be. As long as I am in dialogue with my appetites, Christ's definition of

22 Mk 9:25c.

23 Ro 7:19–20. "For the good that I would I do not: but the evil which I would not, that I do. Now if I do that which I would not, it is no more I that do it, but sin that dwells in me."

my "me-ness" becomes slowly dissipated and I become just another indistinguishable, human animal, a plastic, provisional personality, entirely driven and tossed by the whims of social context, as Peter was. All life is a process of either entering into a permanent, conscious dialogue with Christ or a permanent, unconscious dialogue with the appetites. Either I become divinely domesticated as the only-begotten, unique image of Christ is formed in me, or I become wild, driven spontaneously and completely by the appetites of nature's laws working in me. All life is a process of becoming conscious of myself as Christ would have me, or becoming unconscious.

In Peter and in Paul, Mark sees the perfect opportunity to describe the universal exodus of every soul: from unconscious bondage to our appetites, to a testing in the wilderness of indecision, and then finally to an unequivocal eisodus (entrance) into the promised kingdom, in which we rest from our works in the righteousness of Christ and work out our consciousness of who we are in him. Thus Mark takes us through the stages of belief of the universal man and woman by means of these typological, Synoptic characters: from the dumbfounded fear and amazement of Herod; to the partially converted, epileptic psychology of Peter, torn between unbelief and belief; to the fully converted, unequivocal, never-look-back spirituality of Paul, who, like blind Bartimaeus, eventually threw off every stitch of worldly pride and comfort so that he might know Christ and be known of him.

When Peter found himself in the precincts of freedom, he "came to himself."[24] When Paul let go of every vestige of his own heritage,[25] he achieved the prize of the high calling of Christ to his soul. He achieved the confident self-knowledge that John belabors in his epistles. Late in his ministry, Paul says, "For I know whom I have believed, and am persuaded that he is able to keep that which I have committed unto him against that day."[26] Paul more fully knows who Christ is. In the end, Paul did not mortify his flesh. He mortified his unbelief. And Paul more fully knew who he himself was, although he was not altogether sure of

24 Acts 12:11.
25 Phil 3:7.
26 2 Tim 1:12.

who he would *become*. His knowledge was not an epileptic struggle between belief and unbelief, but a confident waiting to see what he would become in Christ. As John says of the fully converted, "Beloved, now are we the sons of God, and it doth not yet appear what we shall be: but we know that, when he shall appear, we shall be like him; for we shall see him as he is."[27]

Mark knows why Matthew portrayed Peter as typological of Israel's unbelief: Peter continued to deny Christ for almost forty years of wandering and equivocation. The Jerusalem church's witness to Christ was finally, completely neutralized. Jesus was just another dead prophet. And "the way" had become just another esoteric cult within Judaism that looked at the Pauline converts as second-class citizens of the kingdom of God. The Jerusalem church betrayed Paul's ministry just as they had all betrayed Christ. Peter's authority and his bland syncretism with the Judaizers was gradually eroding the remnants of Pauline orthodoxy. The gospel of Paul looked as if it were ready to collapse. So Matthew stepped in to tell the whole truth about Peter's betrayal.

Mark, of course, saw this was all true about Peter. But Peter had become a scapegoat for *every* unbelief. People began to externalize their own spiritual apostasy upon the head of Peter. Mark saw how hard it was for the Jerusalem church to understand the conversion of Paul. Now Mark also sees that the universal church is beginning to misunderstand the moral collapse of Peter. Mark says, "Yes, Peter is guilty of all these despicable characterizations. But we must realize that he is typological of an unbelieving generation. We are *all* guilty of these despicable characterizations. And the sooner we admit this, the sooner we can get on with the labor of entering into God's rest of Pauline belief apart from works."

If we say that we are not like Peter, we lie and the truth is not in us.[28] Jesus tells Peter that he minds the things of men. Paul tells the church of God to "set their mind on things above."[29] But how do we achieve this change of mind? How does one get from unbelief to belief? Mark takes us more deeply into the Pauline dilemma—the inner struggle

27 1 Jn: 3:2.
28 1 Jn: 8.
29 Col 3:2.

against sin in Romans 7. Mark's thematic variations upon Matthew's pericopes surrounding Peter's confession transposes this Pauline dilemma into the context of John's Gospel: "I know that the belief that empowers me to be a son of God can only be possessed by a son of God. Therefore how can I be born from above by means of something that I do not possess?" I can be *given* belief indiscriminately as the determinists say. But John the Baptist has already destroyed this argument: "And think not to say within yourselves, We have Abraham to our father: for I say unto you, that God is able of these stones to raise up children unto Abraham."[30] If Paul is right, that God has had mercy on all,[31] then that means he gives the freedom and power to believe to everyone. He enlightens everyone who comes into the world.[32] Christ descends into the depths of hell and preaches to the spirits in prison.[33] Those who have sat in darkness have seen a great light.[34] Christ calls every soul out of darkness into his light.[35] Those who reject this call are condemned.[36] Those who do not reject this call will be saved.[37]

Our belief saves us. We are empowered to believe as the *logos* confronts our souls. And every soul has heard this call.[38] If a soul had not heard the call of Christ and had not been empowered to believe by the spirit of Christ, then he would be guiltless.[39] Through the inner dialogue of the soul with Christ, she sees that she is wretched, miserable, poor, blind, and naked. It is a stormy love affair. But eventually the soul cries out, "Lord, I see—help my blindness." In Mark, the father of the epileptic boy therefore says, "Lord, I believe—help my unbelief."

---

30 Mt 3:9.

31 Ro 11:32. 32 Jn 1:9.

33 1 Pe 3:19. "By which also he went and preached unto the spirits in prison..."

34 Mt 4:16.

35 1 Pe 2:9.

36 Jn 3:19. "And this is the condemnation, that light is come into the world, and men loved darkness rather than light, because their deeds were evil."

37 Lk 9:50. "And Jesus said unto him, Forbid him not: for he that is not against us is for us."

38 Ro 10:17–18.

39 Jn 9:41. "Jesus said to them, If you were blind, you would have no sin."

Who will separate us from this salvation of Christ? Will the determinist separate us, saying that God has a secret psychosis which damns souls from the foundation of the world, Christ never giving these souls the freedom and power to believe? Will the legalist separate us, saying that if our behavior is not sufficiently good, then no amount of belief can save us? The message of the Synoptic template is that a grain of mustard seed is all that is required to save us. Just a bit of smoking flax. What kind of behavior will flow from faith this small? Perhaps it will be nothing more than to give a cup of cold water to a righteous man. God demonstrated in the Old Testament that he would not destroy a city if even one righteous soul lived there. Jesus says that God will not destroy any soul in which one grain of belief still lives. That is good news.

Mark is telling us that belief is a complicated thing. The fall and eventual rehabilitation of Peter is proof of this. Mark is saying that the alternatives in the parable of the sower are not as simple as they first appear, because every soul experiences every alternative. In the course of its own life, the soul turns away from the *logos* in rebellious misunderstanding, then Satan plucks away the seed—yet Christ continues to woo her, renewing seed. The seed begins to grow, but it is often detached from the root of Jesse as we attempt to avoid the disapproval of the world. We detach from our budding relationship with truth and seek to root ourselves in worldly acceptance instead. But even as Christ re-roots us and the seed begins to grow again, it is often choked by our own gluttonous appetites.[40]

Paul calls this divine patience "longsuffering." He says that one of the reasons that Christ had mercy on Paul's own rebellious soul is so that this longsuffering could be demonstrated to other disobedient souls. Though the event of our conversion seems to happen all at once, the drama of our conversion begins long before we finally begin to open the door of our souls and continues long after our first pitiful attempts at repentance. Paul specifically says that God does not come in one moment. The complete change of mind that "repentance" (**μετανοια**) entails takes time: "Or do you despise the riches of his goodness and

40 Mk 4:19.

forbearance and longsuffering; not knowing that the goodness of God is leading you to repentance?"[41]

Sometimes it doesn't. Sometimes belief begins to grow upon the hardened exterior of unbelief but permanently tears away the moment that this belief is tested. Sometimes belief grows among a tangle of competing beliefs, and nothing of *any* substance ever grows; the soul is then simply overcome by natural processes, which in the human soul are deformed natural appetites. Whether or not the soil of a human heart will allow the seed of God to germinate and bear fruit is something that must be carefully watched by a patient husbandman.

We may decry an equivocal response to Christ as Matthew has done. But Mark is saying that we are *all* guilty, in some respect, of this equivocal response. Although blind Bartimaeus is typological of the unequivocal response of Paul, Mark is nevertheless saying that, in the end, the difference between Peter's equivocal response and Paul's unequivocal response is *relative*. As late as his imprisonment in Rome, Paul admits that, in a fundamental sense, he himself has not fully apprehended Christ's call.[42]

In his Gospel, Mark says that to understand the difference between the response of Judas Iscariot and the response of Paul of Tarsus is just a beginning. Unless we understand the psychological *stages* of belief, we will never be able to understand the absolute difference between the denial of Judas and the denial of Peter. Without this understanding, we will never understand the moral collapse of Peter or his final rehabilitation.

We will never be able to understand the Jamesean/Pauline controversy about faith and works. And we will not understand why virtually everyone deserts Paul in the end. They had all been so highly praised for their faith, even by Paul. But in the end, there was nothing. For many years, Peter yielded precisely this. Nothing. Yet a patient husbandman never gives up. Mark saw something that no one else saw. Mark explains: eventually, the seed grows, we know not how. "First the blade, then the ear, after that the full corn in the ear."[43] Unless belief endures to the end, it cannot be saved. Most importantly, unless Mark's

41 Ro 2:4.

42 Phil 3:7–14.

43 Mk 4:27–28.

Roman audience understands these things, they too will deny Christ in the Roman amphitheater and all will be lost in a final moment of faithless fear.

10

The Fall and Rehabilitation of Peter

We have said that the primary intent of Mark was to present a psychology of belief to a congregation about to be tested in the amphitheaters of Rome. His case study: Peter. He attempted to balance the scathing exposé of Matthew with the tentative predictions in Luke and John that Peter's conversion would one day be complete. Mark does not shrink from recording Christ's censure upon Peter that Luke avoids: "But when [Jesus] had turned about and looked on his disciples, he rebuked Peter, saying, Get thee behind me, Satan: for thou savourest not the things that be of God, but the things that be of men."[1] But as we understand Mark's commentary concerning belief, we understand that he is making Peter typological of our own unbelief. Matthew has made a powerful case for the emptiness of Peter's confession; Mark has made a powerful case for the emptiness of our own: "I believe—help my unbelief." And it is in this context that we must honestly face the limitations of Peter's first epistle.

We do this with the Old Testament; why not the New Testament? Who would think that the Song of Solomon or Ecclesiastes or Proverbs could stand alone as a sort of divine oracle, recorded by human auto-

1 Mk 8:33.

matons in an altered state of religious consciousness, from which homogeneous truth can be extracted? Of course they don't stand alone. They must be placed in the context of the larger whole before they can be properly understood. In Job, the pious speeches of Eliphaz, Bildad, and Zophar appear unassailable. They are good sermons from start to finish, yet they are theologically defective when placed within the larger argument of Job.

Also, as we are confronted by the vast range of material in the Old Testament, both in literary type and historical setting, we realize that revelation is an ongoing, unfolding, progressive thing. The author of Hebrews confirms this: "God, who at sundry times and in diverse manners spoke in time past unto the fathers by the prophets, hath in these last days spoken unto us by his Son."[2] Why the build-up? Why not send the Son in the first place? In John's Gospel, Jesus tells us why: "I have yet many things to say unto you, but ye cannot bear them now."[3] The Mosaic laws about divorce illustrate that this is as true corporately as it is individually: "Moses because of the hardness of your hearts suffered you to put away your wives: but from the beginning it was not so." Then Jesus takes us to the next level: "I say unto you, Whosoever shall put away his wife, except it be for fornication, and shall marry another, committeth adultery."[4]

Just as the Old Testament materials cannot be properly understood unless they are properly placed within their literary, historical, and theological settings, neither can the New Testament. If we are prepared to see that revelation is ongoing, interconnected, and unfolding in the Old Testament, then we must be prepared to see this process in the community dialogue of the New Testament. The New Testament materials are not like the Delphic Oracles. They are as ordinary and interconnected as nature herself, just as Jesus was conceived within the womb of an ordinary, natural woman. And we must read them as ordinary, interconnected literary materials or we will be unaffected by their divine authority. The flowers in the field do not spring forth, fully formed in a moment of time, and they do not stand alone. When they mature, they require bees to take the pollen from one

2 Heb 1:1–2a.

3 Jn 16:12.

4 Mt 19:8–9.

flower to the next—an entirely extrinsic process. The bee is unconscious of its crucial role in the growth and reproduction of the flower.

Standing alone, the book of James seems woefully incomplete. But the book of James is crucial in understanding Paul's categorical rejection of the Judaizing argument concerning justification apart from the works of the law. James very truly said that: "... as the body without the spirit is dead, so faith without works is dead also."[5] The spirit of revelation seems to be saying the same thing about the process of the revelation of the New Testament: without the dissonance of James and Paul, the argument of the New Testament apostolic community, which stretches interconnectedly across several authors, is unintelligibly lifeless. Paul, of course, will have an incompleteness of his own, and we will have to look elsewhere for his conclusion.[6]

One apostolic conversation pollinates another. Sometimes directly. Sometimes in ways that are beyond the comprehension of the apostles themselves. And if what they are saying is true, this is not their conversation anyway. The conversation and the unpredictable spiritual pollination between one another is a providential process which is completely beyond their ability to predict or to control. Without Matthew's exposé of Peter's fall from grace, we could not possibly understand the significant limitations of Peter's first letter, or even why it was written. And we would have had no reason to look elsewhere for its conclusion. Luke predicts that Peter will be restored. John predicts that Peter will be restored. Mark gives us the theoretical basis for Peter's restoration. But what we should most like to know is this: how does this story turn out? *Is Peter restored to grace?*

If God could use Pharaoh and a hard-hearted and stiff-necked nation to proclaim his truth and glory, and could place a central Messianic prophecy in the mouth of the high priest who slew his only son, why couldn't he use a hardened member of the Judaizing party and a partially converted disciple to help put the "finishing touches" on

5 Jas 2:26.

6 Paul does not say, "*you* know in part." He says, "I know in part." "For now we see through a glass, darkly; but then face to face: now I know in part; but then shall I know even as also I am known" (1 Cor 13:12).

the "spiritus corpus"—the New Testament materials? Again, as with much of the Old Testament, if these documents are taken out of the context of the larger matrix in which they are historically embedded and set up on their own, their significance and meaning are immediately obscured. Popular religion sometimes concedes the principle of differing levels of clarity in "Scripture," but it is not prepared to say which places in the Scriptures are less clear than others. Nor is it prepared to say *why* they are less clear. In the household of God, there are vessels of gold and vessels of clay. Peter lost his leadership position and so often found himself betraying Christ and arguing with God because he stood in a theological box. The thesis of this chapter is that it is not until the writing of his second letter that Peter moves outside of that box.

The Judaizers, seeking to synthesize the law with the gospel of Christ, clamored for the death of Paul, who was determined to lead his people out of mere Judaism into an apparent wilderness of justification by faith alone apart from the works of the law. Eventually, Paul is martyred. But what of the remnant? Will Timothy, Paul's heir apparent, like Joshua many years before, lead them to a final "sabbath rest" that Paul was unable to do, in the face of this powerful ecclesiastical counter-reformation? Could this exodus be swallowed up in a flood of theological words?[7] Could a compromise be struck between the Judaizers and the Paulinists? Could the most scandalous aspects of the Pauline gospel be officially condemned as antinomianism[8] and the Mosaic law quietly reinterpreted back into the Pauline Gospel? Indeed, many Roman Catholics and Protestants even today find no final conflict between the Jamesean and Pauline theologies of justification. Surely a bland edict could be written by a respected church official that would harmonize the two, peaceably resolving all the nasty conflict between the Judaizers and the Paulinists and restoring the Judaizing rite of circumcision of the Gentiles to its proper place?

7 Re 12:15. "And the serpent cast out of his mouth water as a flood after the woman, that he might cause her to be carried away of the flood."

8 It is evident that Paul is addressing this charge in Romans. To the charge that he has taught "Let us do evil, that good may come" (3:8b), he rhetorically retorts, "What shall we say then? Shall we continue in sin, that grace may abound? God forbid. How shall we, that are dead to sin, live any longer therein" (6:1–2)?

Peter's first letter is just such a bland edict. In isolation, the speeches of Eliphaz the Temanite appear to praise God. But in a much larger context, they curse Job. Thus in the larger context, 1 Peter functions like Balaam's initial "curse" of faint praise.[9] Balaam knows that he cannot openly curse the Israelites, but he simply cannot do without the political honors that Balak might confer. Peter knows that he cannot curse the Paulinists, because God himself told him, "What God hath cleansed, that call not thou common."[10] But the Jamesean faction is offering Peter a tremendous opportunity to repair the political damage that Matthew's exposé has surely caused, and to regain the kind of respect afforded him of his once glorious career in the earliest days of the Church. Peter seizes the opportunity.

A Vessel of Clay

If "James is an epistle of straw,"[11] Peter's first letter is a vessel of clay. Though Mark is a very intentional and close structural and phraseological synthesis of Matthew and Luke, it is full of theological originality, pathos, and psychological color. In contrast, Peter's first letter is a mosaic of vocabulary, signature phrases, and idea fragments of other "pillars of the faith," and seems to be nothing more than an ordinary homily urging conservative conformity to the status quo. Now that Silvanus has gone over to Peter,[12] he (apparently) calls upon Silvanus to produce an encyclical which seemingly attempts to be all things to all people, combining an essentially Jamesean theological program with a depolarized (if not bland) restructuring of Pauline theology. Conveniently, 1 Peter reuses a structural template of Titus

9 Balaam says merely, "Balak the king of Moab hath brought me from Aram, out of the mountains of the east, saying, Come, curse me Jacob, and come, defy Israel. How shall I curse, whom God hath not cursed? or how shall I defy, whom the LORD hath not defied" (Nm 23:7–8)?

10 Acts 11:9.

11 Martin Luther says this in his preface to the earliest editions of his New Testament (1522).

12 1 Pe 5:12. "By Silvanus, a faithful brother unto you, as I suppose, I have written briefly, exhorting, and testifying that this is the true grace of God wherein ye stand." Perhaps this transfer was necessitated by the recent death of Paul; perhaps Silvanus, like Mark years before, broke from Paul over his gospel to the Gentiles.

for his work.[13] (See Table 10 below.) Peter provides the basic Jamesean theological outline (see Table 11 below), variously colored with the theological nuances of John, with Silvanus himself (presumably) negotiating the phraseology and theological concepts of Paul and Hebrews (see Table 12 below).

Table 10. The Titus Template of 1 Peter. Structural linkages appear in both Titus and 1 Peter, many of them in the same order (bolded).[14]

	Titus	1 Peter
1	**an apostle of Jesus Christ (1:1)**	**an apostle of Jesus Christ (1:1)**
2	**God's elect...which God...promised (1:2–3)**	**elect according to the foreknowledge (1:2)**
3	**But hath in due time manifested his word through preaching (1:3)**	**which are now reported unto you by them that have preached (1:12)**
4	**that they may teach young women... to be obedient to their husbands...that the word be not blasphemed (2:4–5)**	**Likewise ye wives be in subjection...and...not afraid with any amazement (3:1–6)[1]**
5	**Young men likewise exhort to be sober (2:6)**	**Likewise ye younger, submit yourselves unto the elder (5:5)**
6	In all things showing thyself a pattern of (2:7)	being examples to the flock (5:3b)
7	In all things showing thyself a pattern of good works: in doctrine showing uncorruptness, gravity, sincerity, sound speech, that cannot be condemned; that he that is of the contrary part may be ashamed, having no evil thing to say of you. (2:7–8)	Having your conversation honest among the Gentiles; that, whereas they speak against you as evildoers, they may by your good works, which they shall behold, glorify God in the day of visitation. (2:12)

13 This template, perhaps, is coming from Silvanus, who very well could have written Titus for Paul.

14 Table footnotes are found at the end of the chapter.

	Titus	1 Peter
8	**Exhort servants to be obedient unto their own masters, and to please them well in all things; not answering again (2:9)**	**Servants, be subject to your masters with all fear, not only the good and gentle, but also to the forward. (2:18)**
9	For the grace of God that bringeth salvation hath appeared to all men (2:11)	grace that is to be brought unto you at the revelation of Jesus Christ (1:13b)
10	Looking for the blessed hope and the glorious appearing (2:13)	Blessed be the God…hope…revealed (1:3, 5)
11	**teaching us that, denying ungodliness and worldly lusts, we should live soberly, righteously, and Godly in this present world (2:12)**	**Dearly beloved, I beseech you as strangers and pilgrims, abstain from fleshly lusts which war against the soul (2:11)**
12	Who gave himself for us, that he might redeem us from all iniquity and purify unto himself a peculiar people, zealous of good works (2:14)	redeemed…a peculiar people (1:18, 2:9)
13	**Put them in mind to be subject to principalities and powers, to obey magistrates, to be ready to every good work… (3:1)**	**Submit yourselves to every ordinance of man for the Lord's sake; whether it be to the King, as supreme…(2:13)**
14	**To speak evil of no man, to be no brawlers, but gentle, showing all meekness unto all men (3:2)**	**Honor all men. Love the brotherhood. Fear God. Honor the King. (2:17)**

Within this "Titus Template," Peter's first letter incorporates the theological ethos of James. (See Table 11 below.) Italicized words are the same or very similar; bolded words or phrases are used only by James and 1 Peter.

Table 11. The Jamesean Theology of 1 Peter

Unifying Theology	James	1 Peter
Peter and James are still addressing the Jews and not the universal church, in which the "wall of partition" between Jew and Gentile has been broken down.	James, a servant of God and of the Lord Jesus Christ, to the twelve tribes which are **scattered** abroad (1:1)	Peter, an apostle of Jesus Christ, to the strangers **scattered**[2] throughout (1:1)
The word (logos) saves and restores the soul. "O taste and see that the LORD is good" (Ps 34:8).	Wherefore **lay apart** all filthiness and superfluity of **naughtiness**, and receive with meekness[3] the engrafted **word**, which is able to save your souls… Of his own will begat he us with the word of truth (1:21, 18)	Wherefore **laying aside** -all **malice**, and all guile, and hypocrisies, and envies, and all evil speakings. As newborn babes, desire the sincere milk of the **word**, that ye may grow thereby (If so be ye have tasted that the Lord is gracious.)…Being born again, not of corruptible seed, but of incorruptible, by the word of God (2:1; 1:23)
"He had done no violence, neither was any deceit in his mouth" (Is 53:9b). In Peter's Lame Man Sermon: "God…hath glorified his servant[4] Jesus; whom ye delivered up, and denied him in the presence of Pilate, when he was determined to let him go. But ye denied the Holy One and the Just, and desired a murderer to be granted unto you; And killed the Prince of life."[5]	Ye have condemned and killed the just; and he doth not resist you. (5:6)	Who did no sin, neither was guile found in his mouth: Who, when he was reviled, reviled not again; when he suffered, he threatened not; but committed himself to him that judgeth righteously (2:22–23)

Unifying Theology	James	1 Peter
"Surely he scorneth the scorners: but he giveth grace unto the lowly" (Prv 3:34).	But he giveth more grace. Wherefore he says, **God resisteth the proud, but giveth grace unto the humble... Submit yourselves therefore to God. Resist** the **devil**, and he will flee from you. Draw nigh to God, and he will draw nigh to you. Humble yourselves in the sight of the Lord, and he shall lift you up (4:6–8,10).	Likewise, ye younger, **submit** yourselves unto the elder. Yea, all of you be subject one to another, and be clothed with humility: for **God resisteth the proud, and giveth grace to the humble.**[6] Humble yourselves therefore under the mighty hand of God, that he may exalt you in due time. Be sober, be vigilant; because your adversary the **devil**, as a roaring lion, walketh about, seeking whom he may devour: Whom **resist** steadfast in the faith (5:5–6; 8–9)
	Your riches are corrupted, and your garments are motheaten. Your gold and silver is cankered (5:2–3)	Forasmuch as ye know that ye were not redeemed with corruptible things, as silver and gold (1:18)
	Cleanse your hands, ye sinners; and *purify* your hearts, ye double *minded* (4:8).	Seeing ye have *purified* your *souls*[7] (1:22)
Allusion to Ps 66:10: "For thou, O God, hast proved us: thou hast tried us, as silver is tried." There are many other OT references to the proving of faith through trials.	My brethren, count it all joy when ye fall into divers temptations; Knowing this, that the **trying** of your **faith** worketh patience.) Be patient therefore, brethren, unto the coming of the Lord. Behold, the husbandman waiteth for the precious fruit of the earth, and hath long patience	Wherein ye greatly rejoice, though now for a season, if need be, ye are in heaviness through manifold temptations: That the **trial**[8] of your **faith**, being much more precious than of gold that perisheth, though it be tried with fire, might be found unto praise and honour and glory at the

Unifying Theology	James	1 Peter
	for it, until he receive the early and latter rain (1:2–3; 5:7)	appearing of Jesus Christ (1:6–7)
"Hatred stirreth up strifes: but love covereth all sins" (Prv 10:12).	Let him know, that he which converteth the sinner from the error of his way shall save a soul from death, and **shall hide a multitude of sins** (5:20).	And above all things have fervent charity among yourselves: for charity **shall cover the multitude of sins**[9] (4:8).
	good conversation his **works** (3:13)	Having your **conversation honest** among the Gentiles: that, whereas they speak against you as evildoers, they may by your good **works** (2:12)
	From whence come wars and fightings among you? come they not hence, even of your lusts that *war* in your *members* (4:1)?	abstain from fleshly lusts, which *war* against the *soul* (2:11b)
In many places James shows a keen concern for the unprofitableness of riches.	For if there come unto your assembly a man with a gold ring, in goodly apparel, and there come in also a poor man in vile raiment (2:2)	Whose adorning let it not be that outward adorning of plaiting the hair, and of wearing of gold, or of putting on of apparel (3:3)
"Come, ye children, hearken unto me: I will teach you the fear of the LORD. What man is he that desireth life, and loveth many days, that he may see good? Keep thy tongue from evil,	If any man among you seem to be religious, and bridleth not his *tongue*, but deceiveth his own heart, this man's religion is vain. But the tongue can no man tame; it is an unruly *evil*, full of	For he that will love life, and see good days, let him refrain his *tongue* from *evil*, and his lips that they speak no guile Let him eschew evil, and do good; let him seek peace, and ensue it.

Unifying Theology	James	1 Peter
and thy lips from speaking guile. Depart from evil, and do good; seek peace, and pursue it. The eyes of the LORD are upon the righteous, and his ears are open unto their cry. The face of the LORD is against them that do evil" (Ps 34:11–16a).	deadly poison...And the fruit of righteousness is sown in peace of them that make peace (1:26; 3:8,18).	For the eyes of the Lord are over the righteous, and his ears are open unto their prayers: but the face of the Lord is against them that do evil (3:10–12).
	Take, my brethren, the prophets, who have spoken in the name of the Lord, for an example of suffering affliction, and of patience. Behold, we count them happy which endure. Ye have heard of the patience of Job (5:10–11)	But rejoice, inasmuch as ye are partakers of Christ's sufferings... For even hereunto were ye called: because Christ also suffered for us, leaving us an example, that ye should follow his steps (1:13a; 2:21)
"The voice said, Cry. And he said, What shall I cry? All flesh is grass, and all the goodliness thereof is as the flower of the field: The grass withereth, the flower fadeth: because the spirit of the LORD bloweth upon it: surely the people is grass. The grass withereth, the flower fadeth: but the word of our God shall stand for ever" (Is 40:6–8).	But the rich, in that he is made low: because as the flower of the grass he shall pass away. For the sun is no sooner risen with a burning heat, but it withereth the grass, and the flower thereof falleth, and the grace of the fashion of it perisheth (1:10–11).	For all flesh is as grass, and all the glory of man as the flower of grass. The grass withereth, and the flower thereof falleth away (1:24).

1 Peter also displays a striking affinity with the language of Paul and with the author of Hebrews. Italicized words are the same or very similar; bolded words or phrases are used only by these authors.

Table 12. Pauline/Hebrewine Signature Phrases and Idea Fragments in 1 Peter

Paul	Hebrews	1 Peter
By whom we have received grace and apostleship, for **obedience** to the faith among all nations, for his name (Ro 1:5). God hath from the beginning chosen you to salvation through **sanctification** of the Spirit and belief of the truth (2 Thess 2:13b).	And to Jesus the mediator of the New Covenant, and to the **blood of sprinkling**, that speaks better things than that of Abel (12:24). Follow peace with all men, and **holiness**, without which no man shall see the Lord (12:14).	Elect according to the foreknowledge of God the Father, through **sanctification**[10] of the Spirit, unto **obedience**[11] and **sprinkling of the blood**[12] of Jesus Christ: Grace unto you, and peace,[13] be multiplied (1:2).
And the peace of God, which passeth all understanding, shall **keep** your hearts and minds through Christ Jesus (Phil 4:7).		Who are **kept**[14] by the power of God through faith unto salvation ready to be revealed in the last time (1:5)
	The Holy Ghost this **signifying**, that the way into the holiest of all was not yet made manifest, while as the first tabernacle was yet standing (9:8).	Searching what,[15] or what manner of time the Spirit of Christ which was in them did **signify,**[16] when it testified beforehand the sufferings of Christ,[17] and the glory that should follow (1:11).
	And these all, having obtained a good report through faith, received not the promise: God having provided some better thing for us, that they without us should not be made perfect... which at the first began to be spoken by the Lord, and was confirmed unto us by them that heard him (11:39–40; 2:3b).	Unto whom it was revealed, that not unto themselves, but unto us they did minister the things, which are now reported unto you by them that have preached the gospel unto you with the Holy Ghost sent down from heaven; which things the angels desire to look into (1:12).[18]

Paul	Hebrews	1 Peter
Having the understanding darkened, being alienated from the life of God through the **ignorance** that is in them, because of the blindness of their heart (Eph 4:18). And be not **conformed** to this world: but be ye transformed by the renewing of your mind, that ye may prove what is that good, and acceptable, and perfect, will of God (Ro 12:2).		As obedient children, not **fashioning**[19] yourselves according to the former lusts in your **ignorance**[20] (1:14)
Be kindly affectioned one to another with **brotherly love** in honour preferring one another (Ro 12:10; 1 Thess 4:9)	Let **brotherly love** continue (13:1).	Seeing ye have purified your souls in obeying the truth through the Spirit unto unfeigned **brotherly love**[21] (1:22; 2 Pe 1:7)
	For the **word** of God is **living** and powerful (4:12).	Being born again, not of corruptible[22] seed, but of incorruptible, by the **word** of God, which **liveth** and abideth for ever (1:23).
	offer up sacrifice (7:27; 13:15)	As newborn babes, desire the sincere milk of the **word**[23] that ye may grow thereby: **If so be**[24] ye have tasted that the Lord is gracious. To whom coming, as unto a living stone, disallowed indeed of men, but chosen of God, and precious, Ye also, as lively stones, are built up a **spiritual**[25] house, an holy priesthood, to **offer up** spiri-

Paul	Hebrews	1 Peter
		tual **sacrifices**,[26] **acceptable**[27] to God by Jesus Christ (2:2–5).
As it is written, **Isaiah 28:16a** Behold, I lay in Sion… **Isaiah 8:14** a stumblingstone and rock of offence (Ro 9:33)		Wherefore also it is contained in the scripture, **Isaiah 28:16** Behold, I lay in Sion… (2:6) **Isaiah 8:14** And a stone of stumbling, and a rock of offence[28] (2:8).
	people of God (11:25)	**people of God**[29] (2:10)
	confessed that they were *strangers* and **pilgrims** on the earth (11:13)	I beseech you as *strangers*[30] and **pilgrims**, abstain from **fleshly**[31] lusts, which war against the soul (2:11; 1:1)
Let every soul be subject unto the higher powers. For there is no power but of God: the powers that be are ordained of God…For rulers are not a terror to good works, but to the evil. Wilt thou then not be afraid of the power? do that which is good, and thou shalt have **praise** of the same… Render therefore to all their dues: tribute to whom tribute is due; custom to whom custom; fear to whom fear; honour to whom honour (Ro 13:1, 3, 7).		Submit yourselves to every ordinance of man for the Lord's sake: whether it be to the king, as supreme; Or unto governors, as unto them that are sent by him for the punishment of evildoers, and for the **praise**[32] of them that do well. (And who is he that will harm you, if ye be **followers**[33] of that which is good? (3:13) For so is the will of God, that with well doing ye may put to silence the **ignorance**[34] of foolish men: As free, and not using your liberty for a *cloke of maliciousness*,[35] but as the servants of God.

Paul	Hebrews	1 Peter
		Honour all men. Love the brotherhood. Fear God. Honour the king (2:13–17).
Exhort servants to be **obedient** unto their own **masters**, and to please them well in all things; not answering again (Tim 2:9)		Servants, be **subject** to your **masters** with all fear (2:18)[36]
	By faith Moses, when he was come to years, refused to be called the son of Pharaoh's daughter; Choosing rather to suffer affliction with the people of God, than to enjoy the pleasures of sin for a season; Esteeming the reproach of Christ greater riches than the treasures in Egypt (11:24–26)	For even hereunto were ye called: because Christ also suffered for us, leaving us an example, that ye should follow his **steps**[37]...Forasmuch then as Christ hath suffered for us in the flesh[38] (2:21; 4:1a)
yet now hath he reconciled in the body of his flesh (Col 1:21–22)	So Christ was once offered to **bear** the **sins** of many (9:28)	Who his own self **bare** our **sins in** his own **body**[39] (2:24)
Wives, **submit** yourselves unto your own **husbands**, as unto the Lord (Eph 5:22).		Likewise, ye **wives**, be in **subjection** to your own **husbands** (3:1)
But he is a Jew, which is one inwardly; and circumcision is that of the heart, in the spirit, and not in the letter; whose praise is not of men, but of God (Ro 2:29).		But let it be the hidden man of the heart, in that which is not corruptible, even the ornament of a meek and quiet spirit, which is in the sight of God of great price (3:4)

Paul	Hebrews	1 Peter
Recompense to no man **evil for evil** (Rom 12:17; 1 Thes 5:15)		giving honour unto the wife, as unto the weaker vessel, and as being **heirs together**[40] of the grace of life; that your prayers be not hindered. **Finally,**[41] be ye all of one mind, having compassion one of another, love as brethren, be **pitiful**[42], be courteous. Not rendering **evil for evil**[43] or **railing** for **railing**[44] **contrariwise**[45] blessing (3:7b–9b).
	So Christ was *once* offered to bear the sins of many (9:28)	For Christ also hath *once* suffered for sins, the just for the unjust (3:18)
For as ye in **times past** have **not believed** God, yet have now obtained mercy through their unbelief (Ro 11:30)	By faith *Noah,* being warned of God of things not seen as yet, moved with fear, **prepared an ark** to the saving of his house; by the which he condemned the world, and became heir of the righteousness which is by faith (11:7).	Which **sometime** were **disobedient,**[46] when once the longsuffering of God waited in the days of *Noah,* while the **ark was a preparing**, wherein few, that is, eight souls were saved by water (3:20).
	For Christ is not entered into the holy places made with hands, which are the **figures** of the true; but into heaven itself, now to appear in the presence of God for us (9:24)	The like **figure**[47] whereunto even baptism doth also now save us (not the putting away of the filth of the flesh, but the answer of a good conscience toward God), by the resurrection of Jesus Christ (3:21)

Paul	Hebrews	1 Peter
For he hath put all things under his feet. But when he says all things are put under him, it is manifest that he is excepted, which did put all things under him. And when all things shall be subdued unto him, then shall the Son also himself be subject unto him that put all things under him, that God may be all in all (1 Cor 15:27–28).	Thou hast put all things in subjection under his feet. For in that he put all in subjection under him, he left nothing that is not put under him. But now we see not yet all things put under him (Heb 2:8).	Who is gone into heaven, and is on the right hand of God; angels and authorities and powers being made subject unto him (3:22).
Let this mind be in you, which was also in Christ Jesus (Phil 2:5) How shall we, that are dead to sin, live any longer therein (Rom 6:2) Therefore, brethren, we are debtors, not to the flesh, to live after the flesh (Ro 8:12) The night is far spent, the day is at hand: let us therefore cast off the works of darkness, and let us put on the armour of light. Let us walk honestly, as in the day; not in **rioting** and drunkenness, not in chambering and **wantonness**, not in strife and envying (Rom 13:12–13).		arm yourselves likewise with the same mind: for he that hath suffered in the flesh hath ceased from sin; That he no longer should live the rest of his time in the flesh to the lusts of men, but to the will of God. For the time past of our life may suffice us to have wrought the will of the Gentiles, when we walked in *lasciviousness*,[48] lusts, excess of wine, **revellings**,[49] banquetings, and abominable **idolatries**[50] (4:1–3)

Paul	Hebrews	1 Peter
Now ye are the body of Christ, and members in particular. And God hath set some in the church, first apostles, secondarily prophets, thirdly teachers, after that miracles, then gifts of healings, helps, governments, diversities of tongues. Are all apostles? are all prophets? are all teachers? are all workers of miracles? Have all the **gifts** of healing? do all speak with tongues? do all interpret? But covet earnestly the best gifts: and yet shew I unto you a more excellent way (1 Cor 12:27–31).		As every man hath received the **gift**[51] even so minister the same one to another, as good stewards of the manifold grace of God (4:10).
oracles of God (Rom 3:2)	oracles of God (5:12)	oracles of God (4:11)
And our hope of you is stedfast, knowing, that as ye are **partakers** of the **sufferings**, so shall ye be also of the consolation (2 Cor 1:7).		But rejoice, inasmuch as ye are **partakers** of Christ's **sufferings**; that, when his glory shall be revealed, ye may be glad also with exceeding joy (4:13)…and also a partaker of the glory that shall be revealed (5:1b)
For what have I to do to judge them also that are without? do not ye judge them that are within? But them that are without God judgeth. Therefore put away from among yourselves that wicked		For the time is come that judgment must begin at the house of God and if it first begin at us, what shall the end be of them that obey not the gospel of God (4:17)?

Paul	Hebrews	1 Peter
person (1 Cor 5:12-13). In flaming fire taking vengeance on them that know not God, and that obey not the gospel of our Lord Jesus Christ (2 Thess 1:8)		
God is faithful, by whom ye were called unto the fellowship of his Son Jesus Christ our Lord (1 Cor 1:9; also 1 Cor 10:13).		Wherefore let them that suffer according to the will of God commit the keeping of their souls to him in well doing, as unto a **faithful Creator** (4:19).
And every man that striveth for the mastery is temperate in all things. Now they do it to obtain a corruptible crown; but we an incorruptible (1 Cor 9:25).	Now the God of peace, that brought again from the dead our Lord Jesus, that **great shepherd** of the sheep, through the blood of the everlasting covenant (13:20)	And when the **chief Shepherd** shall appear, ye shall receive a crown of glory that fadeth not away (5:4).
Submitting yourselves **one to another** in the fear of God (Eph 5:21). *Put on* therefore, as the elect of God, holy and beloved, bowels of mercies, kindness, *humbleness* of mind (Col 3:12)		Yea, all of you be **subject one to another**,[52] and be *clothed with humility* (5:5)
That I may know him, and the power of his resurrection, and the fellowship of his **sufferings** (Phil 3:10a)		Whom resist stedfast in the faith, knowing that the same **afflictions**[53] are accomplished in your brethren that are in the world (5:9).
Called...to glory (1 Thes 2:12; 2 Thes 2:14)		**Called...to glory** (5:10; 2 Pt 1:3)

Paul	Hebrews	1 Peter
By whom also we have access by faith into this **grace** wherein we **stand**, and rejoice in hope of the glory of God (Ro 5:2).		By Silvanus, a faithful brother unto you, as I suppose, I have written briefly, exhorting, and testifying that this is the true **grace** of God wherein ye **stand** (5:12).
"**Christ Jesus**" is a title apparently coined by Paul, who uses it 55 times. The title is employed in 3 other places: once in Hebrews, twice in 1 Peter. "**Appearing of Christ**" is only used once by Paul, but Peter uses it 3 times in 1 Peter. Paul prefers the Matthean technical term "parousia" (used 14 times), to which Peter switches in his second letter (used 3 times). Paul links **faith** and **hope** 7 times. This linkage occurs elsewhere only in 1 Peter—once (1:21).		

What is Peter's first letter about? What is his theological perspective? Considering the massive but selective importation of so much theological jargon and so many idea fragments from Paul and from Hebrews without theological development, it is difficult to say. If he is not saying anything in particular, then why has he written? One thing is sure: if we are to understand what Peter's first letter is about, we must confine ourselves to the theological ideas which *Peter* develops, and not assume the theological ideas underlying the jargon which he has so often imported from other authors and which he leaves undeveloped.

This is especially true in that the ethos of his letter resonates so closely with James, which seems to be working at such cross-purposes with the radical ideas of Pauline theology and of the theology of Hebrews which underlie this jargon. For example, in contrast with Paul and Hebrews, except for two mentions of "Jesus" and "Christ" and a slight co-mingling of his name with "Lord" (used thirteen times), one would never know from James that a lamb has recently been slain for the sins of the world and has been resurrected for our justification, saving us from the judgment to come. Now imagine Peter's first letter, stripped of its Pauline and Hebrewine jargonistic importations. It seems to begin an elaboration upon the suffering servant motif of Isaiah 53, but it ends (theologically) with a bland, Elijah-like prophet who, as Socrates and so many prophets of Judaism, suffered and died for the sake of truth on behalf of the people of Athens, the nation of Israel, and us—the "just for the unjust."[15]

Matthew's Gospel gives evidence that after almost three decades, Peter does not fully understand why Christ must die to save us. Peter's first letter gives evidence that after almost four decades, Peter still does not fully understand this. Indeed, James' epistle still insists that the word can save us.[16]

But if the word of God can save our souls, what need was there for Christ to die? The primary theme in 1 Peter is suffering (**πασχω**) for righteousness' sake. But how is the suffering of Christ of any more significance than the prophecy of Caiaphas, that Jesus must become a sort of "scapegoat" sacrificed for the stability—if not the very survival—of the nation?[17] The author of Hebrews acknowledges that there have been many prophets which have assumed this messianic role: "By faith Moses, when he was come to years, refused to be called the son of Pharaoh's daughter; Choosing rather to suffer affliction with the people of God, than to enjoy the pleasures of sin for a season; Esteeming the reproach of Christ greater riches than the treasures in Egypt."[18] "And others had trial of cruel mockings and scourgings, yea, moreover of bonds and imprisonment: They were stoned, they were sawn asunder, were tempted, were slain with the sword: they wandered about in sheep-skins and goatskins; being destitute, afflicted, tormented; Of whom the world was not worthy."[19]

But what makes the suffering of the prophet from Nazareth any different from these? "Just for the unjust" is a phrase that will mean

---

15 A phrase only Peter has used.

16 Jas 1:21. "Wherefore lay apart all filthiness and superfluity of naughtiness, and receive with meekness the engrafted word, which is able to save your souls."

17 Jn 11:49–50. "And one of them, named Caiaphas, being the high priest that same year, said unto them, Ye know nothing at all, Nor consider that it is expedient for us, that one man should die for the people, and that the whole nation perish not."

18 Heb 11:24–26.

19 Heb 11:37–38.

nothing more than Caiaphas' prophecy unless it receives theological development elsewhere.[20]

At the end of his Gospel, Luke has Jesus explain to two of his disciples why it was necessary for the Christ to suffer. Although suffering is often mentioned in Peter's epistle, and there is much suggestive jargon about Christ's blood from other sources, Peter gives no clear reason why Christ should suffer. In his first letter, Peter does not use "cross" or "crucifixion," he does not acknowledge Christ as the unique "Son of God,"[21] and he altogether avoids the centrality of Christ's death to *our* life.[22] We must therefore conclude that phrases like "sprinkling of the blood of Jesus Christ," "ye were...redeemed by...the precious blood of Christ," "Who his own self bare our sins in his own

20 For example, Paul's statement in Ro 5:8, "But God commendeth his love toward us, in that, while we were yet sinners, Christ died for us," has been given definition by clarifying statements before: "Christ died for the ungodly" (5:6) and "[Jesus] was delivered for our offences, and was raised again for our justification" (4:25), and by clarifying statements after: "being now justified by his blood, we shall be saved from wrath through him" (5:9) and "by the righteousness of one the free gift came upon all men unto justification of life" (5:18). These constructions in Paul's letter to the Romans greatly clarify what Paul means when he says, "Christ died for us." And in the rest of the Pauline corpus, his theological constructions have been so varied and graphic that there is no doubt we are now far above a Caiaphastic meaning of Christ as the scapegoat of ordinary historical processes or even Peter's "just for the unjust." Paul's forensic argumentation augments his broad yet clear development of justification, the process whereby the righteousness of Christ becomes *our* righteousness. "Christ our passover is sacrificed for us" (1 Cor 5:7). "For he hath made him to be sin for us, who knew no sin; that we might be made the righteousness of God in him" (2 Cor 5:21). "Christ hath redeemed us from the curse of the law, being made a curse for us: for it is written, Cursed is every one that hangeth on a tree" (Gal 3:13).

21 **μονογενης** (only begotten), a term so central to the theology of John (Peter's first preaching partner), is never found in the mouth of Peter. **πρωτοτοκος**. (first-born), a key theological title for Christ in Paul, Hebrews, and John, is also never found in the mouth of Peter. In Mt 16:16, Peter says to Jesus, "Thou art the Christ, the Son of the living God." Mark begins his Gospel with this phrase yet does not put it into the mouth of Peter. Peter merely says, "Thou art Christ." Luke agrees; he records "Christ of God." In a synagogue in Capernaum, John records yet another, weaker, Petrine confession: "And we believe and are sure that thou art the Holy One of God" (Jn 6:69). Four times Peter calls Jesus **παις** ("servant" or "child") of God (in dialogue recorded by Luke in Acts), but never again does he call him "Son of God." This is an important omission.

22 Which is the core idea in Paul's crucifixion theology.

body on the tree," "that we, being dead to sins, should live unto righteousness: by whose stripes ye were healed," left undeveloped and surrounded by the decidedly non-Pauline theological context of James, have no ultimate meaning beyond "suffering for righteousness' sake."

Peter had refused the cross of Christ at Caesarea; he had slept through the transfiguration and at Gethsemane, and had refused to have his feet washed by Christ. Peter refused to allow Christ to die peacefully and obediently and so drew his sword. The Lord called on Peter's loyalty, suddenly, at cockcrow, and Peter failed him.[23] The Lord came suddenly to the shore of Lake Tiberius to look in on Peter's bishopric, for Peter was failing him.[24] Peter at first refused his call to the Gentiles in order to preserve his sacramental purity.[25] Peter refused to be loyal to that call by betraying his fellowship with the Antiochian Christians in order to maintain the purity of his reputation with the Jamesean Party at Jerusalem.

When Mark went over to Peter after Paul was executed, he very probably found Peter still entangled with the errors of Judaizing Christianity. Paul says, "And the other Jews dissembled likewise with [Peter]; insomuch that Barnabas also was carried away with their dissimulation. But when I saw that they walked not uprightly according to the truth of the gospel..."[26] Mark had already gone through his own final catharsis and died to the righteousness of Judaism and had reconciled with Paul as a new man in Christ. How Mark must have longed for the full conversion of Peter. He has seen history slip through his fingers. He remembered the days of glory—almost thirty years ago—when Peter was strong and clear and led his Church with a mighty hand. He preached boldly, was imprisoned, and worked many mighty works in the name of Christ. His stubborn loyalty to ritual purity and Judaizing Christianity had slowly choked his soul. Spiritually retarded, he supped continually on the "milk of the word" when he should have been feasting upon its meat.[27]

---

23 Mk 13:35. "Watch ye therefore: for ye know not when the master of the house cometh, at even, or at midnight, or at the cockcrowing, or in the morning."

24 Jn 21.

25 Acts 10:14.

26 Gal 2:13–14.

One might easily imagine Mark and Silvanus exchanging painful glances as Silvanus dutifully crafted much of 1 Peter. Would the "sifting" and conversion of the "first" apostle ever be complete? Mark, the interpreter of Peter, says yes: "After that he put his hands again upon his eyes, and made him look up: and he was restored, and saw every man clearly."[28]

How did the final conversion of Peter happen? No one knows. Except Mark. And he's not saying. Beyond the clear statements that he has embedded in his Gospel, he is as silent as Balaam's faithful friend.

A Vessel of Gold

Peter's first epistle appears to have been an attempt to contain the still-fermenting blood of the "new promise" in the worn-out wine-skins of a Judaized Christology. The resulting awkward synthesis produces an ambiguous Christ and an ambiguous program of suffering. These ambiguities suddenly resolve in 2 Peter. But it is not just the resolution of ambiguity we see in 2 Peter. For here is a confident, full-bodied pastoral epistle which speaks authoritative words of crucial encouragement to a disoriented and scattering flock. The tremendous differences of tone,[29] content, and theological orientation between 1 and 2 Peter are so pronounced that many in the early Church doubted continuity of authorship. But a linguistic analysis shows that the author of 1 Peter is the same as the author of 2 Peter. (See Figure 3 below.)

---

27 Heb 5:12. "For when for the time ye ought to be teachers, ye have need that one teach you again which be the first principles of the oracles of God; and are become such as have need of milk, and not of strong meat."

28 Mk 8:25.

29 For example, compare 1 Pe 3:10, "For he that will love life, and see good days, let him refrain his tongue from evil, and his lips that they speak no guile," with the motive power of 2 Pe 3:11: "Seeing then that all these things shall be dissolved, what manner of persons ought ye to be in all holy conversation and godliness." Perhaps even more to the point, Peter unhesitatingly indicts those who are ravaging his flock: "But it is happened unto them according to the true proverb, The dog is turned to his own vomit again; and the sow that was washed to her wallowing in the mire."

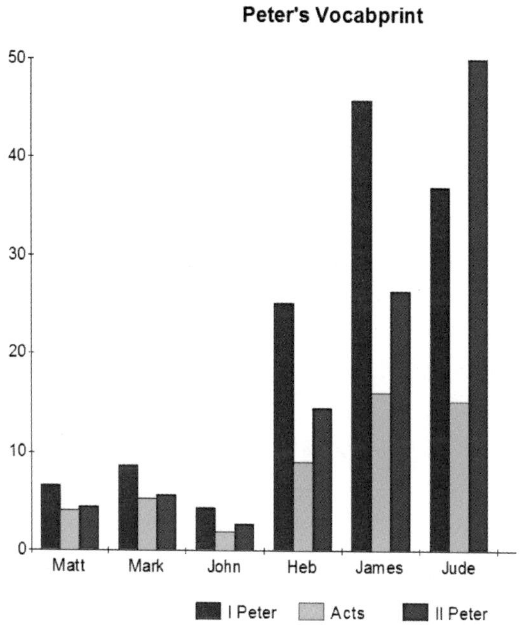

Figure 3. Peter's Vocabulary Print

Since 1 Peter displays such an affinity for the phraseology of Paul, the verbiage of 1 Peter, Peter's verbiage in Acts, and 2 Peter was compared to other authors. One point was assigned for each word that was used by any author and Peter, regardless of what other author might have already used that word. In an attempt to minimize "noise," only those words which occurred thirty-five times or less were considered. Two points were assigned if a word was shared only with Peter. Finally, the word correlations are adjusted in ratio with the differing lengths of each literary sample. The architecture is almost identical.

Jude flips the architecture because he very closely utilizes 2 Peter as a template for his work, and this almost drives 2 Peter off the chart in relation to the other authors.[30] Additionally, all letters which come

30 The proof that Jude is quoting Peter and not Peter quoting Jude was derived from research directly connected with the writing of this book, but which is beyond the scope of the present discussion.

from Paul and Luke (Paul's presumed amanuensis[31]) were eliminated since it would obscure phraseological correlation between more neutral authors. Of course we can see the high correlation between 1 Peter and Hebrews and James as the tables above suggest would be the case, but the striking correlation between 1 Peter, Peter's verbiage in Acts, and 2 Peter can be seen by the repeating *pattern* in each of the comparisons.

This phenomenon may be seen more easily by imagining that 1 Peter, Peter's verbiage in Acts, and 2 Peter are three separate authors: A, B, and C. Furthermore, let it be imagined that authors A, B, and C had a profound effect over each of the other authors along the x axis: Matthew, Mark, John, Hebrews, and James. The figure would be showing that each one of these authors was more or less influenced by the ABC author group. But this would require that every one of these x axis authors, who shared differing amounts of vocabulary, each filled his vocabulary "palette" with isometric proportions of each author (A, B, and C); that is, Matthew took mostly red, least of green, and a median amount of blue. Hebrews, who took proportionately more of the ABC author group, filled his palette similarly, and so on. This is statistically inconceivable. If the flow of influence in this thought experiment were reversed, i.e., authors A, B, and C were all *borrowing* from all the x axis authors, there would still be an unaccountable isometric stratification of the linguistic behavior of each of these authors which would also be inconceivable, unless some unifying hypothesis was found to account for this phenomena. The obvious solution: authors A, B, and C are the same author.

The really remarkable thing about Figure 3 (above) is that it shows that on the level of mere vocabulary, 1 Peter and 2 Peter are almost identical, even though 1 Peter is a conscious process of importing Jamesean and Hebrewine quotes and phrases and 2 Peter is not. Although 2 Peter is still closely associated with the phraseology of James, the theological ethos and tone of this epistle has changed completely.

In 2 Peter the *thematic* linkage with Paul is now clear. His central section is a bitter denunciation of the false prophets and false

31 Essentially, this means that Luke was Paul's secretary for many of his epistles. The proof for this will be demonstrated in a second book, *From Exodus to Eisodus*.

teachers within the church. Who are they? They look very much like the nemesis of Paul—the Judaizers. Following Paul closely here, Peter says that they are "...chiefly them that walk after the flesh in the lust of uncleanness, and despise government. Presumptuous are they, self-willed, they are not afraid to speak evil of dignities."[32] Peter's "despise government" is cognate with Paul's "unruly" (Tim 1:10). "Self-willed" is a word used only in Tim 1:7.

There is also a strong thematic linkage between the entire judgmental section of 2 Peter—where false teachers smuggle in false teachings, and with deceitful words and powerful fleshly lusts bewitch those who had been making progress in the truth—and 2 Tm 3:6-8: "For of this sort are they which creep into houses, and lead captive silly women laden with sins, led away with divers lusts, Ever learning, and never able to come to the knowledge of the truth. Now as Jannes and Jambres withstood Moses, so do these also resist the truth: men of corrupt minds, reprobate concerning the faith."

Indeed, it is very probable that this section, 2 Timothy 3, has strongly influenced the formation of 2 Peter.

Table 13. Thematic Similarity between 2 Peter and 2 Timothy

Thematic Emphasis	2 Peter	2 Timothy
An emphasis on the reliability of Scripture	Knowing this first, that no prophecy of the scripture is of any private interpretation. For the prophecy came not in old time by the will of man: but holy men of God spake as they were moved by the Holy Ghost[54]	All scripture is given by inspiration of God, and is profitable for doctrine, for reproof, for correction, for instruction in righteousness

32 2 Pe 2:10

Thematic Emphasis	2 Peter	2 Timothy
And an emphasis on following the apostolic teaching, not Jewish myths	For we have not followed cunningly devised fables, when we made known unto you the power and coming of our Lord Jesus Christ, but were eyewitnesses of his majesty	But thou hast followed my doctrine, manner of life, purpose, faith, longsuffering, charity, patience…Hold fast the form of sound words, which thou hast heard of me, in faith and love which is in Christ Jesus…And they shall turn away their ears from the truth, and shall be turned unto fables
Both authors intend to "stir up" their charges by way of remembrance…	This second epistle, beloved, I now write unto you; in both which I stir up your pure minds by way of remembrance	Wherefore I put thee in remembrance that thou stir up the gift of God, which is in thee by the putting on of my hands
Since their time of departure is near	Knowing that shortly I must put off this my tabernacle, even as our Lord Jesus Christ hath shewed me	For I am now ready to be offered, and the time of my departure is at hand
An emphasis on the seductiveness of heterodoxy	Who privily shall bring in damnable heresies, even denying the Lord that bought them	Having a form of godliness, but denying the power thereof
An Old Testament example is given of those who, through false religious power, resisted the true religion and the true authority	Which have forsaken the right way, and are gone astray, following the way of Balaam the son of Bosor	Now as Jannes and Jambres withstood Moses, so do these also resist the truth
An emphasis on seductiveness of evil behavior	Having eyes full of adultery, and that cannot cease from sin; beguiling unstable souls: an heart they have exercised with covetous practices; cursed children	But evil men and seducers shall wax worse and worse, deceiving, and being deceived

Thematic Emphasis	2 Peter	2 Timothy
An emphasis on the degenerating situation for the church in the last days	Knowing this first, that there shall come in the last days scoffers, walking after their own lusts	This know also, that in the last days perilous times shall come
Deceit opportunistically works through lust	For when they speak great swelling words of vanity, they allure through the lusts of the flesh, through much wantonness, those that were clean escaped from them who live in error	For of this sort are they which creep into houses, and lead captive silly women laden with sins, led away with divers lusts
The present world is an entanglement to the business of godliness	For if after they have escaped the pollutions of the world through the knowledge of the Lord and Saviour Jesus Christ, they are again entangled therein	No man that warreth entangleth himself with the affairs of this life; that he may please him who hath chosen him to be a soldier
Having destroyed (καταφθειρω) their minds, they have destroyed themselves	[They] speak evil of the things that they understand not; and shall utterly perish in their own corruption	…so do these also resist the truth: men of corrupt minds, reprobate concerning the faith

There is a spurious Jewish tradition which makes Jannes and Jambres the sons of Balaam. This could explain why Peter has reached for a more concrete Old Testament example: Balaam, the son of Bosor, who is a type of all those who have "forsaken the right way." An even more plausible explanation for Peter's choice of Balaam is that Balaam is a type (τυπος) of Peter himself. And Peter knows it. Peter has stood paralyzed between heaven and hell: first confessing Christ, then denying him. As Balaam was called to curse the children of Israel three times, so did Peter fail Christ at Gethsemane three times and curse Christ through denial three times. And so did Peter fail the flock of Christ three times. He failed them by going back to his trade and was remonstrated by Christ. He failed the Antiochian Christians and was remonstrated by Paul. He now realizes that 1 Peter is a vessel of clay that carries no blood to the common fellowship. He has failed the flock three times.

But now, somehow, Peter has seen the angel of the Lord, standing in his way, ready to slay him with the sword. Someone or something finally got through to him. Was it the death of Paul? No. That was not enough. 1 Peter appears to have been written in spite of Paul's messianic death. Was it the publication of Hebrews? No. He has already imported its jargon into 1 Peter, stripped of its revolutionary fervor.[33] Was it Silvanus? Perhaps. Chances are, it was Mark. Someone had to wake Peter up. Peter was like a man half awake, half asleep. He did see, but not clearly. Peter was a proud, impulsive man who was in bondage to an insatiable lust for the approval of other men. Christ said precisely this of him. Of all the hurtful, destructive lusts of men, this was the most powerful.[34]

And this was also the downfall of Balaam. The circumcision party had strongly urged Peter to curse the Paulinists. Though Peter refused to do this with his mouth, as Balaam at first refused the emissaries from Balak, he nevertheless did so with the political silence and Jamesean theology which is 1 Peter—just as Balaam did by entertaining a second visit from Balak's emissaries, even though God had unequivocally obviated the possibility that they could have anything more to say to convince Balaam to curse Israel. So Balaam played a game of hypocrisy. He would flatter God with his mouth and secretly pursue his lust for the approval of the king of Moab.

The account seems confusing to modern ears. First God tells Balaam to go. Then he sends an angel to kill him for going. This confusion is not rooted in the mind of God. It is rooted in the duplicitousness and equivocation of Balaam. The author of Numbers knows exactly what is going on here. Why else would he have put in the mouth of Balaam these words: "God is not a man, that he should lie; neither the son of man, that he should repent: hath he said, and shall he not do it? or hath he spoken, and shall he not make it good" (Nm 23:19)? No, the author of Numbers knows what the problem is with Balaam. But Peter didn't.

33 Much more will be said of this in *From Exodus to Eisodus*.

34 Jude 1:16 specifically cites this lust: "...walking after their own lusts; and their mouth speaketh great swelling words, having men's persons in admiration because of advantage."

Until now. He had already been given an explicit vision on the rooftop of Simon the Tanner. But as James had wisely observed: many are the men to whom God reveals their true self, yet as soon as they turn away from this divine vision of self-knowledge, forget who they really are.[35]

Perhaps Mark mocked Peter's self-constructed legend of spirituality, which had rationalistically taken his passions and had transformed them into virtues. Peter's proud righteousness lay in his Jewish purity derived from non-association with contaminated, common, defiled, Gentile men. Peter felt that his impulsiveness was *intrinsically* spiritual. This should be easy to understand for the modern age, which is saturated with charismatic fervor, which places reason in direct opposition to feeling, and which is thoroughly imbued with an abiding conviction that impulsive behavior is divine. And it surely is. This is an ancient belief. It is more ancient than Bacchus himself. In doing service to those whose approval he craved, he assumed that he was in service to his God.[36]

God brought the Paulinists out of the Egypt of the Old Covenant with the strength of a unicorn.[37] And there was no force on earth and no curse of any false prophet that would stop them from entering the Sabbath rest of God's righteousness, his peace, and his joy—even *after* the death of its Moses. "So when Peter saw that it pleased the Lord to bless the Paulinists, he went not to conscript the silver pen of Silvanus, but himself lifted up his eyes and saw the new heavens and new earth in which dwells nothing but righteousness,"[38] even now, in images only half-seen heretofore, dancing before his uncomprehending eyes in the process of being made.

---

35 Jas 1:23b–24: "…he is like unto a man beholding his natural face in a glass: For he beholdeth himself, and goeth his way, and straightway forgetteth what manner of man he was."

36 Jn 16:2. "They shall put you out of the synagogues: yea, the time cometh, that whosoever killeth you will think that he doeth God service."

37 Nm 23:22.

38 24:1–2. "And when Balaam saw that it pleased the LORD to bless Israel, he went not, as at other times, to seek for enchantments, but he set his face toward the wilderness. And Balaam lifted up his eyes, and he saw Israel abiding in his tents according to their tribes; and the spirit of God came upon him."

Now Peter had completed the same circuit which Balaam had completed: "He hath said, which heard the words of God, which saw the vision of the Almighty, falling into a trance, but having his eyes open."[39] Peter had heard the very voice of God from the cloud – "this is my beloved Son" – and had denied him. He had received the vision in a trance atop the house of Simon the Tanner about God having cleansed all the animals that the Levitical laws had put under the ban of uncleanness, urging him to accept the Pauline teaching that God had now broken down the partitioning wall of Leviticus between Jew and Gentile. For a time he endured in this belief. He then promptly forgot the vision and denied the Antiochian Christians.

But now, his eyes are opened. He now sees the just, clothed with the righteousness of Christ, streaming out of old Israel to the promised New Jerusalem. He now sees the angel of death which bars his way to curse them. He now realizes that nothing will save him. Not his purity. Not his impulsiveness. Not his clever syncretism. Only the prayers of Christ would save him.[40] And so they did.

Here is where Peter diverges from Balaam, son of Beor. For Balaam was eventually slain by the overwhelming hosts of Israel, killed as a common soothsayer. But Peter was permitted to turn again, by the prayers of Christ, through the longsuffering of God. It was, after all, faith as a grain of a mustard seed, which grew very slowly in the ground for almost forty years: we know not how. The important thing is that that seed germinated and produced fruit. The Morningstar *did* rise in Peter's heart. Venus had shown him how to love Christ after all these years of god-talk. Peter is now zealous that the children of the New Covenant make an entrance into the Promised Land (1:11).

This is the kind of explanation that can account for the radical differences between 1 and 2 Peter. These differences in Peter are the result of a final, cathartic conversion to the theological position of Paul, fulfilling the prophecy of Christ himself. Indeed, it is quite possible that Peter himself acknowledges this conversion in highly idiosyncratic

39 Nm 24:4.

40 Lk 22:32. "But I have prayed for thee, that thy faith fail not: and when thou art converted, strengthen thy brethren."

phrases which can only be construed as autobiographical: "But he that lacketh these things is blind, and cannot see afar off, and hath forgotten that he was purged from his old sins" (1:9). "We have also a more sure word of prophecy; whereunto ye do well that ye take heed, as unto a light that shineth in a dark place, until the day dawn, and the day star arise in your hearts" (1:19). "The Lord is not slack concerning his promise, as some men count slackness; but is longsuffering to us-ward, not willing that any should perish, but that all should come to repentance" (3:9).

2 Peter is not pandering and platitudinous. There is no ambivalence and non-offensive, inclusive, Pauline god-talk. 2 Peter is not meandering; it is electric with motion and judgment—*krak und blitz*. He names names. He comes down on the side of Paul. More importantly, Peter comes down on the side of the Pauline gospel. The purposes of 1 Peter was to "exhort" and to "witness to the truth." The purpose of 2 Peter is unequivocally defined and twice repeated: Peter means not just to exhort the church to "gird up the loins of the mind" (1 Pe 1:13) but to give a wake-up[41] call to the sincerity of the mind (2 Pe 1:13, 3:1). No longer are just the "scattered strangers" addressed (1 Pe 1:1). Now, his epistle is to *all* those who have by faith obtained like precious promises (2 Pe 1:1, 4).

Peter no longer avoids the Pauline titles for Christ, eight times calling him "Lord" (compared to a perfunctory mention in 1 Pe 1:3). After almost forty years, Peter again confesses Christ as the Son of God: "For he received from God the Father honour and glory, when there came such a voice to him from the excellent glory, This is my beloved Son, in whom I am well pleased" (1:17). Peter also embraces Christ as "savior" (**σωτηρ**), repeating the title five times.

Peter greatly strengthens the idea of "righteousness," alluding clearly to the "righteousness of God and of our savior Jesus Christ" (1:1) and the "way of righteousness" (2:21). Noah is now not typological of the individual conscience (1 Pe 3:21), but an exemplar of righteousness.

---

41 The NKJV has "stir up," but the word is always used in connection with waking someone up from sleep. For example, Mk 4:38 says, "And he was in the hinder part of the ship, asleep on a pillow: and they *awake* him, and say unto him, Master, carest thou not that we perish" (indicating considerable intensity in this wake-up call).

(2 Pe 2:5). And the "antithesis of righteousness" (**αδικια**) will now be judged. Just as Sodom and Gomorrah were condemned, the unrighteous (**αδικος**) will receive the "reward of unrighteousness." Damnation is reserved for false teachers, their heresies, and their ways (2:1–2), as it is for all the ungodly (**ασεβης**) and those who malign the writings of Paul (3:16).

Peter enjoins a *specific* spirituality with considerable intensity, centering on the word **σπουδαζω** (to be diligent). Paul says that he must "give diligence" to "… be found in him, not having mine own righteousness, which is of the law, but that which is through the faith of Christ, the righteousness which is of God by faith" (Phil 3:9). This aligns with 2 Pe 3:14: "Wherefore, beloved, seeing that ye look for such things, be diligent that ye may be found of him in peace, without spot, and blameless." Since 2 Peter appears to be primarily directed against the Judaizers, the chief threat is that the basis of our righteousness "move away" (Gal 1:6) from being "in Christ." If this happens, we are "fallen from grace" (Gal 5:4). To ensure that this does not happen, we must "give diligence" to make our calling and election sure (1:10), i.e., that our faith is "in his promises," the knowledge of which will produce "fruit" (1:8).

2 Peter now includes the idea of the "parousia," referring both to the first coming of Christ (1:16), the second coming of Christ (3:4), and the coming of the day of God (3:12) when the elements will be dissolved. Peter's own party, perhaps, scoffed at the parousia of Matthew and Paul: "Knowing this first, that there shall come in the last days scoffers, walking after their own lusts, And saying, Where is the promise of his coming? For since the fathers fell asleep, all things continue as they were from the beginning of the creation"(3:3–4).

Peter's spiritual program also includes a strong emphasis on judgment (**κρισις**), which was entirely lacking in 1 Peter. It will be a fiery day of judgment and damnation of ungodly men (3:7) in which the heavens will pass away with a great noise and the elements themselves will be dissolved by fire (3:10). Peter fully embraces the Matthean[42]/Pauline[43]/Johannine[44] "thief" of the parousia: " But the day

42 Mt 24:43.

43 1 Thess 5:2.

44 Re 16:15.

of the Lord will come as a thief in the night; in which the heavens shall pass away with a great noise, and the elements shall melt with fervent heat, the earth also and the works that are therein shall be burned up" (3:10).

Peter now greatly strengthens his explanation for the crucifixion of Christ: he now fully acknowledges that we are "bought with a price" (2:1).[45] It is through knowledge of God and of our Lord Jesus Christ that we escape the pollutions of the world (2:20) and that grace and peace (1:2) and all things that pertain to godliness (1:3) come.[46] To grow in knowledge of our Lord and Savior Jesus Christ is the last thing that Peter told the fledgling church to do (3:18). Peter intimates that he who has forgotten these things, "...is blind, and cannot see afar off, and hath forgotten that he was purged from his old sins" (1:9). Peter says that it is ultimately against these ideas of salvation that heresy is directed: "But there were false prophets also among the people, even as there shall be false teachers among you, who privily shall bring in damnable heresies, even denying the Lord that bought them, and bring upon themselves swift destruction" (2:1). But mere knowledge of the "way of righteousness" will not save us. Repentance (**μετανοια**) will (3:9).

And it is in this venue that Peter repudiates his program of a limited salvation for the lucky few: "The Lord is not slack concerning his promise, as some men count slackness; but is longsuffering to us-ward, not willing that any should perish, but that all should come to repentance." In this sentence we also, perhaps, get a hint of Peter's view of his own conversion. Christ has been longsuffering with Peter. Paul is the chief of sinners, but Peter is the chief of intransigents. He now embraces what he did not mention in 1 Peter: repentance.

---

45 "For ye are bought with a price: therefore glorify God in your body, and in your spirit, which are God's" (1 Cor 6:20). "And they sung a new song, saying, Thou art worthy to take the book, and to open the seals thereof: for thou wast slain, and hast redeemed us to God by thy blood out of every kindred, and tongue, and people, and nation" (Re 5:9).

46 The Pauline argument is this: God gives us knowledge of himself. If we turn away from that knowledge, then our minds become darkened and the knowledge that we do have becomes perverted and twisted (Ro 1:28). If we believe (*pistis*) that knowledge, even more is given to us (see especially Col 3:10, but also Eph 4:13, Phil 1:9, and Col 1:9).

Peter now also gives much needed reasoning about *why* we should live godly lives though they result in nothing but suffering and persecution, since he had offered nothing before but a nebulous future vindication. Peter now says: "Seeing then that all these things shall be dissolved, what manner of persons ought ye to be in all holy conversation and godliness" (3:11)? His reasoning is much the same as in Hebrews. God has given us *promises* (and God cannot lie).[47] It is to these promises that Peter now clings: "Whereby are given unto us exceeding great and precious promises: that by these ye might be partakers of the divine nature" (1:4). Primarily, God has promised to return for his own (3:4). If there be any delay, it is because of the longsuffering of the Lord which waits for our repentance. Finally, the promise is not for a nebulous "restitution" as in 1 Peter. Now the promise is that there will be a new heaven and a new earth in which righteousness dwells (3:13).

This certainly is a new Peter. 2 Peter does not directly say, "I have undergone a significant spiritual metamorphosis—I see much, much more clearly now." But there is plenty of circumstantial evidence that 2 Peter was written shortly after a such a final conversion experience. Without this conversion explanation we cannot understand why Peter had previously answered God from Simon the Tanner's roof in the way that he did. When God commanded him to "kill and eat" Peter said, "Not so Lord, for I have never eaten anything either common or unclean" (Acts 10:14). What was the explanation for this absurdity? Did Peter think that God was testing him by commanding him to do something contrary to a previously issued law? Perhaps Christ *was* divided (1 Cor 1:13) in his thinking about the propriety of his own law.

No. The source of the foolishness in Peter's question was much simpler. Peter *himself* had become so habituated to the authority of the rabbinic tradition, which had set itself up as a rival authority to God, that he could not see the utter foolishness of what he had been saying.

47 Hebrews uses this word "promise" (επαγγελια) 13 times. "Wherein God, willing more abundantly to shew unto the heirs of promise the immutability of his counsel, confirmed it by an oath: That by two immutable things, in which it was impossible for God to lie, we might have a strong consolation, who have fled for refuge to lay hold upon the hope set before us" (Heb 6:17–18).

What else could explain why he couldn't see why Christ did not warrant a fleshly tabernacle at the Transfiguration, why Christ should die, why worldly violence was forbidden and that his words of bravery were empty – betraying Christ for a morsel of security and warmth and public approval,[48] why he went fishing instead of feeding Christ's sheep, and why he cruelly betrayed the Antiochian Christians? Because his thinking was weighted down with a kind of topsy-turvy establishment theology, which had resulted in all kinds of absurd interpretations of the Scriptures that left the people to strain at gnats and swallow camels, to tithe the mint and ignore the need for mercy, and to crucify the very Lord of glory.

2 Peter stands at the end of a protracted spiritual catharsis, in which Peter finally understands the significance of the "divorcement of Israel" and of how the new wine of Pauline righteousness *cannot* be placed in the old wineskins of the Jamesean compromise with Judaism. As Peter realizes the extent and significance of the Judaizing infiltration and entanglement within the fledgling "Christian" community and the progress of its deconstruction of Pauline theology, he reacts decisively and gives a scathing denunciation against those false prophets *and* false teachers. With the death of Paul, the Pauline bishopric has collapsed. The Judaizing party rises like a storm within its drifting and disorganized remnants, devouring its sheep from within as the increasing Roman persecutions are crashing in upon its gate without.

Peter now knows the truth. He knows the truth about Christ. And he knows the truth about himself. Peter speaks as Bishop now. Because something more than Pauline jargon will be needed to rescue the church from the coming storm. On the eve of the most terrible persecutions the church has ever known, Peter is now fully transformed.

---

48 Many apologists for Peter explain that he was simply caught "off guard" by the young woman who asked if he was with Jesus of Galilee. After such a momentary lapse of resolve, most people would say to themselves after such a slip: "I feel awful! That was shameful behavior. I wish I could do that over again." But this happens a second time, in which Peter "denies with an oath" that he even knows Christ. And then it happens a *third* time, in which Peter curses and swears that he does not know Christ (Mt 26:69–75). Matthew is making it very clear that this is not a momentary lapse of judgment on Peter's part. No. This is an intentional denial.

As Christ predicted, Satan has "sifted him as wheat." He finally has the spirit to "strengthen his brethren." The tendrils of Pauline theology had heretofore everywhere surrounded his heart of rock (*petros*). But now the raw truth had broken through to its very depths. The seed has finally produced some fruit, just as Mark had said. For the survival of the church, he hurls himself into the sea to quiet the storm. This is good news. This is very good news.

Footnotes from Tables

1 Which itself seems lifted from a 2 Tim 2:9–15 template.

2 Excepting John's one use of this word in a similar context, only James and Peter address the diaspora.

3 The word James uses here is **πραυτης**. It is only used by James and in 1 Pe 3:15.

4 The word is **παις** and not **υιος**. Therefore it should be translated as "child" of God or "servant" of God, not "son" as the AV has done.

5 A title unique to Peter. "Prince" itself is only used four times. Hebrews uses it for two other titles: "Prince of our Salvation" and "Prince of our Faith." Peter again calls him a prince by saying that God elevated him to his position (5:31). So we are not here speaking of "Prince of Life" in the Johannine sense, in which Christ is our life and he is the life of men. But Peter is no doubt making reference to the suffering servant prophecy in Is 53:4–9: "Surely he hath borne our griefs, and carried our sorrows: yet we did esteem him stricken, smitten of God, and afflicted. But he was wounded for our transgressions, he was bruised for our iniquities: the chastisement of our peace was upon him; and with his stripes we are healed. All we like sheep have gone astray; we have turned everyone to his own way; and the LORD hath laid on him the iniquity of us all. He was oppressed, and he was afflicted, yet he opened not his mouth: he is brought as a lamb to the slaughter, and as a sheep before her shearers is dumb, so he openeth not his mouth. He was taken from prison and from judgment: and who shall declare his generation? for he was cut off out of the land of the living: for the transgression of my people was he stricken. And he made his grave with the wicked, and with the rich in his death; because he had done no violence, neither was any deceit in his mouth."

6 A quotation from the Septuagint.

7 James **διψυχος**; Peter **ψυχη.**

8 Both James and Peter only use this word and both in connection with faith.

9 **καλυψει πληθος αμαρτιων.**

10 Only these three authors use this word, **αγιασμος**, which denotes "holiness" or "sanctification."

11 Only these three authors use this word, **υπακοη.**

12 Only 1 Peter and Hebrews combine these two words. **ραντισμος** is only used here.

13 "Grace to you and peace" is seemingly a Pauline signature introductory phrase. John uses it once in the introduction to Revelation, but Peter uses it in the introduction to both of his letters.

14 An unusual military word, **φρουρεω**, used by both authors to describe the security of the believer in God. The word is used only by Paul and in 1 Peter.

15 It is uncertain what Peter might mean by: "Searching what, or what manner of time the Spirit of Christ which was in them did signify, when it testified beforehand the sufferings of Christ, and the glory that should follow." If we were confined to Phil 1:19, we might conclude that these men were simply invoking the spirit of Christ in the same way as "team spirit." But Paul's discussion of the "Spirit of Christ" in Ro 8:1–11 makes it clear that he uses this phrase in a technical, non-figurative sense.

16 The common word, **δηλοω**, was used to express the common idea that the Holy Spirit was active in Old Testament times as the revealer of Christ. Used only by these three authors.

17 A phrase used only in 2 Cor 1:5 and 1 Pe 1:11, 4:13, and 5:1.

18 The common idea is that the prophets did not receive the complete promise, which is now being announced through apostolic preaching.

19 **συσχηεματιζο**, used only by Paul and Peter.

20 This term, **αγνοια**, is used only by Paul and Peter. It occurs two other places in the NT: once in a sermon of Paul, once in a sermon of Peter.

21 **φιλαδελφια** (*philadelphia*), used only by these three authors.

22 This word, φθαρτος, is used only by Paul and Peter.

23 **λογικος** is used only by Paul and Peter (1/1).

24 **ειπερ** is used only by Paul and Peter (5/1).

25 **πνευματικος** is used only by Paul and Peter (20/1).

26 Only 1 Peter and Hebrews combine these two terms (**αναφερω** and **θυσια).**

27 **ευπροσδεκτος** is used only by Paul and Peter (4/1).

28 Both authors use the same two Isaiah quotations in the same order.

29 Only 1 Peter and Hebrews use this phrase (**λαω του θεου**).

30 Peter uses a different word here (**παροικος**), emphasizing temporariness; Hebrews uses **xenov**, emphasizing foreignness.

31 This distinctive word, **σαρκικος**, is used only by these three authors: once by Peter and in Hebrews, 8 times by Paul.

32 **επαινος** is used only by Paul (9) and Peter (2).

33 This is a very important word for Paul (**μιμητης**), who used it 5 times in virtually the same sense. Heb also uses it once in the same sense. A key difference is that Peter's is following an inanimate "good" while Paul and Hebrews always have a personal object.

34 **αγνοσια** is used only once by Paul and Peter.

35 Paul has **εν προφασει πλεονεξιας** (a "pretence for covetousness," 1 Thess 2:5).

36 Eph 6:5 uses different words for "servants," "obedience," and "masters," but it too couples this imperative with "fear": "Servants, be obedient to them that are your masters according to the flesh, with fear and trembling, in singleness of your heart, as unto Christ."

37 **ιχνος** ("steps") is used only by Paul.

38 The idea in Hebrews is that the suffering of the prophets was to suffer the reproaches of Christ, which is the central theme of 1 Peter. In Hebrews, the prophets are used as an example; in 1 Peter, Christ is the example. And in both cases, the suffering of the prophets and our suffering is in lieu of the pleasures of sin.

39 "In the body" (**εν τω σωματι**) is a phrase used only by Paul.

40 **συγκληρονομος**, used only once by these three authors.

41 **το δε τελος**, a phrase only used by Paul (twice).

42 **ευσπλαγχνος**, used only once by Paul and Peter.

43 This phrase (**kakon αντι κακου**) is used only by Paul (twice).

44 **λοιδορια**, used only by Paul (once).

45 **τουναντιον** is used only by Paul (once).

46 This phrase is used only by Paul and Peter (once).

47 Only Hebrews and 1 Peter use this word **αντιτυπος** ("antitype"). The author of Hebrews says that the tabernacle is an antitype of the heavenly tabernacle into which Christ has entered with his own blood to purge our conscience (9:9). The order is reversed in Peter, but the connection is the same: Baptism is an antitype of the Noahic flood, whereby the world, like our conscience, was cleansed of sin.

48 The word that both use here is **ασελγεια**. This word is used only by Paul, Peter, and Mark.

49 Riotings and revellings is **κωμος**, used only by Paul and Peter.

50 This word—**ειδωλολατρεια**—is used only by Paul (3 times).

51 **χαρισμα** is a Pauline signature word. Peter uses it only here; Paul uses it 16 times.

52 **αλληλοις υποτασσομενοι.**

53 **παθεμα**, used only by these three authors. In this usage, the context is the same.

54 Which also has a very strong affinity with Gal 1:12. "For I neither received it [Paul's gospel] of man, neither was I taught it, but by the revelation of Jesus Christ."

Conclusion

Jesus said that no sign will be given to this generation except the sign of Jonas.[1] We cannot underestimate the significance of this. Jesus did not say that he *was* Jonah, but that he was greater than Jonah.[2] We may then gather from this that the typology of Jonah is now normative for what is happening in the final generation of mankind. How long is a generation? Forty years? Forty thousand years? No one knows. All we know is that this is the final generation. Jesus says, "O ye hypocrites, ye can discern the face of the sky; but can ye not discern the signs of the times?"[3] What is the sign of the times? The "sign of Jonas," Jesus says.

It is not just Matthew's Gospel that is written in this genre. According to Christ, the final chapter of history is written in this genre. And the more we look at the apostolic drama, the more and more it appears to conform to the typology of Jonah. The apostolic cadre was called to preach the gospel to the world: not to the "world of the Jews," but to the *whole* world, which was primarily Gentile. Generally speaking, they refused this call. Matthew constructs a powerful case that makes Peter typological of this tragic refusal. Although all three other Gospels appear to be moderating this judgment against Peter, Matthew does not relent. At Jesus' final meeting with the disciples in Galilee, Matthew makes his final editorial comment: "Then the eleven disciples went away into Galilee, into a mountain where Jesus had appointed them. And when they saw him, they worshipped him: but

---

1 Mt 16:4. "A wicked and adulterous generation seeketh after a sign; and there shall no sign be given unto it, but the sign of the prophet Jonas."

2 12:41. "The men of Nineveh shall rise in judgment with this generation, and shall condemn it: because they repented at the preaching of Jonas; and, behold, a greater than Jonas is here."

3 16:2b–3.

some doubted."[4] Who? Matthew doesn't say. But the verb he uses, **δισταζω**, occurs only one other time in the New Testament: in Matthew's account of Peter's failure of faith. "O you of little faith," Jesus says to Peter, "why did you doubt?"[5]

Then a new man is called in to take on the role of Jonah. Although he is completely outside the "official" apostolic cadre, he is a Hebrew of the Hebrews; concerning the law, a Pharisee; concerning zeal, an ardent persecutor of heresy; concerning the righteousness of the Mosaic law, blameless.[6] Just as Jesus struggled with his destiny in the garden of Gethsemane, so too did the Apostle Paul struggle with his. As Jonah was sent to the Ninevites, so Paul was sent to the Gentiles.[7] Thus the typology of Jonah is the frame of reference for our understanding of the Gospel of Matthew, the life of Christ, the apostolic drama, the life of Paul, the life of Peter, the development of the Christian church, and the course of the world unto the end.

4 Mt 28:16–17.

5 14:31b.

6 Phil 3:5–6.

7 Acts 22:21. "Depart: for I will send thee far hence unto the Gentiles."

Epilogue

Jeremiah once said that "the heart of man is deceitfully wicked above all things–who can know it?"[1] I had long known this was true of me. My prayer to God for answers about why Christendom was breaking up and how the Synoptics had become thoroughly discredited in the world as witnesses to the Christ of history turned out to be an answer not so much about Christendom or the world, but about me. Though I had specifically asked for an answer that would leave me and my personal, existential world out of the story, at every point where the answer came, I realized that I was indeed part of that story.

The problem, ultimately, was not Christendom. Nor was it the modern, secular science of biblical criticism. The problem was me. The problem was not that I had mindlessly absorbed a defective religion from my cultural experience. The problem was that I had mindfully nurtured a primary, co-dependent interest in its collapse. If Christianity is weak, I am strong. And Christianity would need me to flatter and defend her. My life could proceed as a happy blend of bourgeois immorality and ambiguous moralism. As the research moved inexorably forward, I further realized that I was trapped in a kind of divine courtroom. Every time I learned something about Matthew, or about any of the men of flesh and blood who wrote the New Testament materials, I found out something about myself. Every time I came upon something that the world would have preferred to remain unsaid, I came across something about myself that I would have preferred to remain unsaid. Gradually, I resisted less and less as I realized that there was no point in defending the indefensible. Why was I behaving as if I had something to lose when I had so stridently confronted God as if I had nothing to lose?

---

1 Jer 17:19.

As soon as I lost this one thing, I had everything to gain. As I had struggled to understand what Matthew was doing in his Gospel, I very slowly began to understand that the reason why I had had such difficulty in understanding him was that my many internal presuppositions about how language worked greatly restricted what was possible for him to say. For example, Matthew was not allowed to put representational speeches in the mouth of Christ. (Where did I get that rule?)

But there was a larger, global restriction to which my research had been confined. The church had said that the New Testament materials were an aggressive act of revelation from God. But the world began to say that the revelation of the church was in conflict with reason. In time, the church and the world worked out a compromise, in which the world would allow the church its authority in matters of religion and the church would allow the world its authority in matters of reason. Thus there was an unspoken assumption that the mechanics of New Testament composition and transmission should not be understood scientifically; such a project would be irreligious. My research showed me that the New Testament was not a passive menagerie of community myth; it was a blaze of communication so hot you could hardly stand next to it without getting burned.

And the New Testament itself stood within a world that was ablaze with communication. It was not just the content of the New Testament that was the message; the media itself was also the message. The very drama of the post-ascension church was part of that message. The whole typological history of Israel was part of that message. Even the drama of my own personal, individual history was part of the message. And the whole evolutionary, created order was the media for the message.

I had stumbled upon a theory of language that would brook no détente between the frigid categories of reason and revelation. The theory began with Socrates' challenge to "know thyself." It ended with the Christology of John: *Christ is language*. The apostolic community of authors assert that Christ begins a dialogue with the human soul from the very beginning. Even though we are children born of a terrible moral catastrophe that took place long ago, even though we are yet enemies of God, Christ nevertheless begins this conversation.[2]

Every infant already knows a little history. He cries because he already knows, in part, the tragedy of the fall. An infant laughs because he already knows, in part, what is funny. The infant is too young to have been taught these things by human intervention.[3] Yet he must have heard it somewhere before. He knows these things because he is immersed in the amniotic fluid of the ordinary speech of God.

God can speak to us in ordinary speech and ordinary literature because the creator of the ordinary world became an ordinary man. "And the Word was made flesh, and dwelt among us…[4]" The New Testament materials clearly assert that *all* man's knowledge must be revealed by God. The ordinary man understands the weather in the very same way that he understands prophecy: "[Jesus] answered and said to them, When it is evening, you say, it will be fair weather: for the sky is red. And in the morning, it will be foul weather today: for the sky is red and lowring. Hypocrites—you can discern the face of the sky; but to discern the signs of the times you are not able."[5] The New Testament materials assert that the ordinary man can understand the world around him because all of his senses have been created by God, created to hear and see and taste and touch the logic of the cosmos or the songs of the stars.[6]

Zen Buddhism claims that a flower does not talk. That's because in Zen Buddhism, there is nothing to say. But this is not the language the-

2 Ro 5:10. "For if, when we were enemies, we were reconciled to God by the death of his Son, much more, being reconciled we shall be saved by his life." Also 2 Cor 5:20: "Now then we are ambassadors for Christ, as though God did beseech you by us: we pray you in Christ's stead, be ye reconciled to God."

3 The inspiration for this illustration comes from Jean Piaget's *The Child's Conception of the World* (London: Routledge and Kegan Paul, 1928).

4 Jn 1:14a.

5 Mt 16:3.

6 The senses, therefore, exist on a continuum. Each sense is attuned to a particular range of the "music" or "speech" of the cosmos. The divisions between the senses are true but are often unnecessarily compartmentalized as different in kind instead of degree. For example, if our optical apparatus worked at a low enough frequency we would "see" sound. Likewise, if our hearing were sufficiently extended we would "hear" colors. With the sense of touch we "hear" the very quantum, aggregate structural "vibrations" of the laws of other "substances" in our environment.

ory of the Psalmist. He claims that the world is ablaze with communication: "The heavens declare the glory of God; and the firmament shows his handiwork. Day to day utters speech, and night unto night shows knowledge."[7] The logic that his senses reveal is more than mere order and stability. The logic that his senses reveal is *beautiful*.

Mathematics, music, and physics all make the same speech. However plausible a scientific theory, even if it seems to have passed the rigors of the scientific method, if it is not *elegant*, the scientist will immediately know that there is something wrong with it. The New Testament materials tell us that God created the ear and all the other senses, the emotions, the conscience, the memory, and the rational processes of the mind in order to "hear" that speech. And they tell us that the logic of that speech is elegantly beautiful.

Through the senses and the mind we hear and see the beauty of the cosmos – whether it be the smell of black humus or the mathematical proportions of a black hole. The universe is beautiful because it bears the impress of inexpressible beauty. Our souls must embrace the beautiful because we are hopelessly in love with the beautiful. The Gospels do not coax us to love our own souls. They coax us to love our neighbor's soul. We *must* love our own souls because they too are beautiful. They are beautiful because they bear the impress of inexpressible beauty. The souls of human beings cannot repudiate reason and beauty any more than the fetus can repudiate the womb. The alternative to reason and beauty is not only absurdity and ugliness. The alternative to reason and beauty is a hellish insanity of weeping and gnashing of teeth. That which is beautiful is in the eye of the beholder because it is also everywhere outside the beholder.

And that beauty is Christ. The New Testament claims that Christ is the intersection between God and man, between flesh and spirit, between the infinite and the finite, between the creator and what has been created. John is emphatic about this. He says that when we reach out and touch Christ, we are touching God. John does not say that Christ merely speaks the words of life. John says that Christ *is* the word of life: "That which was from the beginning, which we have heard,

7 Ps 19:1.

which we have seen with our eyes, which we have looked upon, and our hands have handled, of the word of life."[8]

The reason that we can know ourselves is because from the beginning, Christ begins to tell us who we are. The reason that we can understand the language of another is because we both are having the same conversation with Christ. The reason that we may understand the world around us is that the world is being spoken into existence by the same voice that is speaking our soul into existence. The reason that we may understand the mind of God is because the Son of God tells us what he is thinking. And the reason that we can understand and know the truth of apostolic preaching is because we have heard what they are saying somewhere before.

The study of what the Synoptic authors had been doing in terms of genre opened a Pandora's box of possibility for me. Engulfed by this language theory, I knew I had to go on with the research. And this study left me standing on the precipice of Hebrews – the object of my original study concerning my troubling lack of forgiveness. What would happen if I applied these mechanics to Hebrews? Could I find some definitive answers about the author of Hebrews? If the theological basis of my forgiveness ultimately rested upon the argument presented in Hebrews, wasn't it essential that I understand – or at least make every attempt to understand – the relationship between the author of Hebrews and the historical Christ? The answer to that question became a second book: *From Exodus to Eisodus*.

At length what I found in the research about the author of Hebrews left me holding yet another key which looked very like something that could be tried in unlocking the enigma of John's writings. Who was John? Who was he writing to? What was he saying? What was his relationship to all the other authors of the New Testament materials? Why was he so different? How are the Johannine writings related to each other? And most importantly, what was his relationship to the historical Christ? The answer to these questions became a third book: *A Vesture Dipped in Blood*.

Through this study of the Synoptic Gospels, I discovered that I didn't need to be afraid of sailing off the edge of the world anymore if I approached the New Testament materials scientifically. Jonah assum-

8 1 Jn 1:1.

ed that there was such a place, but he was wrong. And so was I. The real problem with studying the New Testament materials is that I had placed mental restrictions upon what the New Testament was allowed to say to me. Once I threw those mental and theological restrictions overboard, the storm ceased and the seas calmed. No longer encumbered with the high and mighty office of Lord Protector of Revelation from the supposed threats of worldly reason, I was completely free to attend to the ordinary business of sailing. And I discovered that Christ is both revelation *and* reason. And that there was no need to protect him - or me.